Praise for Fir  .ity

What a treat to be taken not only on spiritual journey but on a geographical adventure, too, as Weiss traces his life from Uruguay through Argentina, Cuba, then onto the United States.

World War II, brothels in Old Havana, and de-segregation in the South all play a part in the story. Through it all, there is an intelligent and gracious spirit at play, as Weiss finds a way in even the toughest situations to land on his feet with his faith intact.

A lively thought-provoking read.

Bonnie Dwyer, Editor, Spectrum

Weiss is a master at transforming traditional Christian beliefs and values to personal convictions and moral imperatives. What starts as an intellectual autobiography by an ordinary Christian on a spiritual trek, becomes a guidebook by an extraordinary teacher on a moral/ethical highway. Journeying with him from South to North America, from the East Coast to the Midwest, the reader gradually becomes the author's spiritual and intellectual compatriot. The author's encounters easily become those of the reader, who has plenty to learn along the way: from the challenges of graduate-level biblical studies to the contentment of academic integrity. FINDIG MY WAY IN CHRISTIANITY is a worthwhile companion to all who wish to make their life journey more meaningful."

Abraham Terian

Professor Emeritus of Early Christianity, St. Nersess Armenian Seminary

In a story that moves over seventy years from the confines of an Adventist childhood in Uruguay to a department of theology in a Roman Catholic college in Notre Dame, Indiana, this book charts a remarkable personal journey in which the borders and textures of faith broaden and deepen with each new encounter. The relation between faith and culture, faith and politics, faith and personal experience are explored with an even and generous hand by a man who has known the margins and the inner circles of a surprising number of worlds and has found welcome and truth in unexpected places. The vision of Christianity that emerges from this narrative is compelling and inspiring.

Charles H. Cosgrove
Professor of New Testament Studies and Christian Ethics,
Northern Seminary

This is not just a memoir of one man's spiritual journey, but rather a deeply theological work of intercultural encounter, growth, and grace-filled moments. Dr. Herold Weiss's Finding My Way in Christianity is a parable for our time of openness to the world and to the deepest resources provided by scholarly exploration for reading the Scriptures.

From its earliest times, Christianity has valued the witness of notable lives formed by the faith. Dr. Weiss's journey reaches across and through many cultures and constellations of meaning, and breathes the universality of the Christian message. This is ultimately the story of a life well lived, shaped by encounters with others (both inside and outside the Adventist community) who gave flesh to Gospel values and, ultimately, direction to an author in search of his home.

It is a narrative of richly-textured recollections, and a tale beautifully written and captivatingly told.

Joseph M. Incandela, Ph.D.
Associate Dean of Faculty and Joyce McMahon Hank Aquinas
Chair of Catholic Theology
Saint Mary's College

Fascinating and illuminating. Weiss tells how a follower of Jesus moved from a world-denying sectarianism into a rich and affirming dialogue with classical and contemporary culture, modern scholarship, and other faith communities. Yet he has retained a deep affection for ordinary people and strong ties with the faith community that shaped his early years. A must read for those who tussle with issues of faith, worship, and authority.

Alden Thompson, Ph.D., Professor of Biblical Studies
Walla Walla University

This engaging and heartfelt memoir is a capstone to Herold Weiss's long and distinguished career as a theologian, professor of religious studies, and biblical scholar. It is a vivid personal story that spans centuries, nations, continents, and cultures and, in the process, offers a varied and unique view of the immigrant experience. It is also an inspiring story of intellectual and spiritual integrity. In his faith-filled refusal to accept easy answers and his unwavering commitment to ask uneasy questions, Professor Weiss shows his readers the personal cost of Christian discipleship. Through his own experience, he demonstrates the power of love to transform the person and the world and makes clear the challenges and benefits of crossing religious divides. For those who hope to be, in his words, "agents of justice and peace, bridges that allow for the free transit of peoples and ideas in God's world for the benefit of all of God's creatures," this compelling testament is essential reading.

Gail Porter Mandell, Ph.D.
Bruno P. Schlesinger Chair Emerita in Humanistic Studies, St. Mary's College

This book tells a compelling and moving story of faith seeking understanding within the context of an American apocalyptic community. It is also a very personal account of how context, culture, and education rub up against the norms and mindset of a conservative religious movement. The lucid descriptions of personalities and places makes for interesting reading. It is a story of an intellectual, journeying between two ethnic cultural worlds—Latin American and American—and multiple religious worlds to form a broad ecumenical vision. It is a critique of the best and worst of sectarian exclusivism. And it chronicles the often uncharted path from a sectarian movement to the platform of a world class educational institution—Notre Dame—while yet maintaining loose ties to sectarian roots specially the Sabbath—less as a doctrine to be defended but as an experience seen as a "boon to humanity". The result is an eclectic but broad religious vision that is able to hold in tension and integrate opposite traditions into a synthesis of meaning and accommodation that finds its ultimate expression in a meaning led life. A remarkable story of courage, honesty, intellectual risk that embraces a journey of faith beyond proposition to real life experience characterized by love, justice and peace.

Edwin I. Hernandez, Ph.D.
Research Fellow at the Center for the Study of Latino Religion,
at the University of Notre Dame
Senior Program Officer at the DeVos Family Foundations

About the Book

Finding My Way in Christianity: Recollections of a Journey is a story of dealing with the differences within the Christian community that is both personal and theologically reflective. With a diverse cross-cultural background, exceptional theological education, and fascinating personal experience, author Herold Weiss is uniquely qualified to write about this topic.

This notable book outlines the author's experiences starting in Montevideo, Uruguay and moving through various educational experiences and teaching positions. It is no accident that the chapter titles reflect geographical locations, as the journey through space provides an illuminating metaphor for the faith journey that accompanies it.

Some of the people you meet in this book will make you angry. Others will make you thankful to be a Christian. Some will evoke your sympathy even as you seek to understand why they acted as they did. All of them will help give you some insight into what goes into a successful journey of faith. You can read Finding My Way in Christianity either as an interesting story or as theological reflection. The author's experiences will resonate with many of us who have experienced the divisions within the Christian community and dealt with those who would silence dissent. Dr. Weiss' story comes primarily within one denomination, but it follows outlines that will be familiar to many.

If you find yourself on a journey of faith, you owe it to yourself to read *Finding My Way in Christianity*.

Finding My Way in Christianity

Recollections of a Journey

by

Herold Weiss

Energion Publications
P. O. Box 841
Gonzalez, FL 32560
www.energionpubs.com

Energion Publications
P. O. Box 841
Gonzalez, FL 32560

ISBN10: 1-893729-80-X
ISBN13: 978-1-893729-80-3
Library of Congress Control Number: 2010936867

This book is dedicated

to

the memory of my parents,

Daniel Weiss
1895-1955

María Riffel de Weiss
1903-1963

who

created the conditions and

sent me on my way

Contents

Preface

The idea for this book circulated in my head for a long time. I began to put words on paper, however, when the American electorate gave George W. Bush a second term in office. The election demonstrated the power of biblical fundamentalism on American religion. Jewish and Christian conservatives guided by peculiar readings of the Bible succeeded in transposing their doctrinal views into national politics. Evangelical Christians with definite apocalyptic views had established their predominance in American Christianity and were giving the impression that anyone who did not share their views could not possibly be a Christian. Against this background, I wished to contend that Christianity has taken, and can take, a spectrum of forms. Here I limit myself to present the one I have found most helpful.

My argument for a Christianity that is open, pluralistic and biblical is couched in a narrative of my spiritual journey. It is not my intention to denigrate or to ridicule fundamentalism. Neither am I telling the story of a dramatic conversion experience that turns on the lights and takes me out of darkness at a spectacular moment in my life. This is the story of a very consistent and slow awakening to the leadings of God toward a vision of God's workings in the world that serves the main objectives that, as far as I can tell, God has for humanity, not just the few elect: justice and peace on earth.

Acknowledgments

Writing a book is not quite a lonely endeavor. The author is most of the time accompanied by his self-doubts, frustrations with his own short comings and realizations of very slow progress. Why he keeps at it is a question he does not wish to entertain. Is he responding to a selfish need or to a need felt by others? The final product of his efforts ultimately comes from him. If it turns out that the book is considered praiseworthy, however, it would be wrong to assign all credit to him alone. Its shortcomings, on the other hand, are due only to him.

Throughout the narrative that follows I refer to many who have exerted a strong influence on my becoming the Christian person I am. I will not identify them here. Still, I wish to formally acknowledge my debt to all of them. Here I will single out those who have been particularly helpful in the writing of the book. My first readers and supporters have been my two sons. Herold Eduardo (Dito), and Carlos Orval. Dito immediately suggested literary allusions I should exploit. Carlos took it upon himself to help me find better ways to say in good English what I wanted to say.

Three colleagues from Saint Mary's College read the manuscript and offered suggestions and criticisms. Terence Martin read the chapters as they were being written. As the reader will learn, he has been a dependable friend and sounding board for many years. Gail and Dan Mandell read an earlier version of the whole book with care and a willingness to help. An old friend from college days, Dean Kinsey, also read the text and offered suggestions. The help received from these friends certainly made for a much better book.

Finally, I wish to specially thank my editor and publisher, Henry Neufeld, and his copy editor, Aaron Bergh. They did an excellent job further improving the style and asking for needed elucidations. Needless to say, without their enthusiasm for the manuscript it would not be now seeing the light of day.

Acknowledging my debts makes clear that after all authors don't work alone. It must be admitted, besides, that while writing authors are always in the company of their intended audience. It is my pleasure, therefore, here to pay my debt to my future readers, who were always with me in my imagination making demands from me, most clearly of all, without a doubt, my wife Aida. She was the first to read and perceptively criticize an advance copy.

1

Montevideo

My brother Klinton and his friend Bubby Ernst did not want me along. I surmised they were up to something and wanted in. It was about four o'clock on a Sunday afternoon dedicated to a cookout with the Ernsts, who lived in a modest house with a nice yard and a bountiful vegetable garden in Maroñas, a Montevideo suburb with a well-known thoroughbred racetrack. The families had finished eating an expansive noon meal and everybody was settling down for conversation or a nap. My brother and his friend, however, were sneaking out. Even if not fully aware of what was going on, I wanted to join them. So, seeing them leave in a quiet way, I followed. They quickly tried to talk me out of it, but I was not to be dissuaded. We had walked about four or five blocks and were entering an open field when we faced a small ditch. Klinton and Bubby, who were about eight, easily jumped and continued on their way. I was about five and afraid to jump. They, of course, were not about to help me. They continued without looking back, happy to be rid of me.

Downcast by my lack of courage, I decided to return to the Ernst home. Soon my surroundings were totally unfamiliar. I was lost.

Sunday afternoon in Uruguay is when families are home enjoying themselves, often just sitting in front of their houses talking, sipping mate, listening to music and just being friendly. A young man saw me crying in the middle of the street and approached me.

"What's the matter?" he asked.

"I am lost. I want to get to the Ernst home," I replied.

Neither he nor any of the neighbors sitting in their front porches knew the Ernsts. So this young stranger decided to take me to the local police station nearby in Maroñas. I was not too happy with that idea, and by the time we got there I insisted that I did not want to stay. I told my rescuer that I wanted to go home, and I knew my home street address. Taking pity on me, my protector took my hand and guided me to the street car stop. To go from Maroñas to my home on Bahia Blanca street, we had to take two streetcars and ride on them for over an hour. Once the second streetcar got to our neighborhood, I told my rescuer where we had to get off, and then how to get home walking. Of course, when we got there we found no one. For a while we were both disconcerted. A locked, empty house had not been what I had in mind when I refused to stay at the police station. My benefactor had agreed to take me home, but he was not expecting the rest of my family to be in Maroñas, where we had just come from I could not ask him to wait with me until the unknown time of their return. On the other hand, going all the way back to Maroñas with him was out of the question. In my eagerness to get home I had forgotten all about my family. Facing the locked door of our house, their absence was overwhelming. Then, I remembered that our friends the Smelings lived three houses down the street. My rescuer took me there and left me with them. By this time it was already getting dark. The Smelings gave me supper and put me to bed. Even though I wasn't in my own bed, I felt secure. To this day I don't know the name of the man who found me that Sunday afternoon. He took me all the way to Maroñas, and then brought me all the way back to my neighborhood. He found me distraught and crying, and left me in a comfortable, secure place.

Back at the Ernsts, it was not until my parents were ready to start the journey back into the city that anyone realized that I was missing. Immediately, they all went into the neighborhood looking for me. The dark of night had settled in and I was not to be found.

2

Around midnight, my exhausted mother decided to go home with my two sisters, Lylian and Evelyn. My father and my brothers, Ewaldo, and Klinton, kept walking the streets and asking strangers about a lost little boy. Finally, around one o'clock in the morning someone went to the police station. There they were told that, yes, a young man had come in with a lost little boy, but that he had taken him home to the city. Hoping for the best, my father and brothers headed for home. Streetcars did not run often in the very early morning hours. By the time they got home it was about 4 o'clock. After some reflection among themselves, they decided to knock at the Smeling home to see if I was there. I had finally been found, but it had been a very long afternoon and night for my parents.

The situation did not lack some deep irony. I had been lost, but my suffering as a lost little boy was actually very short-lived. A stranger came to my rescue and made me feel safe. Thus, as far as I was concerned, I was going home helped by this very friendly and strong young man. That night I did not go to sleep in my own bed, but I was very secure and comfortable sleeping in a bed in the home of our friends and neighbors. My parents, and my brothers and sisters, however, had a very bad time. For hours they had been desperately looking for me, imagining the worst and suffering the torments of second thoughts that made them feel guilty for my being lost. In these circumstances, everyone tries to say something that hopefully will reduce the pain of others, while in their own minds they are harboring nightmares. This family story cannot be reduced to that one day. With its multiple overtones, it encapsulates the saga of my life. It is this larger tale I wish to tell.

My father, Daniel Weiss, had been born on a farm in the Argentine province of Entre Ríos in 1895. As a young man he was sent a few kilometers away to a school recently established by American missionaries. At the school, he studied to become a book keeper. Later, when he was 25 years old, he married his cousin, María Riffel, who was not quite eighteen. When they moved to Montevideo, they already had two boys and a girl: Ewaldo, Lylian, and Klinton. I was born a couple of years after their arrivals, and Evelyn was born two years after mine. We were a relatively happy family, living on modest means. We did not enjoy luxuries; neither did we lack essentials.

As children, we had to devise our own games with apricot or cherry seeds, and to fabricate the balls with which to play soccer with worn lady's stockings and a small piece of rubber from a discarded tire at their core. The most valuable thing in the home for us children was a twenty volume encyclopedia set produced by Jackson Publishers called: El Tesoro de la Juventud. I imagine it had been translated from an English original. Before I could read, I spent long hours looking at its black and white pictures. Once I could read, I had to take turns with my siblings for our favorite stories. Klinton, Evelyn and I would sometimes read together, or try to tell stories to each other. I envied Klinton's ability to invent really interesting tales.

Mother was a wonderful cook. She prepared the rich central European dishes she had eaten at her home growing up. They required large amounts of sweet cream, butter and cottage cheese. Through the years, however, she had established friendships with women from different backgrounds, and had become quite proficient in the preparation of Spanish, Italian, and Lebanese dishes. All her dishes began with fresh basic ingredients. Even for her pasta dishes, she prepared the dough, extended it with a roller, let it dry by hanging it for an hour, and cut it by hand to the desired width. Rice and meat packed grapevine leaves, a delicacy we all loved, required a visit to a neighbor with a grapevine in his yard. At home we had a parlor where visitors were received and where my brothers and sisters practiced for interminable hours at the piano. Undoubtedly, however, the kitchen was the heart of the place, and the delicious aromas emanating from it gave its warmth a special lingering effect.

Montevideo in the thirties was a lovely city enjoying the rewards of farsighted political and social reforms that transformed Uruguay in the second decade of the century. The presidencies of José Batlle

4

Ordóñez, an enlightened intellectual who ended the cycle of civil wars that marred the history of Uruguay during the nineteenth century, transformed the small republic into a modern state. Under his leadership, several far-reaching initiatives were introduced in order to create a responsible middle class, and for Uruguay to cease being an economic puppet of foreign interests. Laws providing for pensions, farm credits, unemployment compensation and the eight-hour workday were passed. The constitutional revision of 1917 established the separation of church and state, and eliminated the death penalty from the judicial code. The country spent more on education than on the army, and the latter consisted of volunteers. Secondary education became free and easily available in all corners of the country. The University in Montevideo encouraged the admission of women. Electoral reforms guaranteed universal suffrage and proportional representation in the legislature. As a result of these initiatives, Uruguay had a wonderful reputation around the world and was considered one of the most advanced societies in the Americas.

Since its inception as a buffer between the two South American giants, Argentina and Brazil, Uruguay had charted a rather liberal course for itself. For one, it kept close ties to secular movements in France. Its educational system was patterned after the French, and its university promoted all types of student unrest in support of different causes. Still, its exports of wool, meat, hides and grains had established a healthy middle class and a lively intelligentsia. Culturally and commercially, Uruguay kept closer ties with Europe than with the United States. On national holidays it was not uncommon for marines from a British ship to take part in the downtown parade. Montevideo looked to Paris as its academic beacon. Native sons who sought to study abroad dreamt of the Sorbonne. In his famous little book, Ariel (1905), José Enrique Rodó contrasted the cultures of North and South America and pronounced the enlightened development of the life of the spirit as pursued in Latin America superior to the materialistic mercantilism of the North. Cultural mores valued the life of the senses and the emotions which find expression in the arts, particularly poetry and painting, but also in the way interpersonal relations are conducted. Friendships are based on deep fellow feelings which can weather emotional strains with reliance.

Montevideo had beautiful, well-kept parks with striking monuments. Not far from our home, at the Parque de los Aliados, was the famous monument to "La carreta". It represents a life-size two wheel wagon pulled by three pairs of oxen with their driver on horseback at its side. As the wheels are half buried in the mud, it is obvious that opening the country's interior had not been easy. At the Parque de las Acacias, the companion monument to "La diligencia" is of a life-size bronze representation of a stage coach. The basic pre-industrial vehicles for the transportation of goods and people are thus immortalized as the instruments that facilitated the establishment of a nation. Downtown a third monument, "La raza", has a white man, a Native American and an african slave blended into a human mass that exerts itself lifting the national flag. On the other hand, also at the Parque de los Aliados, the careful observer may find "El indio muerto". A native lies prone on the ground arching his body back and to the side, showing a knife stuck in his heart. In this way the nation admitted, long before it became politically correct, that its rise also had a tragic underside. All in all, reverence for the past gave Uruguayan society its enduring character, best preserved in folkloric music and poetry.

My parents had gone from Argentina to Montevideo in 1933, when my father was named secretary-treasurer of the Uruguayan Mission of the Seventh-day Adventist Church. At the time, the church had fewer than 500 members in the whole country, and the offices and church building in Montevideo were a rather dilapidated barn-like structure in a working class barrio on Avenida Arenal Grande. I was born in 1934 at our home on calle Urquiza, half a block from Avenida Garibaldi and the Instituto Crandon, a school run by American missionaries. As soon as my parents arrived in Montevideo, they enrolled my older brother and sister, Ewaldo and

Lylian, at the Crandon. Eventually, I also was enrolled and attended first and second grades on this Methodist island.

In my imagination the Crandon remains a magical place. The instructional building was a two-story Tudor structure covered with ivy on the outside walls. It had a large patio for recreation on one side, and formal gardens between the building and the tall iron fence protecting the property from the heavy traffic on the sidewalk and the street. The classrooms had wooden floors, large blackboards and closets for instructional aids. That was the only building I knew that had central heating, a very welcomed luxury during the chilly Uruguayan winters. At the center of the building was a gymnasium where the students played basketball and volleyball and did gymnastics. None of these things were found in a Uruguayan public school. I learned to read English with American books which told me about Jack, Jane and Spot, who lived in small town America where fall leaves create an enchanting world in which children played with robins and squirrels, creatures that did not even exist in my world. This fenced in, secured little place, paradoxically, may have played a significant role in enlarging the horizon of a rather timid little boy.

I did first and second grade in 1941 and 42, when everyone at the Crandon was fully committed to an allied victory in Europe. Uruguay remained neutral for a long time as the war raged, only to declare war on Germany when the fall of the Third Reich was a matter of weeks. Well before this time, German businesses were boycotted and the most famous pastry shop, Los anillos del Rhin, had its front windows smashed with stones more than once. The city fully awoke to World War II suddenly when on December 14, 1939, the pocket battleship Admiral Graf Spee entered the port and requested a fifteen day reprieve to repair damages suffered in a naval battle with three british cruisers just off the River Plate estuary. Uruguay, a neutral nation at the time, granted the Germans 72 hours. Since it was not enough time to do all the repairs and maintenance the ship required, her skipper, Hans Langsdorff, decided to scuttle her. In the afternoon of December 17, a series of explosions broke some windows in parts of the city and destroyed the ship just off the break waters of the port. Knowing that in Argentina his crew would have a much friendlier reception, Langsdorff arranged for them to cross the river to Buenos Aires. He then wrapped himself in the flag with the black eagle, rather than the Swastika, and shot himself at his hotel room. Later, on visits to the Spanish colonial fort at the top of the little promontory that gives the capital its name, I would look at the turret of the Graf Spee rising above the waters of the river just a few hundred yards from shore and imagine the battle she had fought, visualize the seas she had crossed and ponder the tragedy of its end, wondering whether it had been in honor or dishonor. As it turned out, I later learned that the captain had disobeyed strict orders not to engage enemy warships. His mission was only to sink merchant ships.

Talk around the dinner table at home would occasionally center on the sinking of the Graf Spee. Even though my parents belonged to families who had left Germany in the eighteenth century, they spoke and read German well, and had a healthy sense of national pride. What Germany was engaged in under Hitler, however, was strongly condemned. Reconsidering the tragedy of the Graf Spee at home, it never failed to be remarked that Langsdorf had wrapped himself in the flag of the Kaiser. It was necessary to point out that he had been a career officer, not a Nazi.

I grew up conscious that I was a member of two disliked minorities, one cultural and one confessional. On the one hand, I could not deny that I had German blood running in my veins. My Lutheran ancestors had left Germany looking for new horizons in the East. On my father's side, they had gone to Volhinia after the partition of Poland and settled in Rozchyshche, about 16 miles northwest of Lutsk in what is now Ukraine. Two of my great-great uncles were Lutheran pastors in Volhinia. Around 1890, my great-grandparents, Valentin and Katarina Weiss, together with most of their children, took a train to Bremen and then a ship that took them to Porto Alegre, Brazil. My grandfather José Weiss, at age 26,

8

had just married Carolina Feder before he left for the new world with his parents. Since they were unfamiliar with Brazilian crops, they traveled on covered wagons pulled by oxen for three months to eastern Argentina where they settled eventually in Entre Ríos province. There they could grow the crops they had harvested in the rich Volhinian soil: wheat, flax, oats, barley and rye. They also had a herd of milking cows and large chicken houses. In Entre Ríos several small towns had been settled by German immigrants who had come encouraged by the Argentine Immigration Act of 1876.

On my mother's side, the story was not dissimilar. The Riffels left Germany for the banks of the Volga in the late eighteenth century and went to Entre Ríos around 1876, also via Brazil. My mother's grandfather, Jorge, said good bye to his brother at the port of Hamburg and took a ship bound for Porto Alegre. His brother, Frederick, took one bound for Galveston, Texas. Eventually he settled in Kansas to do the farming he had learned to do in Russia. A few years after their separation, Jorge decided to visit his brother in Kansas. It turned out to be a fateful trip. While in Kansas, the brothers attended evangelistic tent meetings by a German Adventist preacher. Elder Louis Conradi's sermons converted the Lutheran Riffels into Seventh-day Adventists. Full of his new faith, Jorge Riffel returned to Entre Ríos to spread the Adventist Gospel to the Germans in Aldea Jacobi and other nearby communities. Soon after his return, and at his insistence, the Adventist leaders in Battle Creek, MI, sent the first pastor to South America, and the first Adventist Church in the continent was soon established in my great-grandfather's home in 1898. José Weiss and his wife Carolina eventually became members.

Growing up as an Adventist of German extraction in Montevideo made me quite aware that I did not fit in the world around me. Even though Uruguay and Argentina had a substantial number of non-Spanish immigrants, before the new wave of immigration from Eastern Europe after World War II, the population was overwhelmingly Hispanic. The next largest segment of the population was italian, primarily from the southern towns that had been ruled by the Spanish Bourbon kings for centuries. Uruguay had encouraged immigration, and there were significant Swiss, German and some Russian colonies in the interior. But Montevideo was by and large a latin town, with aspirations of echoing Paris. At home, during the war years, we all rooted for the Allies. My father and mother had been born and raised in Entre Ríos speaking German at home, and the oldest children in the family who had spent time with the family in Entre Ríos knew German. Growing up in Montevideo during World War II, I did not learn German at home, and all the children made sure that our parents did not speak German with each other in public.

I have been forever grateful that my parents had the foresight to send their children to the Instituto Crandon, an institution fully committed to progressive education. I have the distinct impression that this decision was primarily taken by my mother. She had been raised in a home with a higher economic lifestyle and had a vision of the good things life could offer. It was, after all, quite unusual for Adventist parents to send their children to another denomination's school. In their defense my parents argued that Adventists had historical connections with Methodism. Ellen G. White, the denomination's prophet and major foundational force, was a Methodist who joined the Millerites who expected the second coming of Christ, first in 1843 and then on October 22, 1844. Many of the early Adventists came out of the Holiness Movement that flourished in Methodism in the early nineteenth century. The Adventists also adopted their ecclesiastical structure from Methodism. On the other hand, Methodists were among the first evangelicals in America who took science seriously and therefore were open to an evolutionary understanding of human origins. They enjoyed the theater, the cinema, dancing, and the drinking of alcohol. All of which were forbidden among Adventists, as well as coffee and tea. When Coca-Cola became the soft drink of choice in the late thirties, Adventists also proscribed it, since it was thought to contain some drug in its secret formula. Rumor had it that it was the coca used by the natives of Perú and Bolivia, which Adventist missionaries in the region were having a hard time preventing new converts from using. On account of all these issues it was difficult for me to establish close friendships with my classmates at the Crandon.

In 1935, my father and the new president of the uruguayan adventist mission, Pastor Pedro Brouchy, bought a large parcel of land next to the Hospital Italiano fronting on Plaza Italia, one of Montevideo's traffic hubs. They planned for and constructed a new church, a more representative, art deco building, sacrificially built with the rather meager offerings of Uruguay's small Adventist constituency. The church was dedicated in 1940. The building had four floors. Besides the sanctuary on the main floor, there was an apartment for the president of the mission on the second floor, and rooms for the mission offices on the third. In the basement, only half a floor below ground, there was a large social hall and behind it two large rooms.

In one of these rooms, in 1943, the church decided to establish a church school. The son of the secretary-treasurer of the mission could not attend the Instituto Crandon once the church opened its own school. Thus, I did third grade in a one-room school with about 10 students in different grades. Our teacher was Catalina Genover, a young Cuban woman who had been thrown out of her home by her father, together with her sister, after the two of them became Adventists. After this traumatic experience, the sisters went to Argentina and studied at the Adventist College in Puiggari, Entre Ríos. Her first job was to be our teacher in the newly opened classroom in Montevideo. Miss Genover was an excellent teacher and quickly made me forget that I was no longer at the lovely Crandon. Besides, in her classroom we did not have to be "on guard" about evolution or other such things. The physical plant of this school, no doubt, left much to be desired, especially when it came time for recreation. In the back there was a very small tiled patio, encased by rather high walls on all sides. There our Cuban teacher taught us to play baseball with a tennis ball and a broom

11

stick. Years later, when I came to the States and tried to play the game, I soon realized that what we had played in that small patio was a far cry from the real thing. Not only were the bat and the balls poor imitations, but the rules of the game had been adapted to our cramped quarters. Still, somehow, I must confess that that little school and its teacher left in me a lasting impression of the value of discipline and persistence in spite of poor circumstances.

One of the highlights of that year was the visit of Pastor James McElhany, president of the General Conference of Seventh-day Adventists with central offices in Takoma Park, Maryland. The news that the president of the General Conference was coming was announced with awe and expected with unusual reverence. The aura surrounding such a personage was overwhelming to a little boy who imagined the General Conference officers as holy men who had been appointed by God as performers of the Divine Plan on earth. When Elder McElhany finally arrived, Adventists from every church in Uruguay had come to Montevideo. The newly built Iglesia Central was packed and people strained in the aisles and the back doors to see the man of God preaching with the help of a translator. Many had to resign themselves to hearing the sermon through speakers installed in the basement. Among them, of course, were all the children who were ordered to leave room for the adults. Still we could see the visitor from the Promised Land to the north from a short distance coming in and going out of the church. We were all sure, after that historic visit, that of all the General Conferences presidents, Elder McElhany must be, after James White (the husband of the prophet, and the first), undoubtedly the best. We had been privileged to have among us a man led by the Spirit of God.

Going to school in the church basement gave my religious development a new twist, but it was not the most enduring. The moments of worship at home, especially at the opening and the closing of the Sabbath, gave my life its spiritual foundation. Every evening after supper, Bibles and the Sabbath School Lesson Quarterly were brought to the table, and we all took turns going

12

over the questions of the day by reading the Bible texts and the supplementary readings in the Lesson Quarterly. The Lesson Quarterly, which is studied by Adventists around the world in their own languages each day of the week and then reviewed together at the Sabbath Schools on Sabbath mornings, is, undoubtedly, the most important formative element in the denomination. In our home, study of the Sabbath School lesson after the evening meal was a regular feature of every day. The seven of us were together studying the Bible and praying.

As their denominational name emphasizes, Adventists keep the seventh day of the week holy. Like the Jews, they consider the day to begin at sunset on Friday and to end at sunset on Saturday. During the holy hours of the Sabbath, special care is to be taken to avoid any secular activity. Today many Adventists routinely do things on the Sabbath that would have been unthinkable when I was growing up. In general Adventists are unfamiliar with the many Sabbath regulations promulgated by the Rabbis before the fifth century and still available in the Mishnah and the Talmud. Adventists are as critical of what Christians cavalierly identify as "Jewish legalism" as most protestants. But there are many similarities between the way in which we kept the Sabbath, and Jewish Halakah. Cooking, traveling, buying or selling, sports and entertainments were all forbidden. Even the subjects one could engage in conversations with others were to be carefully chosen. Both the beginning and the end of the Sabbath were marked by family worship. These devotionals would last longer than on the other evenings of the week, and included singing a number of hymns. At home we always had a piano and all my brothers and sisters learned to play. As it turned out, of the five of us I was the only one without any talent for playing an instrument. Klinton actually graduated from a piano Conservatory in Buenos Aires, and Evelyn, my younger sister, eventually obtained an M.A. in piano performance (and a PhD in musicology) from Michigan State University. Evenings spent singing around the piano as a family created precious memories that go as far back as I can remember,

13

especially for sundown worship at the beginning and the end of the Sabbath. I must confess, though, that many times Sabbath afternoons were interminable. There were not many activities we could safely undertake.

One of the most vivid and enduring images of my childhood was observing how my father, after breakfast and before leaving for work, would return to his bedroom and kneel by himself beside the matrimonial bed for what seemed to me to be extremely long prayers. I often wondered why he had so much to talk about with God. Exactly what went on during those conversations was never discussed, but I imagine that all five of his children were featured prominently in them.

In 1944 my father was called to become the secretary-treasurer of the Central Conference in Argentina with offices in Paraná. Thus in January of that year the family left Montevideo on one of the passenger boats that made the river crossing between Montevideo and Buenos Aires. The boat left one city at about ten o'clock at night and arrived at the other about seven o'clock the next morning. We made the trip in third class. My father, my two brothers and I each had a sleeping bunk way below deck in a large room with about 40 other men. There was another such room for the women. A few days later we took another passenger boat that went up the Paraná River to Corrientes, and then up the Paraguay River to Asunción. We were on board only as far as Paraná, a trip which, with some stops along the way, took almost two days. On this ship we enjoyed the luxury of private cabins. I still carry with me the indelible images of the beauty of the Paraná's delta. Once our ship left the Río de la Plata behind and began to slip among innumerable islands one could see houses of humble fishermen on stilts. At times we would pass by a fisherman checking his line and letting fall into his boat large "dorados" and "surubís". The hooks were attached to lines about four feet long that hung from a wire that had been suspended under water from one bank to the other. In his small boat the fisherman would just bring the suspended wire up and pull his boat along, checking on all the

14

hooks. The shipping channel was marked by colored buoys. Every once in a while a rather wide boat with its sides barely appearing above the water would be coming down river loaded with oranges or wood.

Even though my birth in Montevideo had been rather accidental, I remained forever attached to the city of my birth and to the liberal traditions of uruguayan culture. My citizenship gave me some definite advantages. For one, I would not have to contend with military obligations. My two older brothers, who were argentine citizens, had to contend with the military draft. For Adventists, who are conscientious objectors, not having to face the pressures of military service and the bureaucratic paperwork associated with exceptions to the bearing of arms was a welcome relief. Going with my family to Argentina, I think, made me even more aware that the liberal, political and educational traditions embedded in Uruguay were to be highly valued. Having to leave Uruguay behind left me with a keen sense of loss, and of pride in my country. On the other hand, I was quite excited with the prospect of now being close to all the members of the family whom I knew only from family lore at the dinner table.

2

Paraná

The personnel needs of the Adventist Conferences in Argentina, Chile, Paraguay and Uruguay are administered by the Union president of the Austral Union, and a small circle of his friends.[1] The appointments are then rubber-stamped by conference committees. The vote would be a "call" to serve in this or that capacity, which the recipient was expected to respond to as one coming from God. It happened that the current secretary-treasurer of the Central Argentine Conference, Ernesto Steger, was called to serve at the Northern Argentine Conference, and my father was called to serve in his place. Thus our family planned to move directly to Parana. Upon our arrival, however, we learned that Steger was refusing to go to the Northern Conference. For a few weeks we wished my father had not accepted his "call". The Conference and the Union tried to persuade Steger to obey the church's call, but he wouldn't budge. In the end, my father was asked to go to Corrientes and serve as secretary-treasurer there until a more permanent arrangement could be made. Since my oldest brother, Ewaldo, had completed his pre-medical course work in Montevideo and planed to enter the medical school at Rosario, my parents decided that while my father went to Corrientes, the rest of the family would spend the year in Rosario, the second largest city in Argentina.

---

1   In the Adventist ecclesiastical structure, the General Conference is made up of Divisions. Divisions are made up of Unions. Unions are made up of Conferences, and Conferences are made up of churches.

We rented a modest house on Jujuy Street, just a few houses from Boulevard Ordóñez. The local Adventist church was a few blocks away on Catamarca Street. In Rosario there was no adventist church school, so my mother decided to enroll Klinton and me at the German school that was open even while the war was raging in Europe. This in itself was a good indication of the difference between Uruguay and Argentina.

My brothers and I experienced a harsh reality check when we enrolled into the Argentine educational system. All of us were required to repeat grades. The medical school took an entire year to decide how many credits it was going to give Ewaldo for his pre-medical course in Uruguay. At the end of the year, he was told that he should return to Montevideo, do a first year of medicine there, then come back to Rosario, take seventeen exams on secondary school subjects having to do with Argentine history, geography and economics, and then start first year of medicine with them. It was not hard for Ewaldo and the family to decide that he should go back to Montevideo and complete his medical education there. In the meantime he had squandered a year of his life. I had to repeat the grade I had already done with Miss Genover.

Repeating third grade at the German school in Rosario created all sorts of tensions within me. My mother, I am sure, thought she was doing the best for me, and, in a very real way, she was. Even though their families had left for Russia two hundred years earlier, both she and my father had strong identity ties to Germany, though neither had any sympathy for the Nazis. They had grown up in Entre Ríos reading a German Bible and attending church where German was spoken. When my mother found out that there was a German school in Rosario, she enthusiastically enrolled Evelyn, Klinton and me. Lyllian was already in secondary school. The teachers and the families of the other students at the German school, whether they sympathized with the Nazis or not, were wholly in favor of a German victory in the war. So, while at the Crandon I had been openly rooting for the Allies, at the German school in Rosario, I soon learned, I could not let my allegiance be known. For a ten year old boy, peer acceptance was a must. I vividly remember the day in 1944 when the Allies entered Berlin and the Germans surrendered. It was as though history had come to an end for everyone at the German school. That day classes were suspended. It was a day of mourning. As far as I know, that was the last year that school was open.

During the year at Rosario our family's budget was stretched tightly. My father's meager church salary was not enough to support two houses: his in Corrientes and ours in Rosario. To ease the economic pinch, my mother gave room and board to two Adventist bachelors. Both were nice, middle aged fellows. They made for very lively conversations at the dinner table. One of them was French, Aimee Fayard, a traveling salesperson for several companies. The other was a Bolivian in the fourth year of medical school, Manuel Ampuero Matta. Both men were very amiable characters, especially Ampuero Matta, who was a typical bohemian student for life. He had already been studying medicine for ten years, but was nowhere near graduating. Also, since Ampuero was separated from his wife, and at the time there was no legal divorce in Argentina, this added another twist to his personal profile, and also left him outside the graces of the church.

In Rosario there was a cinema which only showed news reels and Walt Disney movies and cartoons. Around the dinner table our extended family decided it was not a sin to attend this cinema, even though there was no such consensus at church. Both of our pensionistas took us at one time or another to that cinema, whose name I no longer recall. I also remember going there to see Disney's Fantasia. I was overwhelmed by Leopold Stokowsky and the Philadelphia Orchestra. It made me an orchestra fan forever.

My best friend at the German school, Walter Niebauer, who lived a couple of blocks from my home on Blvd. Ordóñez, convinced my mother to let me go with him to the cowboy serials that played on Friday afternoons at a neighborhood cinema. I don't think I would have received permission if my father had been around, but my mother was more open to culture and the arts.

Walter's mother regularly took me to see cowboy films that cut the story each week when the guy with the white hat was cornered in a barn or behind a big boulder. Once during that year Mrs. Niebauer took Walter and me to a live theatrical performance of Pussyfuz with Boots. These exposures to activities that were not approved by the church made me realize that not everything proscribed by my religion was as it was described. Fascination with the movies made me daydream that one day maybe I could become a matinee idol myself. These dreams created the first real inner tensions in spiritual matters in my life. Only ten years old, I understood that it would be difficult, if not impossible, to be a movie actor and an Adventist. At the time, I could not conceive myself not an Adventist. Therefore, there was no question that those dreams of becoming a movie star, were only distracting fantasies. Their persistence, however, was something that at times disturbed me. It caused me to question the strength of my commitment to the faith. I did not know how to deal with doubts about the reasonableness of what the church required.

In February or March of 1945 we finally moved to Paraná, where my parents rented a house on La Rioja street. The secretary-treasurer of the Central Conference still would not budge from his post. To resolve the situation, the ecclesiastical authorities asked my father to become the manager of the Book Agency that supplied denominational books, magazines and pamphlets to all the churches in the Conference, as well as to the canvassers who sold literature door to door. It was, certainly, a humiliating experience for my father, but, being the marvelous person and Christian he was, he took it in stride and continued to serve his church faithfully and contentedly. His superiors, however, did not reward his good spirit. A few years later they forced him into retirement before he had reached retirement age, or was ready for it. He did not belong to any "camarilla," or clique, in which members took care of each other within denominational politics. As I watched what happened to my dad, I made a solemn promise to God in the privacy of my prayer that I would never become an employee of the church. I could already see that there was constant infighting at the Conference offices, favoritism for friends and relatives, gossip about what someone was doing to someone else. All this made ecclesiastical politics no different from the politics of the nation, and in those years Juan Domingo Perón had begun to project his powerful personality on the political horizon.

Paraná is a prosperous provincial capital perched on the high palisades of the eastern bank of the Paraná River. The city has two centers. One is the Plaza San Martín. The Cathedral, City Hall, the Social Club, the Savoy Hotel and the Teacher's College all faced the square. The most popular activity at this plaza on Saturday nights was the retreta. Soon after sundown men would start walking counterclockwise on the outer perimeter of the square. Women walked in the interior half of the same sidewalk in a clockwise direction. The object was to see and be seen. As soon as you spotted a lovely lady walking around, you had to come up with the appropriate piropo (a playfully flattering phrase) for her. Usually at the next encounter, half a circumference later, she would have something to say in response. Or you could just go to the retreta and walk around talking with your friends. No one walked on the retreta by himself. On the sidewalks across the street the tables at the bars and confiterías would be full of people also catching the scene. The doors and French windows of the social club would be wide open and the local aristocracy exhibited themselves on plush chairs and sofas smoking cigars, talking, or playing checkers, chess or cards. Luckily for us, the retretas began after Sabbath sundown worship at home.

The other center of town was the provincial Government Building, a solid italianate palazzo that occupied a whole block and had two plazas, one on the North and one on the South. The Adventist church, and the Central Conference offices, were one block from the South plaza of the Government Building, on the corner of Cervantes and Córdoba streets. While we lived in Paraná the church had its services in a hall in the second story of the office building, which had a totally separate entrance, with a large stairway

21

giving access to the hall. After one year, my parents bought a house three doors down the street from the church entrance on Córdoba street. My life soon revolved around my studies and the church next door.

As soon as we had arrived in Paraná my mother learned that there was a music conservatory and a school of beaux arts and enrolled me to take piano and drawing lessons. My efforts at making music proved a total waste of time. I seemed to have no natural ability to play the keys. At the Escuela de Bellas Artes, the curriculum was very old fashioned. The first year was spent at a table copying drawings with a pencil. The second year we worked on an easel doing still life with a pencil. In the third year we did still life with charcoal. In the fourth, one graduated to tempera. In the fifth, oil. Not until the sixth year did students work with live models using charcoal, pencil, tempera or oil. Of course, the live models were properly dressed. I lasted only to year three. Still, my experience drawing at the school alerted me at an early age to the significance of human achievements in the arts. It was a healthy counterweight to the continuous denigration of the human race that was the premise of all the sermons at church and the religious literature at home. The Calvinist notion of the total depravity of humanity after the fall into sin made it a requirement to look with suspicion at any expression of human achievements that did not openly render glory to God. When my mother enrolled me at the Escuela de Bellas Artes, she had to do quite a bit of explaining to other members of the church who looked with suspicion upon my development in that area. Besides, as several church elders pointed out, painters were notorious for their loose sexual mores. Paraná, with its retretas and art schools, was where I went through the excitements of puberty. I was, however, unlike some painters and musicians, a very bashful, introverted kind of guy who agonized in the presence of girls, even though in my daydreams I imagined delightful intimacies.

The first year after our move to Paraná, the church brought in an evangelist to conduct meetings at a public hall close to

22

downtown. He was Victor Aeschlimann, a Chilean of German descent. In Argentina the Catholic Church is the official church. The Constitution specifies that the President, besides being a natural citizen of at least thirty five years of age, has to be a Catholic. Every official state function, like the celebration of Independence Day, or Flag Day, began with a High Mass officiated by the local bishop. In public secondary schools students were taught religion by a Catholic priest. Among the ministries of the national government, there was also a ministry of religion and worship. This meant that religious freedom was a prerogative of the Catholic Church only. For the other religious communities there was only religious toleration. They had to register with the federal government in order to function in the country, and they could only do what the ministry of religion and worship allowed them to do. The knowledge that their registration could be revoked at any time had a big impact on how Protestant denominations, including Adventists, functioned.

To facilitate interest in the lectures, and neutralize prejudices against Protestants, the first three or four lectures dealt with topics of general interest and health matters. Eventually, however, Aeschlimann's lectures turned to the presentation of the Adventist apocalyptic gospel. Every Christian denomination has an effective canon within canonical Scripture. For Lutherans it is Paul's Letter to the Romans. For Catholics, the Gospel of Matthew. For Adventist, the apocalyptic books of Daniel and Revelation. All evangelistic meetings center on the interpretation of these apocalyptic books, which Adventists have always considered to be prescriptive biblical prophecy.

I had, of course, been indoctrinated in this interpretation of Daniel and Revelation at an early age. It has been part of me for as long as I can remember being aware of myself. Sabbath School lessons dealt with it on a regular basis, and Sabbath sermons were exceptional if they did not refer to several texts of Daniel or Revelation. On most occasions, of course, we dealt with these texts among ourselves, as the people who had the key to their interpretation and, therefore, enjoyed a significant advantage over the rest of humankind. The lectures by Victor Aeschlimann in that rented hall in Paraná were the first time I heard what I considered our private possession presented to "outsiders". It was a strange experience, full of conflicting feelings. On one hand, I felt our knowledge of the meaning of these prophecies was too precious a thing to be given out freely. On the other, I tried to put myself in the shoes of the "outsider" who was being told about the Bible's picture of humanity's future, and of the sacrifices he or she would be required to make to be counted among the blessed at the Second Coming. Accepting our version of the Gospel was not easy. In fact, I was assured, it was not supposed to be easy. I was somewhat amazed, therefore, that people who had not been born in the faith would actually join. Deep inside, I could not understand how anyone would accept our interpretation as valid.

Adventists are well known for their use of visual aids in order to illustrate the vision of the statue of Nabuchadnezzar that Daniel and his companions refused to worship, of the four beasts that come out of the sea in the seventh chapter of the book of Daniel, as well as of the fight of the ram and the he-goat in chapter 8. Aeschlimann had bigger-than-life depictions of these monsters on cardboard. By that time I knew all these narratives of Daniel by heart, as well as the Adventist interpretation of them. But when I attended Aeschlimann's lectures I began to sense that there was something manipulative about the interpretation, even though my knowledge of world history was almost non-existent. What the evangelist presented as obvious was thought such only by Adventists. Why was it that what was assumed to be absolutely clear was not accepted by most students of the Bible? Could it be that those who did not identify the apocalyptic symbols as we did were not obtuse but wise?

I had a hard time understanding why these prophecies, according to our interpretation, made reference to events which historians did not consider very important. Still, I felt satisfaction from knowing I belonged to a very special, blessed, minority with a special message to give to the world, even if it was quite esoteric.

In Paraná I completed grade school in public schools and was accepted to the Colegio Nacional for my secondary education. Unlike grade school, where a group of twenty to twenty five students had all the subjects taught by a single teacher, at the Colegio the small group of students was always together in the same classroom under the supervision of a celador, who took care of discipline during breaks and until the professor entered the room. The subjects in the curriculum were taught by different professors who came to the classroom. It happened that on my first day at the Colegio, the first subject was botany, and the professor was Dr. Guzmán, a medical doctor who lived around the corner from my home. His son had been my classmate in fifth and sixth grade, and I had been in his home a time or two. Dr. Guzmán entered the classroom, took the roll call, and stepped to the back of the room. He then called me to the front. I was perplexed. It was our first day of classes. We had not been given a reading assignment for which I could be held responsible. Once I was standing at the front of the class with strangers looking at me, Dr. Guzmán asked me, "What is life?" I explained I did not know that this was our subject for that day. He explained he was not expecting me to have done a special study of the subject. He just wanted to have my answer. I answered, "Life is a gift of God." He said my answer would probably be acceptable in a theology class, but this was a class in botany, an area in biology. He wanted a scientific definition. I had no scientific definition to give him, so I remained silent making it look like I was thinking hard in search of an answer. The minutes passed slowly and everybody was silent. Twenty or thirty minutes passed in total silence. I was still standing at the front of the class wishing I were anywhere but there. Now Dr. Guzmán asked if anyone in the class could offer a definition for life. One or two students made suggestions with which Dr. Guzmán found fault. After some more minutes of silence, he repeated the question to me, still standing at the front of the class. I repeated my original definition, which he again rejected as unacceptable in a botany class. Finally the bell rang. Dr. Guzmán stepped up to the front of the class, turned around to face us all and said, "I want you to know that we will spend the year in this science class studying life, but there is no scientific definition of life." Then he walked out of the classroom.

Of all the hours I have spent in classrooms, both as a student and as a teacher, I think that first hour in secondary school was the most memorable. Dr. Guzman never told us exactly what point he wished to make on that first class. Was it that science has its limits? Was it that theology and science should be kept separate? Was it to emphasize the irony of spending so much time studying something we could not define? Many years later, I have wondered whether Dr. Guzman that day had been brilliant, pedestrian, or pompous. In any case, I have always been grateful to him for having called my attention to one of the most important aspects of life in our times. If you are a person of faith, you must squarely face the necessity of determining how to relate your faith to the knowledge made available by science.

The secondary school curriculum included a religion class twice a week. Students who were not Catholic were offered an alternative class in ethics. During my four years in public secondary schools I found myself in an ethics class with four or five other students who were Protestant or Jewish. The classes in ethics were taught by professors trained in classical philosophy who, for the most part, were conservative Neothomist Catholics. During my first year at the Colegio Nacional I learned about the ethical teachings of Socrates, Plato and Aristotle. The following years we studied the Epicureans, the Stoics and the Neoplatonists. Later we studied some of the Scholastics, Descartes, Kant, Schopenhauer and Nietsche. Of course, we did not read primary sources. It was a matter of taking notes from the lectures given by the professors. I have always been grateful to the school that taught me at an early stage how the perennial questions facing humans who endeavor to live a good life had been answered in the past. These studies certainly influenced the way I was trying to answer some of these same questions in the middle of the twentieth century. They also demonstrated I needed to wrestle with how my faith was to be related to the knowledge made available by reason.

During my second year at the Colegio Nacional, a new student joined our class. He had transferred to the Colegio from the local Catholic seminary. It soon became obvious that he knew more than the rest of us. The educational authorities had dealt him the same card they had given me when I arrived from Uruguay. Because he had not taken some subjects that were part of the national curriculum, he was forced to catch up in lower grades. At the seminary, of course, he had studied theology. My classmates knew I was an "evangelical" who studied the Bible, therefore some of them were eager to have a debate between the seminarian and the evangelical. At the time, I felt comfortable with my ability to explain God's will as expressed in the Bible, so I was confident I could hold my own with Catholics who, according to what I had been told, didn't read the Bible. (It must be remembered that this was Latin America pre Vatican II.) As it turned out, five or six of our classmates arranged for us to go to plaza San Miguel after school for our expected debate. I have no recollection of the content of our conversation, but I remember well what happened. I was able to quote Bible texts, mainly from Daniel and Revelation. He was able to argue his points logically while also quoting Bible texts. I left the encounter totally deflated and perfectly aware that I had not been up to the challenge presented by someone trained not just to memorize, but to think. I had to come to terms with the fact that there was another way of interpreting the Bible which seemed at times more logical than the way I had been taught. I also realized that I needed to rethink my understanding of Catholicism. After all, I had not been challenged by a Catholic theologian with advanced training. I had been talking with a boy, just like me, at most two years older than I. Catholic bashing was an everyday occurrence among Adventists. According to our reading of the prophecies of Daniel and Revelation, Catholicism, and especially the Papacy, is the evil power that persecutes the beleaguered people of God. Here I had faced a peer who had been going to school at a Catholic seminary (where students entered at the secondary level) and had been put to shame by my parochial views. It was obvious that his training in philosophy placed him at a distinct advantage. It was sobering.

Living in Paraná allowed our family to reestablish connections with our extended family. While in Montevideo and in Rosario I had a very hazy idea of my grandmother, uncles and cousins. On my father's side, my grandmother, Carolina Feder Weiss, had died many years before I was born. I got to know my grandfather, José Weiss, when the family took a vacation from Montevideo. I must have been about five at the time, so my memory of that trip was sketchy, even though it included some very strong images. One of them was of an evening when a group of men were talking in front of my grandfather's home about the possibility of war in Europe. What I remember is that everyone was anxious to know what my grandfather thought of the situation. After all, he had left Europe when he was 26; therefore, he was the only one who knew Europe first hand. That was around 1939. When we returned from Uruguay in 1944, he had been dead for a year already. My father's two brothers were now farming the land that had belonged to grandfather. A tenant farmer cultivated the land that my father had inherited. My grandfather had donated a small parcel next to his home for the building of the local Seventh-day Adventist church in Crespo Campo. It was on a dirt country road, with the lands of Uncle Julio and Uncle Santiago around it. This was an hour and a half horse-and-buggy-ride from the town of Crespo, which was a two and a half hours' train-ride from Paraná.

Uncle Santiago and his wife had no children of their own, but they had an adopted daughter, Aurora, who was about five years older than I. Uncle Julio and his wife, on the other hand, had eight children, five girls and three boys. The girls came first, and by the time we came back from Uruguay all but the youngest were already married. The three boys, Arturo, Eduardo and Tito, were roughly the same ages as Ewaldo, Klinton and I. Tito and I were almost exactly the same age, and we became great friends. A few times he came to Paraná to spend a week with me in the city. Most of the time, I would go to spend time in the country with him. We did chores around the farm together. I never learned to milk a cow, but my cousins were experts. In the morning, by the time I got up they were already finishing the milking, which had to be done by seven o'clock. Five neighbors had an arrangement by which one of them would take their milk to Camps, a desolate train stop about three miles away. The train would then take the milk to the Nestle factory at Nogoyá.

Uncle Julio also had about a thousand chickens needing our attention whose purpose was to produce eggs that were sold at the farmer's co-operative at Crespo. In the Summer, there was corn to be harvested and alfalfa to be cut, dried and stored. In the Winter, there was plowing to be done, fences to be mended and the horses' harnesses to be repaired. Of course every week of the year there were chicken houses to be cleaned. I must confess that I really enjoyed spending time in Uncle Julio's farm doing chores, enjoying the open air, the daily contact with animals, the hard work and the wonderful meals prepared by Aunt Amalia and Cousin Nelly. That Tito and I could take long horse rides to bring or take horses or cows from their pastures, or to run errands, was just the icing on the cake.

Grandfather David Riffel, my mother's father, had been a rather prosperous farmer. He was closer to Crespo than Grandfather José Weiss. He and his wife had had sixteen children: thirteen boys and three girls. He had bought the third automobile ever to travel the roads of Entre Ríos. In the twenties he had borrowed a large amount of money and bought land in Santa Fe province, across the Paraná River, with the intention of starting a large lumber operation. He put one of his sons in charge of developing the new venture. Two things conspired against him: the managerial incompetence of his son, and the economic collapse of 1929. To pay his debts, he was forced to sell the land he had farmed for years

29

and the large house in which he had raised his family. With the little money he had left he bought much less fertile land in a rather primitive section of the province and built a much humbler home. Soon afterwards he died feeling defeated and tired. His wife, Grandma Julia, then took over the new residence in Crucecitas, somewhere between Viale and Nogoyá. One of her sons, Uncle Daniel, who had tried his luck at different enterprises in Crespo, now decided to buy some land next to his mother and built a house for his family about one hundred yards from Grandma's home.

No one in Crucecitas, or in Viale, where she went to sell her eggs and buy her groceries, knew my grandmother by her last name. To a few she was Doña Julia, but to almost everybody, and certainly to all the members of her large family, she was "la Mutter" (the mother in German). She had arrived in Argentina at the age of eleven. Before leaving her small Volhynian village she attended school for one or two years, where she learned to read in German. In Argentina she had had to work since being a teenager. Somehow, probably on account of belonging to the Adventist church, she had married the son of one of the most prosperous German immigrants in the region. Now, however, she found herself trying to start all over again from scratch, when she was no longer young, and had given birth to sixteen children in a rural environment. By now her children were all gone, so she had added young adopted girls to her family. I got to know two of them well, Epifania, who was known as "la Fanny," and Juana, a black girl brought by my mother from the Argentine Northeast when she and my father had worked for the church near the brazilian border, before they went to Uruguay. I knew her as "la tía Juana." She was the happiest human being around, always eager to do something to make someone else also happy.

Living in Paraná meant that every year I would spend some time with "la Mutter" in Crucecitas, where I would do chores for her, and also with cousins at Uncle Daniel's home, or with Uncle Julio in Crespo Campo. I soon realized that the Weisses and the Riffels did not see eye to eye on most things. Of the thirteen boys to whom la Mutter gave life, five became Adventist pastors, and two of them climbed up the ecclesiastical ladder reaching administrative positions at the division level. Others were rather active lay leaders. A few were lukewarm Adventists, and one, the one who Grandfather sent to manage the lumber business in Santa Fe, was now the bad apple of the clan. La Mutter was a very independent lady who defied her minister sons by drinking mate two or three times a day and taking Wunderbalsam, a German miracle syrup with a small alcohol content, as medicine for various maladies. This made her suspect in the eyes of "good Adventists." By contrast, the Weisses in Crespo Campo were all very faithful Adventists who studied their Bibles religiously.

When we first arrived from Uruguay, the Seventh-day Adventist church in Crespo Campo was a building from the 1920s. It was a rectangular hall with room for about seventy-five people. Attached to it, making an L, were two rooms used during the week for church school and on Saturdays for Sabbath School classes. The building still stands today as a museum to the Adventist pioneers, and it is the first Adventist church in South America. When Pastor Frank H. Westphal arrived at my great-grandfather's home, the original Adventist community had started near Aldea Jacobi. Later, when the Weisses acquired land closer to the road to Ramirez and my grandfather Weiss donated a plot of land, the church was erected where it was. When we settled in Paraná a new church was being built next to the L shaped structure. This was more of a church building with a nice art deco facade and room for about 250 people. Its dedication in 1944 marked the fiftieth anniversary of the establishment of the first Adventist church in South America. Adventists from all over the Central Conference, the Austral Union, the South American Division, and representatives of the General Conference in Washington, D.C., participated in the event.

Soon afterwards, Theodore Lucas came to Crespo Campo for a Youth Congress. Elder Theodore Lucas was the Youth Leader at the General Conference. The visit of Elder Lucas was even more impressive than the visit of Elder McElhany had been a few years

31

before. For one thing I was no longer a little boy; by now I was a sprouting teenager. Of course he also had the aura of coming from that Enchanted Land to the north where everyone is religious and the leaders of the Church at the General Conference posses an aura of holiness not seen among common mortals. Elder Lucas stayed for several days and preached a series of sermons, and as a youth leader he was most effective. Even though we conferred on him a magnificent aura on account of his position, he had an uncanny ability, even through a translator, to let everyone know that he was a normal human being. His sermons left us all certain that the Second Coming of Christ would take place within, at the most, the next five years. We had made reference to the "signs of the times", but not too much to fulfilling prophecies. Still, we had prepared ourselves spiritually to meet the Lord in the air as He descended upon the earth. The reality of the imminence of this cosmic event was unquestionable. The concluding sermon of the Congress was a consecration service. When Elder Lucas made the call, we all, full of the Spirit, stood and committed our lives to Christ. Then the lights were turned out and a torch was lit by Elder Lucas at the pulpit, while little candles were passed around. As the torch was passed along, every one lit their own candle as it came by. Those lighting their candles committed themselves to finishing "the work" before Christ came. It was at that youth congress that I became convinced I needed to spend my life in service to Christ. My baptism a few years later, at the large pool of water created by a beautiful waterfall on a little tributary of the Arroyo Ensenada, came and went as a natural event in the course of things.

At Crespo Campo everyone was conscious they were members of the first Adventist church in South America. The services were conducted in German and, even after a year at the German school in Rosario, I did not understand everything that was said. Still, I would get the gist of it. There was no doubt about the earnestness and the fervor of the believers. In that farming community, besides the families of my father's two brothers, there were the families of David, Enrique, Roberto, Daniel and José Weiss, all my father's cousins. Two Schmidt, two Bernhardt, and one Roscher families, together with all the Weisses, made the core of that church. What I remember most vividly about those services are the German hymns sung with a contagious enthusiasm and abandoned gusto while accompanied by a decrepit little harmonium made in Chicago, Illinois.

One of the daughters of Uncle Julio, Alicia, married a Brazilian who had come to study nursing and theology in the Adventist College and Sanatorium at Puiggari. Alicia was also a student nurse there, and after both graduated they went to Brazil. There they worked as medical missionaries on a small boat that went up and down the San Francisco River, stopping on its banks wherever someone needed medical assistance. They lived eight months of the year on their boat. Neither one of them had an advanced degree in medicine or in dentistry, but in that hinterland they treated all kinds of tropical diseases and extracted teeth with amazingly good results. Soon the people who lived along the river would recognize the sound of their motor and post a flag on the bank of the river as a signal for them to stop. Every six years Alicia and Pablo Seidel, would come to Uncle Julio's home on furlough and we would all listen eagerly to the many stories they would tell of God's blessings in their work, as well as stories of encounters with yacarés (a smaller South American crocodile), anacondas, poisonous snakes, pirañas and giant ants. Their stories sparked the desire to do my service for Christ on a mission boat on one of the many large rivers of South America. I was conflicted, however, by my oath not to work for the denomination, and I did not quite envision myself as a pastor. In time I became interested in the possibility of working among the isolated Indian tribes that lived on the banks of the tributaries of the Amazon river in Peru and Ecuador.

In Crucecitas I became enthralled by my cousin "el Pibe," Uncle Daniel's oldest boy. He was a bit younger than my brother Ewaldo and had been named after him. His full name was Ewaldo Valentin Riffel, but no one remembered that. To everyone throughout the course of his life he was "el Pibe." Pibe is an Argentinian word for a young boy. It is more or less the equivalent of "botija" in Uruguay, "chamaco" in Chile, "chamarro" in Mexico, etc. Unlike Ewaldo, who was very busy studying medicine, el Pibe did not have a care in the world. After third grade he decided that he did not need further schooling since he had already learned basic grammar and arithmetic. From then on, he was self-taught. He was happy working on the farm, but at night he was a voracious reader.

He had not only rebelled against a formal education, but had also rebelled against the Church. He was his own person. No one, especially his parents could tell him what to do. In some ways, however, he was a most dutiful son. He was a very healthy and strong young man with no fear of hard work, and he worked faithfully for his father in whatever was asked of him. At this time Uncle Daniel rented land from some of the neighbors and had a revolving herd of cattle. He would go to auctions and buy cattle, bring them to fields he rented to fatten them, and then sell them to the meat packing plant. The herds had to be moved by a couple of riders on horseback in journeys that took several days. El Pibe, even though only eighteen or twenty, would be responsible for the herds on the march. On the farm, he would do most of the plowing and sowing. For all these labors both the Riffels in Crucecitas and the Weisses in Crespo Campo relied on horses. All my uncles needed to have a herd of around twenty five horses to do the farm work. I enjoyed being out in the fields with my cousins, but my favorite was el Pibe.

He did not have any of the religious restraints that kept me walking on the straight and narrow. On the week-ends he would take his most beautiful horse and go to the homes of friends. On Saturday nights he would be at some dance in a bar at some crossroad. He cut a rather handsome figure and was quite popular with the ladies. This, at times, got him into trouble with other men who were rather jealous or protective. After his adventures he would tell me about them during the week as we looked after recently born calves in the middle of some field, or while we harvested alfalfa into a large stack in the corner of another. He was the typical Don Juan who enjoyed telling of his exploits more than actually carrying them out. I was, undoubtedly, a jealous listener.

What I liked most about el Pibe was that he knew every tango played on the radio. The Weisses in Crespo Campo did not have electricity, but at the houses of both la Mutter and Uncle Daniel in Crucecitas there was a wind mill that charged six volt batteries in series. With them it was possible to have lights at night and listen to the radio. El Pibe had heard them all. After listening to just a couple of the initial bars, he could tell the name of the tango, the author of the lyrics, the composer of the music, and identify both the orchestra and the singer you were listening to. I admired and envied this ability of his. He could do this with the tangos and with the milongas, valses, and folkloric pieces. Besides, he could also sing well. Thus out in the fields, el Pibe taught me to sing tangos, milongas and valses, some of which have stayed with me till this day. This, however, was not considered to be something a good Christian should be doing. According to orthodox Adventism, such music belonged to the kingdom of Satan, and Christians were supposed to shield themselves from these songs that were allurements of the Devil. No such music was ever heard in a Weiss home. I was always conscious that el Pibe was a "bad" influence on me, but I could never break the power of his personality over me.

As a healthy young man, el Pibe had a very strong sex drive and the reputation that goes with it. When we lived on La Rioja street in Paraná, it was a well known fact that a couple of blocks away, at 60 Missiones street, there was a brothel. Many times when el Pibe came to Paraná, I would walk with him to the house and go to a beautiful square nearby and wait for him to come out. I was always amazed that his visits to Misiones 60 usually took less than ten minutes. Of course, I was at the time entering my adolescence and awakening to the life of the body. The example of el Pibe was, undoubtedly, exciting. But I must confess that I was never tempted to go with him into the brothel. At the Colegio Nacional, I knew that my classmates were experimenting. Some of them regularly received money from their fathers to go and release their pent up sexual urges. All of a sudden, I also discovered that girls had a special attraction, and some of them were actually somehow attracted to me. My shyness always made it difficult for me to start a conversation with strangers. Even around people I knew, I had never been much of a talker. In the presence of girls, therefore, I felt awkward. I could only deal with them from a distance, and communicated best in my imagination.

It was, therefore, quite a surprise when one day in my second year at the Colegio I found a little piece of paper carefully folded and placed in a crack on my desk. In the morning the classrooms were used by the boys. In the afternoons the girls used the same desks. In a period of a few days, three or four of us in class found missives left for us by the girls using our desks in the afternoon. My correspondence with the stranger began in a rather innocent fashion, but lasted for much of the year. Of course there was much anticipation for the day of our meeting. But my correspondent was playing hide and seek with me. Then September 21 arrived. In Argentina it is celebrated as Spring Day, or Student Day. To celebrate there was a big picnic at the Parque Urquiza, a beautiful park on the embankment that drops to the river basin. In the afternoon the students had the municipal theatre at their disposal and used the occasion to poke fun at the professors in skits and comic acts. It happened that el Pibe had come to town and he was determined to help me meet the author of the love letters left at my desk almost every day for months. Of course, I was curious about the girl whose letters made me spend hours in a reverie. Nevertheless, the encounter never took place, in spite of el Pibe's urgent coaching. Besides my shyness, my strong religious convictions could not envision a sentimental attachment to a non-Adventist girl.

While enjoying my studies at the Colegio Nacional, I continued to have a strong attachment to life on the rippled fields my uncles farmed in the rolling hills of Entre Ríos. Uncle Daniel had the only

36

piece of mechanized equipment working on those fields that belonged to one of my relatives. He owned an old Case steam tractor that powered a harvesting machine. For about a month and a half a crew would harvest the wheat, flax, oats, barley and rye not only in my uncle's fields, but also in the fields of neighbors who did not have a means of harvesting. The tractor had wide metal wheels to move across plowed land. The water for the steam was heated by burning chaff from whatever was being harvested. Since it would burn quickly, two men were needed to keep the fire going, another was needed to look after all the moving parts, keeping them oiled and supervising the operation of the tractor. A large belt transferred power to the harvesting machine once it was set on a field. Two men fed sheaves from the top; two men handled the bags as they were filled, and one was charged with the smooth operation of the harvester. Then there were four or five wagons that brought the sheaves from the field to the harvester, and men walking in the field loading the sheaves into the horse-drawn wagons. Besides, there was a cook and his assistant who had a little trailer as a kitchen. All in all, the harvesting operation employed about thirty men. At the end of the campaign the tractor with the harvester and kitchen wagon would be brought to the barn to be stored till next year. For the grand occasion one or two sheep, thirty chickens, a large batch of potato salad, vegetables, plenty of desserts, and large quantities of soft drinks would be brought out to make a feast for all. My cousins and I would spend any remaining steam in the tractor blowing its whistle.

The most memorable part of those harvesting campaigns were the evenings when Uncle Daniel's fields were being harvested, and the machine and its workers were close to home. Most of them would spend the night sleeping under the stars around the campfire next to the kitchen. Before going to bed, however, they sat around the campfire sipping mate and telling stories. I never attended a youth camp and listened to stories around a camp fire. I think, however, that the stories told in those campfires, especially in church related youth camps, have nothing to do with the ones I loved to hear from those sturdy harvest workers in the grain fields of Entre Ríos. Most of the stories were about twisted love affairs that ended in a duel and a burial. In fact, Crucecitas, where "la Mutter" and Uncle Daniel lived, had received its name because of the many crosses that marked places where people had died along the road, not on account of traffic accidents but, in most cases, of duels with knives over a woman. Next to the gate to "la Mutter's" place there was a cross, and a few yards from the gate to Uncle Daniel's home there was another. Many of the stories told of balls of light that emerged from these burials and ran after someone who happened to pass by at night. Stories about "luces malas" (evil lights) abounded in the folklore of the region, and the way they were told by rugged men under the open sky in the middle of a field next to a threshing machine is one of the most potent memories from my adolescence.

When I spent time in Crucecitas, I would stay at "la Mutter's" home, whose most remarkable feature were the tile floors in the sitting room and the bedrooms. Different patterns were indiscriminately mixed in each room. The results made an unforgettable impression. I never asked why the tiles had been set that way. I have since come to think that when the house was built, after my grandfather's financial collapse, the only tiles they could afford were leftovers from other jobs. The house had a kitchen that was linked to the main structure by a corridor with a grape arbor. It was unusual for me to be the only grandchild in the house. During the summer grandchildren from different sons and daughters would be visiting on vacation. In the evenings, then, we would all be playing well into the night in the orchard and the patio next to the house.

Many mornings when we got up we would discover that "la Mutter" was gone. Some neighbor, at times from rather far away, had come in the night and taken her to his home. Sometimes she would not return for three or even four days. "La Mutter" was famous throughout the region as the best midwife, and she went when she was called not caring whether she was taken to a

38

forgotten hut or an expensive villa. It was a source of pride that my grandmother, who had a third grade education, helped people this way, leaving it up to her neighbors to pay her what they could. Of course, she had experienced sixteen births herself, She had also read German medical books on her own. Between that preparation and many years of experience tending to others, no doubt, she knew what she was doing. During the days of her absences, things around the house continued to run smoothly under the supervision of "la Fanny."

In 1947 Uncle Daniel sold his lands in Crucecitas and bought a business in Segui, a little town on the same narrow-gage railroad tracks that linked Viale and Crespo. By now in her late sixties "la Mutter" was getting to be far advanced in age, given the life expectancy at the time. She had been born in Rozchyshche in 1880. Since another son, Enrique, had a big store in Viale, she sold her house and land and moved to a little house around the corner from her son. Once "la Mutter" settled in Viale, not much time passed before the local doctors asked her to be in charge of the delivery room at the local hospital. Thus, "la Mutter" became the director of the delivery room and the neo-natal ward at the municipal hospital in Viale. Her fame as the best midwife in that part of the world only increased. She will forever be remembered for being the loving and generous person she was, happy to be useful and enjoying the good name she held in the land.

In Segui Uncle Daniel prospered as a middleman in egg distribution. He would buy the eggs produced by the farmers in the surrounding region and sell them groceries. With his truck he would then take the eggs to Buenos Aires, or to a cold storage place in Rosario to wait until the price of eggs rose. This had been the kind of business that Uncle Enrique conducted in Viale for years. Eventually uncles Daniel and Enrique built a factory that produced chicken feed, which they would sell to the farmers whose eggs they bought. El Pibe now became the one who drove Uncle Daniel's truck. At times I would go to spend a few days with my cousins in Uncle Daniel's home in Segui. When my visit was over, I would get in the truck with el Pibe, who was supposed to drop me off in Paraná. A few times, however, I made the trip to Buenos Aires and he would drop me off on the return trip. The whole trip was made shorter by listening to popular music on the radio and singing our hearts out.

By 1950 Klinton decided that he would also study medicine, and our family budget could not afford two sons studying in different cities. Since my father had been forced to retire, we were free to live wherever we pleased, so my parents decided that the whole family would move to Buenos Aires. El Pibe came with his truck and took our furniture to Buenos Aires.

For me it was rather difficult to leave Paraná. I had spent some of the best years there. The Colegio Nacional had excellent teachers, and I had made very good friends. My parents had been able to buy a large house in a nice neighborhood with a large back yard full of wonderful fruit trees. My father had worked hard to enrich the soil in order to have a generous vegetable garden. We also had built a decent court for playing bochas. I had also helped him to build a brick oven where on Sundays we would cook some special breads and a wonderful roast of beef or dorado, a delicious fish from the Paraná river. During this time, playing bochas and working in the backyard I had developed a real friendship with my father, whom I had always admired but had not really gotten close to before. His quiet ways, soft-spokenness and humble integrity made an impression on me as I was beginning to discover the world around me. Paraná, after all, was a rather lazy river town where temptations were not ubiquitous. There I was able to listen to my father and reflect on the wisdom of his ways. Buenos Aires loomed on the horizon as a totally different kind of town, one quite capable of terminating the serenity of life in the provinces.

3

Buenos Aires

When we moved to Buenos Aires, in March 1950, my cousin Arturo secured for us a wonderful house built by the church as a home for the president of the South American Division. He and another medical student lived with us. With the rise of Perón in Argentina and the troubles experienced by the Argentine peso, the Division leadership had decided to move its offices to Montevideo. This meant the office building and the seven homes for the principal officers of the Division were now up for rent. Arturo had been able to secure the best home of all for my parents, and to get my father a part-time job as house keeper at the office building next door. This complex of buildings was in the best barrio in Buenos Aires: Belgrano R. All the foreign business people, mainly British and French, had beautiful mansions in Belgrano R. When the American missionaries looked for a place in which to live and work, they chose to stay close to their own kind, where the foreigners had their mansions. Of course, some Argentinian aristocrats and social climbers, who very much wished to rub elbows with the British and assiduously imitated their ways, also lived there.

Buenos Aires prides itself on being the Latin American Paris, and its inhabitants tend to forget that the city is located where it is. They like to think of themselves as Europeans. Even though the city is sometimes referred to as "la gran aldea" (the large village), on account of its being divided in rather self-contained barrios, it is a rather huge metropolitan center with powerful

41

cultural and political institutions. One of the problems with Argentina is that almost a third of its population lives in the capital or its immediate vicinity. This concentration of political power has not been good for the capital or the provinces. For someone coming from a provincial capital to the big city the transition was exhilarating. Venturing out in the city was always an adventure since it had all the enticing temptations of a metropolis. As a boy in Montevideo I had become adept at using public transportation. When I was eight years old, Klinton and I would take the streetcars to go to the beach almost every day in the summer. In Buenos Aires I had to learn the subway system. Whereas in Paraná I had become confident finding my way through the city on a bicycle, riding a bike in Buenos Aires was a different thing as there was no comparison between the traffic in Paraná and the one in Buenos Aires. Still, it was not long before I felt secure riding my bike twice a week in the heavy traffic, sometimes returning after dark and in the rain. I rode from home in Belgrano R to Palermo, where the conference offices were. I now had a job filling the orders for pamphlets and books coming from the churches and the colporteurs in the Conference. Between classes at the Colegio Nacional in the mornings, my job at the Conference Book Agency in the afternoons, and studies in the evening, my life took a turn toward seriousness.

In Buenos Aires I enrolled for the third year of high school at Colegio Nacional Julio A. Roca, located between Belgrano R and Barrancas de Belgrano, just two blocks from Avenida Cabildo, the main business thoroughfare in this section of town. The Julio A. Roca occupied an old building that was ill suited for this purpose. The classrooms were small and decrepit and the patios for the recess between classes were extremely inadequate. In terms of physical facilities, the Colegio Nacional in Paraná had been much better. I am also inclined to think that the faculty at Paraná was also better, more committed to their students. Our professors in Buenos Aires were people who held two or maybe even three jobs and paid little attention to them. I did third and fourth year at the

Roca, and the only class that I more or less remember was one on ethics, made up of a small group of Jewish students and myself.

During those two years at the Roca I made a furtive escape into what, for an Adventist, was forbidden territory. The jefe de celadores was also the jefe de extras at the Teatro Colón. When the students in a class were not with a professor they were under the supervision of a celador. His responsiblity was to see that the students behaved coming out of the classroom, during the recess and, and while waiting for the next professor. During class time the celadores would do whatever they pleased in a special lounge. Most of them were students at the Law School or the School of Philosophy and Letters of the University of Buenos Aires. Waiting between breaks, they studied for their own classes. The jefe supervised their work, hired and fired them, and solved any disciplinary problem reported to him by a celador or professor. As jefe de extras at the Teatro Colón , the best opera house in Latin America, and one of the best in the world, the jefe de celadores would hire some of the celadores, as well as some students, to work as extras at the Colón. One day I learned that one of my best friends, Enrique Bugnard, was working as an extra in the production of Boris Gudonov by Mussorsky. I immediately became interested in doing something like that. When Enrique was not able to talk to the jefe about me, he told me to just meet him at a specified corner of the opera house at six o'clock.

It turned out to be one of the most exciting evenings in my adolescence. My friend smuggled me through the actor's entrance and took me to the extra's dressing room. There were dozens of trunks full of period clothes for every conceivable personage. I was told to find myself clothes for a soldier, which after some effort I found and put on. Then we had to wait for our cue. Behind the stage I could hear the singing. The Colón stage had a revolving floor so that while one act was being performed in front of the public the props for the next were set up facing backwards backstage. When the curtain came down at the end of the act, the circular stage floor would turn a half circle and the next act would commence at once. Watching all the activity back stage was like living in an enchanted world. Eventually, it was time for me to go on stage. I just followed the soldiers next to me. It was the act in which a messenger brings news from the battle front. To my amazement, this messenger arrived on stage riding on a white horse with leather shoes on his hoofs, so as to muffle the sound of its feet on a wooden floor with empty space underneath. Soon the act was over and with it my luminous acting career had reached its zenith and evanesced. I thanked my friend for the evening, and went home trying to convince myself that I had actually been at the Colón, had seen at close range the workings of the stage managers, the dressing rooms and its bountiful resources, and that I had been on that stage as Boris Christoff sang the part of Boris, and a messenger on horseback had come in and out, all in what seemed to have been a beautiful dream. Returning home in a daze, I thought how I had to keep my intense feelings to myself because they were at odds with our religious mores. As I now write about that unforgettable evening, I am amazed to realize that until today I have told this story only to three or four people.

In those years the Radio del Estado, that is the state radio station, sponsored concerts by the Buenos Aires Symphony Orchestra at the amphitheater of the new Law School. The most remarkable feature of these concerts was that most of them benefited from the direction of European and North American guest conductors. The concerts were free, one of the bread crumbs cast to the cultural elite by a regime that depended on the poorly educated masses for its support. Still, in order to get in you had to have a ticket. Hundreds of tickets, I am sure, were passed around to those with proper connections. The rest of the tickets were given away at the offices of the state radio station beginning at two o'clock on Monday afternoons, for the concert that would take place on Thursday night. It became part of my regular schedule on weeks when there was a concert to go to the radio station on Monday straight from school at noon to get two tickets, the maximum allowed, after having spent two hours waiting in line.

44

Then on Thursday I would listen to the symphony playing great music under the direction of distinguished conductors. Ataulfo Argenta, Antal Dorati, Serge Kousevitsky, and many others had in me an avid listener. The concerts were the highlight of my two years of full time residence in Buenos Aires.

During this period Perón's power was in its ascendancy, and Evita was becoming the big draw at the great concentrations on Plaza de Mayo, in front of the Casa Rosada, the Argentine equivalent to the White House. Already in Paraná I had experienced suppressive police tactics. Once, while participating in a school boycott in solidarity with some workers on strike, I had had to run from the police who tried to arrest a group of us idly talking in a corner in a quiet residential neighborhood. The independent newspaper in Paraná had been closed by the government for long periods because it was not dutifully supportive of Perón's policies. Now in Buenos Aires, it was not unusual to hear that some student had "disappeared", only to re-appear in a sorry state of health two or three months later. We all knew that in public places you had to be careful about what you said to your companion or to a stranger. On the queue waiting for a bus, or while riding a bus, streetcar or subway, conversations had to be reined carefully. It was not unusual for someone to be taken to a police station by a plain-clothes officer only because they had said something that could be construed as critical of the regime. It did not have to necessarily be explicit opposition to what the government was doing. I remember distinctly how nervous my mother became one day because it was already eight in the evening and Klinton had not returned from medical school. By nine he still had not returned and everyone at home was getting really worried. We had heard so many stories of young people being taken in for the most innocent of acts, that imagining the worst was easy. Finally Klinton arrived home about a quarter to ten. He had stayed a bit late at the laboratory at the medical school and then had experienced delays with the street cars. As far as he was concerned it had just been a long, tiring day. But because of the culture of fear in which we lived, we at home had had an agonizing wait.

45

Living in a politically oppressive environment causes all kinds of disturbances in your life. The most obvious, of course, is that you have to learn to live as invisibly as possible, and to be able to say whatever the situation demands without any concern for the truth. In the culture of fear, truth is the first casualty. As it happened, years later after Perón's return from Spain for his second stint as president of Argentina, the army generals took over the country and imposed an even worse period of repression, when thousands really "disappeared," never more to be heard from. The suppression when Evita was still alive in the late forties and early fifties was not quite on that scale. Only a few people "disappeared' for good then. Still, some did, and the knowledge that it could happen with no possible recourse available instilled in one a total sense of defenselessness. The exodus of Argentine intellectuals had begun. It had become obvious that the universities no longer were what they had once been. Students were suspect on account of their intellectual curiosity, and advancement was dependent on participation in the Peronista Party. When the music critic of the daily La Prensa left for the United States, by a coincidence whose details I now have forgotten, we came to acquire the orchestral scores of a large number of classical symphonies that I carried in hand to my Thursday evenings at the concerts.

The summer before moving to Buenos Aires, Klinton and I had done some canvassing with Adventist books. We had sold books in Hernandarias, a small town in Entre Ríos, and then spent three weeks selling Adventist books in Santa Fe, across the Paraná river. Selling books, we believed, was a way of advancing the kingdom of heaven, but it was also the way to earn a little money. Most of the students at the Adventist Colegio in Puiggari, Entre Ríos, paid for their school expenses by canvassing during the summers. The different Conferences and their Book Agencies would count on having students do this work during their summer vacation.

It was the summer before Klinton entered medical school. He had to study for the entrance exam, and the family had to get everything ready for moving. Thus, Klinton and I planned for a half summer of canvassing. Klinton had done this for three summers already. I went with him to learn how it was done. In Santa Fe we started in Reconquista where we did reasonably well. Then we went to Las Toscas, where we stayed with my mother's younger sister, tía Anita. The last little town on the highway before the border with Chaco province is Florencia. We decided that we would spend, at the most, two days there. So we left our aunt's house on the bus to Florencia. When we arrived we found a little hotel where we settled down. We had been told that in Florencia there was only one Adventist family, the Flores. That late afternoon we went to say hello to the Flores. They were delighted to see us, and Brother Flores insisted that we stay with them in their home. He would not allow us to spend the night at the hotel. We insisted we were fine, but he was more persistent. The hotel was only a block from his home, so after a while we relented and checked out of the hotel. We had supper and went to bed. The next day Klinton and I visited everybody we thought could possibly be interested in buying books. We worked hard the whole day and did not make a single sale, not even of a magazine. Discouraged, we went back to the Flores home and made plans to leave early the next morning with the bus that would take us back to Las Toscas. That night it rained very hard and it kept raining all the next day. Florencia was stuck in the mud of northeastern Santa Fe. The dirt roads were impassible. It took six days before a taxi dared to venture South to Las Toscas with Klinton and me and some other passengers. We had spent a whole week as guest of the Flores family, something that no one had planned. But the experience taught me a wonderful lesson about the truth of Christianity. Klinton was a graduate of the Colegio Nacional, ready to embark on his medical career. I had two years of Colegio under my belt. The Flores were educationally deprived. They lived in a small town lost in the Argentine chaco in a house made of adobe, a floor of pressed dirt and a thatched roof. There were no other fellow Adventists with whom to enjoy worship. Occasionally a pastor came by to visit. The week at the Flores home was a revelation of God's love and what the apostle

Paul meant when he said that Christianity is "faith making love effective." Our brothers in Christ had very little, but what they had they shared with us without expecting any reward. I fully learned that week why the New Testament insists that hospitality is one of the primary Christian virtues.

After my first year at the Roca in Buenos Aires, I made plans to canvass in Mendoza during the summer of 1950-51 in order to attend the Colegio Adventista del Plata in Puiggari for my fourth year of high school.

Early one morning, my father and Klinton took me to Buenos Aires' main train station, Retiro, where I boarded the train that crossed the Andes and finished its run in Santiago de Chile. Since I would be working in the vineyards around the city of San Martín in Mendoza, Klinton rode my bicycle to the station while my father and I took my luggage on the bus. We deposited my bike in the car behind the locomotive and I took my luggage with me to my third class wooden bench. I was sixteen years old and this was my first real trip on my own. I would be away for three months.

At San Martin I met my companion for the summer, another student who was also trying to secure his scholarship, Ricardo Sanchez. We worked around San Martín, but had little success for that week, so we got permission to move to a smaller town a few kilometers away. We found a cheap hotel, and with our bicycles we canvassed the surrounding countryside. This was, and still is, beautiful wine country, where the vineyards were cared for by families; therefore each plot was, at the most, fifteen acres. Along the streets that form squares of about a kilometer to the side, the houses are not far apart. Water in this region was very scarce. During the summer it almost never rained. Farmers depended on the water from the thawing of the Andes snows for all their water needs. Over a century of European immigration to this region, Spanish and Italian fruit growers and the national and provincial government carved an intricate system of canals which brought water from the mountains to every little farm in this valley. Besides the canals that carried water for the irrigation of the vineyards and

48

other fruit orchards, there was a small canal that watered the poplars, oaks and elms that were planted along the sides of most country roads, both to give shade in the summer and protection from the winds in winter. I spent many beautiful summer days riding on these dirt lanes and visiting the humble people who cultivated grapes, peaches, apricots and cherries. My sales were not spectacular, but I was doing rather well. The catch was that my clients would not have money to pay for the books until they sold their grapes in late February and March. Therefore, I was taking orders for delivery at the end of the summer. I only had signed contracts. My joy at being in that beautiful countryside with its rows of trees heavy with growing and ripening fruit, riding my bike in the open, fresh air and meeting wonderful, friendly, hospitable people made a most enjoyable time of my summer in Mendoza. While riding from house to house I would be singing or whistling my favorite hymns from the Adventist Hymnal.

Toward the end of January, however, I began to feel tired. Pedaling required more effort than before. I thought that the opposite should be happening. I had been riding dozens of kilometers every day for a month and a half. By now pedaling should have been an easy routine. By the end of the week I did not have enough energy to get out of bed and a doctor was called in. He took a look at me and immediately made a diagnosis. I had typhoid fever. A taxi was summoned and it took me to the hospital for infectious diseases in the city of Mendoza, 50 kilometers away. When I arrived I had a fever of 104 F and I was more or less unconscious for the next four days. When I recovered my senses, I found myself in a long narrow ward with about twenty beds, all their heads against one wall. I had been extremely fortunate. Streptomycin had come on the market a short time before. It brought down my fever, which was checked in about fifteen days. I was so weak, they kept me in the hospital recovering for another fifteen days.

Uncle Jorge, my mother's brother, was a pastor in Mendoza. He took me out of the hospital on a Saturday, Día de la Vendimia

(Grape Harvest Day). He and his wife came by to get me at the hospital after the church service. On the way home we stopped for a while to see the parade of floats from the different clubs, labor unions, and city departments passing by on Main Street. A couple of days later Uncle Jorge took me to the train station, and with my bicycle in the baggage car, I was on my way back to Buenos Aires. The bout with typhoid had been, of course, a close call. I was extremely grateful to God for having survived. As far as I could tell, I had not suffered any permanent harm. But, on balance, my very positive experience of the first part of the summer had been toned down by my brush with death. I returned to Buenos Aires with the words of my nurse at the hospital ringing in my ears. When I was safely recuperating, he said to me, "When you arrived, I didn't think you were going to make it." The fact that I had made it, gave my life a new sense of purpose.

When I got to Retiro, late at night, after a full day on the train, Klinton was there again to take my bicycle home while my father and I took a taxi with my suitcase. It was soon decided that I would not go to the Colegio Adventista del Plata in Puiggari. I was still weak and in need of a special diet. My mother wanted me home to supervise my recovery. Another factor influencing the decision, was that I had not been able to deliver the orders for which I had contracts. An employee of the Book Agency tried to do the deliveries in late February and early March, but he had only been able to successfully deliver about half the orders. In other words, I did not have the funds to spend a year studying at Puiggari.

My bout with typhoid fever when I was sixteen forced me to consider my mortality at a time when most people that age couldn't care less. I am not in the position to evaluate the effects of this on my personality. I would like to think that it made me a bit more serious, more reflective, more aware of the need to use my life wisely than I would have otherwise. It certainly made me think that my life was not my own, and for a believer this became evidence of the grace of God. It probably also had something to do with my eventual decision to study theology. Up until that time I was

50

contemplating the possibility of spending my life as a farmer. I had become enamored with the lifestyles of my uncles in their farms, and was considering studying agricultural engineering at the university in Buenos Aires. This utopian vision of becoming a modern farmer was influenced, no doubt, by Hollywood movies of wonderful farms in North America, where all the benefits of civilization were abundantly evident. Concert pianists came out of these farms just as naturally as county fair champions. Thus my aspirations wavered between a future that seemed right and the temptation to live more fully in this world.

At the time everyone thought typhoid caused you to lose your hair. To prevent this, I was told to cut my hair as short as possible and thus encourage new hair to grow. In Argentina, short hair was the signature of young men doing their obligatory year of military service when they turned twenty. I was sixteen. With my short hair, many thought I was twenty and took me for a draftee. This made for conflicting emotions. I was proud of my Uruguayan citizenship and its privileges. On the other hand, being considered a twenty year old was pleasing and had its luster.

The following summer I made arrangements to canvass in Fray Bentos and Mercedes, two small towns in the interior of Uruguay. This time I worked in town, walking from house to house. In Fray Bentos a large meat processing plant was the main employer. Sea going ships would come up the Uruguay River to be loaded with beef. That summer the plant was not working at full capacity. Only intermittently did ships anchor at the plant. Most people did not have extra money to buy books. Still, I was able to earn a scholarship for the year at the Colegio in Puiggari. In Fray Bentos there was no Adventist church, not even one Adventist family. I spent Sabbaths in private devotions at a secluded beach up the river where a creek spilled its waters into the Uruguay river.

Those Sabbaths alone forced me to give some serious thought to what I was going to do with my life. I was now in the prime of adolescence when all kinds of impulses vied with each other for satisfaction. There was the young woman I had began to date in

51

Buenos Aires, with whom I had been attending the Thursday evening symphony concerts. She was a few years older than I, and therefore was pushing for some serious commitment. I felt that, being this young and with many decisions facing me, it would be foolish of me to settle down then. Going to study at Puiggari meant that I would be taking theological courses, but I still did not want to work for the denomination. Being a pastor was not appealing. Instead, I thought about a degree in agricultural engineering and having a model farm at the family homestead in Crespo. My parents did not have any enthusiasm for dreams of becoming a cultured agronomist. Their hints made clear they would much prefer it if I were to follow my two brothers into medicine. But for me medicine was totally out of the question. I knew I did not have the stomach for working with cadavers in an anatomy lab. Besides, math and science are not my cup of tea. On that lonely beach by the Uruguay River, I would spend hours pondering which direction I should take. What was God's will for my life? By the end of the summer, I had more or less decided not to decide. I would just let God show me the way. Whichever doors opened before me, I would enter.

When the summer was over, I took a bus to Montevideo and spent a day visiting some of the old haunts from early childhood. Then I took the sea plane that took off and landed on the River Plate, connecting Montevideo and Buenos Aires. It was my first plane ride and I confess that on take off I felt that we were not going to make it out of the water. It took forever for the plane to get enough speed to break the pull of friction. It was a good thing that we were not on a normal runway. It could not possibly have been long enough. By contrast, on landing the plane touched the water and came to a rapid stop. As it settled the side windows went under water. Then it popped up and moved slowly toward its anchor. It was an auspicious end to the summer that displaced the previous year's truncated and dangerous experience. This time I was coming back home after a successful summer of canvassing, having earned my scholarship. My family was happy to see me come

52

back healthy and rallied to help me prepare my suitcases to go to Puiggari for the school year.

Hilda, my girlfriend, was sad to see me go for an even longer period of time. I had mixed feelings about the separation. In a way, I thought it might be good to test our relationship. I had a hard time knowing what to do. I did not know her that well after all. She was nice and soft spoken. The fact that she was seven years older than I kept coming up in my mind, and I knew that my parents were very worried about this apparent mismatch. They preferred not to make an issue of it, but had expressed their objection plainly. I imagine that this relationship also fueled my pride in seeming to be older than my years.

Living in a dorm and eating at the cafeteria required some adjustments. You had to watch your language. I soon found out that singing tangos in the showers elicited an appointment with the preceptor, Renee Chaskelis, a Frenchman who was also the assistant choir director and uptight about popular music. Neither the Weisses nor the Riffels were vegetarians. While vegetarianism was recommended by Adventists as the best diet, almost all Adventists I knew ate meat that was clean according to Leviticus 11. In Leviticus, chicken and turkey are in, duck and geese are out. Sheep and cattle are in, pork and horse are out. At the college cafeteria, however, the menu was strictly vegetarian. One of the great advantages of rooming with my cousin Ruben Riffel was that every time he went home he would return with a good supply of empanadas and wurst. Occasionally Ruben would ask a woman in the adjacent village to prepare a roasted chicken for us. We would pick it up and go to the Salto de Andre, a waterfall on a creek with a rather large swimming hole. There we would swim and eat, enjoying both the chicken and the swim even more because both were prohibited activities at the college.

On arrival at Puiggari, I enrolled on the fifth year of the secondary school program. During that fifth year I had to decide what I was going to do. At the Adventist Colegio, besides the regular courses required in the national curriculum for a fifth year, we also took an extra religion course. It was my luck to take Bible Doctrines with Pastor Hector J. Peverini, a descendent of one of the first Adventist families in Argentina. His grandfather had become an Adventist on account of receiving Adventist literature sent by relatives in northern Italy, about the same time that my great-grandfather had returned from Kansas and later brought Pastor Westphal to organize the first congregation in South America. Pastor Peverini was a saintly man who, besides teaching that one course, was also the president of the college. For each doctrine, Peverini gave us a list of proof texts. Ten of the texts had to be memorized. At the beginning of each class he would quiz us on the texts for that day. At the end of the year, for the final exam, we had about three hundred and fifty texts which we were expected to identify as to content. One hundred and fifty we were expected to know word for word. This exercise gave me the sense that I knew what the Bible taught on all important matters. Thinking I had acquired powerful knowledge of God's will and purposes gave me a new sense of myself. This sense of achievement, however, also let me know that there was much more to be known. In the back of my mind, I also knew that many texts were unclear. Some times they required a bit of mental gymnastics to make them prove the intended doctrine. I felt now more equipped with knowledge than when I had my little debate with the former seminarian in Paraná, but I could sense that I still lacked understanding to sustain my faith.

My internal dissatisfaction made me postpone the decision of what to do with my life. Was I going to study medicine as my parents wanted me to? Should I go to the School of Agricultural Engineering of the University of Buenos Aires and become a model farmer, as I had dreamed? Or, was I going to study theology as the other forces inside of me urged me to do? As I asked and wrestled with these questions, the board of trustees at the college authorized a new degree. Until then the only career that students could pursue at Puiggari was theological preparation for ministry, accounting, teaching or secretarial skills. Next door, the Sanatorio

Adventista del Plata prepared nurses. Young ladies, therefore, graduated as Bible workers, teachers, secretaries or nurses. Young men graduated as nurses, accountants or aspiring pastors. This meant that all the graduates, more or less, expected employment within the denominational structure. The expectation was proving unrealistic. More students were finishing the bachillerato and entering state universities to pursue other careers. The board decided that students who wished to study other careers would be much better lay church leaders if they had some basic theological training. Thus a "Pre-University" curriculum was devised, and those taking it would receive a special degree. I saw a door open. The next year I came back to take the pre-university course before entering the School of Agriculture.

To earn my way back for the extra year I had to canvass again and earn a scholarship. This time I made arrangements to spend the summer of 1952-53 in Comodoro Rivadavia, in the Patagonia, a windswept and isolated region that had seen an influx of business after the discovery of oil. Comodoro Rivadavia had become the port for shipping crude petroleum to the refineries up North. The desert plateau that previously saw only sheep was now marked by the towers of deep wells and the camps to accommodate the workforces necessary to keep the fields in production. There was plenty of work, and the salaries were good. In spite of my rather limited abilities as a canvasser, made no better by the sand blasted wind on any exposed skin, I earned three scholarships.

To celebrate my success, I planned to end the summer doing something special. Ruben, my cousin and roommate, was canvassing that summer in Trelew, just a bit north and close to the Andes on the Chubut River. It was a prosperous region where Welsh immigrants developed a flourishing fruit industry, growing primarily apples. At the end of our canvassing campaign, he joined me at Comodoro Rivadavia, and we took an early bus from the Atlantic coast to a town just a few kilometers East of Puerto Aisen on the Pacific coast, arriving late at night. Crossing Patagonia's desolation left us with an indelible impression, a mixture of solitude and loneliness. For the whole day we did not see a sign of human life until we got to the checkpoint at the border with Chile. Then, as soon as we entered Chile and started climbing the Andes, the country was covered with beautiful pine trees and luscious vegetation. All the water brought by the western winds was captured by the Andes and remained in Chile. In Puerto Aisen, Ruben and I took a ship that traveled North in the Chilean archipelago to Puerto Mont. The journey took two and a half days past magnificent scenery with dolphins accompanying our ship. Halfway through the trip, however, the ship came into open water and the waves buffeted it, making it behave like a little canoe. Most of the passengers became seasick. It was strange to go to the dining room and be alone. For me, a full stomach was the best antidote against sea sickness. Ruben and I entertained ourselves on the top deck trying to walk the length of the ship on a straight line following the deck planks. It was almost impossible.

At Puerto Mont we bought a ticket to Bariloche, back in Argentina. The ticket included the bus, the meals, a room overnight, and the boat in Lago Frias, at the Argentine border. By then we were feeling guilty for having such a good time in those beautiful surroundings. Puerto Varas in Chile and Bariloche in Argentina were some of the best tourist destinations in the world. Bariloche was without equal in terms of its location and the many attractions near by. Besides Cerro Catedral, a famous skiing spot, and the Glaciar Tronador, there was the unique forest of the myrtles that inspired a scene in Walt Disney's Bambi. It was easy to feel pampered in Bariloche. We were students with definite financial limitations, but accommodations were not that expensive and the price included full board. The European cuisine, somewhat adapted to Argentine supplies and tastes, left us quite content.

Ruben had left most of his things in Trelew, so we took a bus back there and then hopped the train from the end of the line to Buenos Aires. It was a two and a half day trip back, an unmitigated bore. Spending two glorious weeks basking in the sunshine as carefree tourists, Ruben and I had done very well enjoying the goodness and the beauty of creation. Then we had to take that interminable bumpy ride home.

In Buenos Aires I had to face the fact that just before leaving for Comodoro Rivadavia, when I had told Hilda not to wait for me, she did not hear my message. When I got back, she insisted on seeing me to talk about our future together. I just could not see it, despite many long and torturous conversations. I discovered that breaking up was far more difficult than starting a friendship. I promised myself that in the future, if I ever got involved with another woman I would never, never be the one to break up. I would do whatever I had to do to have her tell me that she could not see a future for the two of us. In fact, my relationship with Hilda had been healthy and pure. In the course of our relationship I had become deeply in love with her. I realized then that the love of God can only be conceived fully when one has experience the love of a woman, and how to love God can only be understood after loving a woman.

The Bible is not reluctant to depict the relationship between God and Israel in terms of deep emotional and sexual language. On account of its constant battle against the Fertility Cults, prominent among the contemporaries of the Old Testament writers, these authors avoided referring to God as father or mother, the prophets use the obvious metaphors provided by nature in their efforts to depict God's interest in having a permanent relationship with Israel. In the Old Testament, rain is not thought of as the result of the sky god impregnating the earth goddess, but Hosea depicts God as the lover who has successfully lured his beloved to a secluded place in the midst of gorgeous vegetation and under the shade of a formidable tree is seducing her by speaking sweet nothings in her ears. It was only after having experienced deep emotional ties with a woman, with no sex involved, that I could really begin to understand the love of God. It is not through love for mother or father that you learn about love. Only the lived experience of love for a woman can make you understand the love of God. This realization gave my relationship with Hilda an added

57

dimension. But, in good conscience, I could not ask her to wait six to eight years for me, especially given our difference in age.

Back at the Colegio Adventista del Plata I was now doing only courses in the theology program. My timing proved to be poor, however. The one professor at the college with a theological turn of mind, Victor Ampuero Matta (the younger brother of our pensionista in Rosario some years before), was on sabbatical. Most of my courses were taught by well meaning pastors with little formal training and even less intellectual curiosity. One interesting course I took was on Old Testament archaeology, by David Rhys, a descendent of Welsh immigrants with serious intellectual concerns. His course provided evidence for the historical accuracy of the biblical accounts. Rhys also taught a course in astronomy, which provided evidence of the wisdom and the power of God. These courses sparked in me the desire to study theology with some seriousness, following in the footsteps of David Rhys. It was obvious, however, that it could not be done in Argentina. Within my Adventist horizon, the only place in which I could further my studies was the United States.

Soon after I had arrived at Puiggari, I learned that Enrique Chaij, a student in his last year of the ministerial course, was making plans to go to the United States to study. His uncle, Nicolás Chaij, was the director of colporteurs in the Inter American Division, and Enrique had asked him if he could colporteur somewhere to secure a scholarship for studying in an American Adventist college. It looked like Venezuela was the place to go. In the Adventist administrative structure, it should be noted, Venezuela, Columbia and Guyana, rather than being part of the South American Division, belong to the Inter-American Division, together with the countries between Panamá and Mexico and all the islands of the Caribbean. I began to dream of going to Venezuela with Enrique.

After some time, we learned there was no room in Venezuela for us as colporteurs. The news left me quite downhearted, but then it occurred to me that I had an alternative route to the States.

My Uncle Andrés was the president of the West Cuba Conference. I wrote to him inquiring about the possibility of canvassing in Cuba in order to earn my way. He answered immediately that the doors were open, both for me and for Enrique. I discussed the new plans for my future with my parents and, to my surprise, they agreed immediately. I had to be accepted by an American college and then apply for a student visa. I knew that if I had a resident visa it would be easier to work in the States in order to pay for my tuition, room and board, but I would also be eligible for the draft, and the situation after the Korean War was still unstable. A student visa, however, required that I show the American Consulate in Buenos Aires that my parents were in a position to support my studies. Getting the visa was the biggest hurdle now. During the winter break in Buenos Aires I started the application. I had to present police reports, medical reports, financial information, a letter of acceptance by an accredited institution in the United States, and two letters of reference. All of this required quite a lot of leg work, and the police report required help from somebody who knew somebody in the Federal Police to get the report within a couple of weeks instead of six months. It seemed that it was God's will that I travel to the United States when the Consulate accepted a simple letter signed by my father declaring his meager financial situation and a few days later granted me a student visa.

When word spread that I was going to study in the United States I became the object of everyone's envy at the College in Puiggari. I was living in a state of euphoria, sensing that I might just be dreaming. Argentina under Perón was a large prison. We lived with our heads down because the ceiling was that low. Only people with connections in the Peronista power structure had a future. In the church, unfortunately, the modus operandi was a version of the secular one. El jefe thought he has absolute power on the body and the soul of his subjects. I was escaping all that. I had a future. I had no clear picture of what that might be, but I knew that I was not going to be restricted by the limited options available in Argentina under Perón. My plan was to leave Buenos Aires on

January 9, 1954, and canvass in Cuba until the end of June. Then I would go to Southern Missionary College in Collegedale, Tennessee. Unquestionably, God was opening doors for me.

4

La Habana

No one was waiting for me when I arrived at Rancho Boyeros airport. According to the letter I had sent ahead I was to arrive on January 14, but I had been delayed in Panama for a day and arrived on Friday the 15th. The offices of the Antillian Union of Seventh-day Adventists were in the vicinity of the airport and I had the address, so I took a taxi. But because it was late afternoon on a Friday, they were closed. Everyone had gone home to make ready for the Sabbath. To my relief, a secretary who lived in the attic of the two-story building heard me ringing the bell and came down, and opened the door. She knew that my Uncle Andrés had been disappointed not to meet me at the airport the day before. She was going to the center of La Habana and would take me to him.

To go into town we immersed ourselves in a crowded public bus. Fortunately, I was traveling light and we were able to get on with my luggage. That bus ride was my introduction to Cuba. Everyone was talking at full volume, and I could understand only one in five words, even though they were speaking Spanish. The trouble was not so much the vocabulary. It was the speed with which they spoke that made it impossible to enunciate syllables fully. I just could not keep up with them. For another thing, they talked to anyone else in the familiar "tu" form, which in Argentina, at the time, was reserved for people with whom you had a close relationship. It gave to the atmosphere in the bus a totally different character. It seemed that every one was immediate family of everyone else. I had much to learn if I was going to be successful as a colporteur in La Habana.

The secretary took me to the large ballroom of the Curro Enrique social club. There I found Uncle Andrés, Aunt Ruth and their son Carlos. They were glad to see I had arrived safely, after worrying about me and waiting for a new directive from me for a day. They were also excited because that evening was the kickoff for the largest Adventist evangelistic crusade in the history of Adventism in Cuba. The featured evangelist was Walter Schubert. He had made his mark already in several countries in South America. Pastors from all over the Inter American Division came to help and learn how to do evangelism. All in all there were about thirty pastors involved in the campaign. Pastor Schubert was actually conducting two campaigns simultaneously. Three nights of the week he would speak at the Curro Enrique Club in La Habana, and the other three nights he would hold forth in a rented theater in Marianao, a suburb of the capital.

I had no idea I was arriving in La Habana at such a propitious time. Actually, I knew Walter Schubert because he was a family friend. He had become an Adventist in his native Germany, and when he was about eighteen or twenty, together with his brother Paul, had traveled to Chile, and in time became a pastor there. He also had married a beautiful Chilean woman. Soon after, his brother Paul left for the United States, but Walter did well in Chile and was called to be president of different conferences in Argentina. Dissatisfied with being an administrator, he had devised a new method for evangelizing and tried it out with success in South America. Now, he had been invited to come to Cuba to hold meetings and teach his new method. By now he must have been in his middle fifties, but he did not lack energy and enthusiasm. Crowds would come to hear him even though he still spoke Spanish with a German accent. Maybe they came in part because of it.

His method was based on an approach that was somewhat devious. To some, it was dishonest. The idea was to advertise lectures that had no direct link to religion and no connection with any particular church. The lectures addressed subjects with contemporary, educational and cultural significance and were presented in a neutral place. Church members were asked not to refer to the church in conversations with other listeners. This was necessary, according to Schubert, because of the strong prejudice the Latin American public had against Protestants in general. In some countries the Catholic authorities would not even allow Protestants to have religious meetings outside their own church buildings. That was what religious "tolerance" actually meant.

After a week of lectures on secular topics, Schubert would address current events and bring in the interpretation of the visions of Daniel and Revelation as historical prognostication. By the end of the second week, his lectures would be fully transformed into evangelism. The campaign in Marianao turned out to be quite successful. At the Curro Enrique Club, the number of those who asked for baptism into the Adventist Church was rather small. Of course, the goal of the campaign was not like that of the campaigns of Billy Graham, who wanted people to make decisions for Christ and go to the church of their choice. Adventist evangelistic campaigns aim at proselytizing.

I could not attend the workshops Schubert had with the pastors, because I had to canvass during the day. I did, however, help in any way I could with the evening meetings, primarily by singing in a quartet that provided musical interludes. One of those who was baptized at the end of the meetings was a prominent doctor who was a professor at the medical school of the University of La Habana. Everyone was particularly excited about this outcome, since the church was eager to attract people of the middle classes.

Selling books door to door was a good way to get to know a place. My territory was the section of La Habana that stretched from the harbor along the Malecón all the way to the Calzada de Monte. This included La Habana Vieja (Old Havana), the Prado with the government house and the attractive Club Asturiano, and the business district with the Sears and Roebuck store and a few large hotels. I was dealing primarily with merchants and professionals.

I soon realized that there was a big difference between Cuba and Argentina in terms of their economic relationship with the United States. Under Perón, Argentina was closed to all imports. Perón wanted to transform the country from an agricultural to an industrial power. To foster national industrialization, he barred all imports. The effect was that those with connections got to open factories protected both from national and foreign competition. Poor quality products were bought because they were the only ones available at home, but they could not compete in foreign markets. In Cuba, by contrast, you could buy anything produced in the United States almost at the same price as in the States. When I left Buenos Aires, I had never watched television. There was one channel in operation and only a few privileged homes had t.v. sets. In my home we had not had an automobile, and almost all the cars on the streets were pre World War II. Volkswagen and Ford were beginning to produce cars in Argentina, but they were not up to the quality of those produced by the same manufacturers abroad. In Cuba, by contrast, t.v. antennas rose from the humblest of roofs in the countryside. Sets were on all day long everywhere, and the latest American cars crowded the streets of La Habana. In fact, almost all the goods for sale in stores and supermarkets were imported from the States. Among professionals and merchants it was rare to find one who had not visited the United States several times.

What surprised me most, however, was the constant denigration of the United States by almost everyone I talked to. I could not understand how there was so much resentment, freely expressed against both Fulgencio Batista, the Cuban president, and the United States that kept him in power. Cuba had a one-crop economy based on sugar cane. Most of the sugar manufacturing and trade was in American hands. Sugar did not bring cash into Cuba. It brought in cars, t.v. sets, refrigerators, washing machines, small appliances, and all kinds of boxed and canned foods. Cubans seemed to be benefiting immensely from their commerce with the States, making their standard of living much higher than that of supposedly richer and larger Argentina. Cubans, however, hated their condition as an economic puppet. While I was in Cuba, from January to June 1954, Fidel Castro was in a Cuban prison on account of his assault on the Moncada army barracks. Some lamented the failure of his daring attempt at rebellion, but no one predicted his future universal fame. I was approached on the street in an effort to enlist me as a volunteer in the forces of liberation against the "Giant of the North," fighting in Guatemala against the CIA's deposition of president Arbenz..

Canvassing in Old Havana and in the area where there were a few hotels made it impossible to avoid the heavy traffic of prostitutes in the streets who catered primarily to American tourists. Thanks in part to the oldest profession, tourism was the second largest industry. Since I was a blue-eyed blonde, they thought I was a tourist and were surprised I could not return their perfect English. In the streets of La Habana beautiful young ladies often came from behind and grabbed me by an arm and tried to talk me into going with them. They were dressed as if they were on their way to the opera. In Cuban eyes, the illegality of brothels in the States had converted La Habana into an American brothel. It was a source of rage that their great city, with its honorable cultural traditions, one of the intellectual capitals of Latin America, was now known for whoring. This was blamed on the Americans who controlled what happened in Cuba.

I was amazed to hear Cuban merchants talk so openly against the government of Batista and its facilitators. Under Perón such talk would have landed you in jail immediately. An inspector of some bureau or another would have come by and closed your business for violating one or another of the new ordinances. In Cuba people would spend hours lamenting the relationship of their government with their closest neighbor, all the time enjoying the standard of living that their proximity to their neighbor gave them. Still, I could not fail to admire the blessing of free speech, something which was sadly missing in Argentina.

While canvassing in Cuba, I lived at uncle Andrés home in barrio La Vívora and attended church a few blocks away. Aunt Ruth was the choir director and wanted me to join, but I was embarrassed by the thought of looking like a nephew who enjoyed special treatment. I did, however, make friends in the church, and discovered that the way in which men and women dealt with each other was much more open than in Argentina. The girls were naturally friendly and easy to be with. In conversations, women would touch your hand and arm in a relaxed manner, which would have been taken to mean something quite different in Argentina of the 1950s. Cuba made me aware that Latin America was not permeated by a common culture, even if it had been colonized by Spain and shared Spanish as its language. The native peoples of the different regions, the kinds of immigration that had taken place after the period of colonization, and the political and economic life of the different republics gave to each a peculiar stamp.

The five and a half months I spent in Cuba also opened my eyes to an issue I had not faced at home. Cubans, I soon found out, were extremely conscious of the color of their skin. The population had the full spectrum of browns possible between white and black, and everyone seemed aware of his or her position in the spectrum. By day, at the level of street life and the business of earning a living, everyone dealt with every one else as best they could. After five o'clock in the afternoon, you went home and continued life inside a social network that was drawn according to the color of your skin. Public functions were the exceptions. It was sad to see people eager to have you meet a relative who was whiter than themselves, but would avoid as much as possible to introduce you to a darker family member.

Once on a train from the Hershey sugar factory (yes, it was owned by the chocolate company in Pennsylvania) to La Habana, I found myself in a car with only one other passenger. I decided to leave my seat and sit next to him to make the trip less boring. He was a bit older than I and was commuting from a company town next to the sugar factory while studying engineering at the

University of La Habana. After we had been talking for a while, he confessed having been taken by surprise when I approached him just to be friendly and talk. He said a cuban white person would have never done that. I was, in turn, quite surprised myself by this. I began to reflect on my friends in the Julio A. Roca in Buenos Aires and in the Colegio Adventista del Plata in Puiggari, and for the first time I considered the possibility that this guy or that may have had some black ancestry.

In Argentina I had been exposed to racial and ethnic prejudices. There had been a current among German immigrants aiming to maintain racial purity. This had become a bit more difficult within the Adventist German community where religious purity challenged requirements of ethnic purity. Within my family some members began the process of hybridity. A cousin of my father and a brother of my mother married two sisters of Spanish ancestry. Both of these fellows were alpha males able to withstand family pressure. By the time I became aware of these things, their marriages had been accepted. I am sure that both wives, however, still had scars from the cold reception they had received from the families of their husbands. In 1950, my brother Ewaldo married Mercedes Merino and her reception into our nuclear family was always warm, even if my mother sometimes was a bit naïve. I still heard members of the extended family express prejudiced notions about my sister-in-law. My generation was beginning to develop a stronger sense that this was South America, not the Old World. Still, in Buenos Aires there was strong prejudice against people of the northwest, near Bolivia and Paraguay, who had flocked to the capital invited by Perón and now provided him with the masses that crowded Plaza de Mayo whenever he needed a demonstration of popular support. They were "cabecitas negras" (little black-heads, referring to their Native American straight black hair).

I was caught off guard by the racial divides in Cuban society. The tensions were not between ethnic, but between racial groups. The amazing thing was that they were as noticeable inside as outside the church. Everyone was quite conscious of the place he or she occupied in the spectrum between black and white. Sometimes there were marked differences in siblings of one family, and these affected the roles they could play in society. Confronting the problem created by the arbitrary classifications based on unscientific definitions of race, I was confused and ashamed. As a child I had experienced the taunts and ridicule of other children on account of my blue eyes and blond hair, but they had been sporadic moments of suffering under abuse. Later I also learned that children can be mindlessly cruel. Coming to terms with the fact that the church had been ineffective in teaching that the image of God is present in all humanity became a theologically important question. Whatever one makes theologically of the effects of The Fall on the image of God in Adam and Eve, one must recognize that Paul understood that all those who are in Christ share in the image of God that is fully available to every Christian on account of the glory of His resurrection that shines now in the lives of those who believe. In Cuba I was challenged to think seriously about the way the Gospel of the Risen Christ is not a dogma but a way to live. My Cuban experience, however, turned out to be inadequate as preparation for the institutionalized segregation I found when I arrived in the Southern United States.

It would be misleading to leave the impression that the Cuba I encountered on my way to the States, which actually made my coming to the States possible, was somewhat dysfunctional. That their political and economic dependency made for a society in continuous crisis was what the Cubans themselves were continually talking about. Still, Cuba was an exciting place, with people who enjoyed the generosity of their tropical paradise. I was constantly amazed at the openness with which Cubans were eager to make me their friend, and the liberality with which they gave of themselves in demonstrations of friendship and hospitality. Traveling across the island I discovered wonderful colonial towns, like Cienfuegos, in the Southern coast, interminable beaches like Varadero, in the northern coast. Fishing in the Laguna de Leche (Milk Lagoon) delivered all that tourist brochures promised, and

68

the valley of Pinar del Rio permanently dislodged the idea that only snow-capped mountains make for memorable vistas. In Cuba, for the first time, I ate mangos, avocados, mameys, guanabanas, anones and fried sweet plantains at a time when such things were not being shipped abroad. It was enough to make one wish the political and economic situation were better so that the island could, indeed, be a tropical paradise.

Canvassing in Cuba did what I had hoped. The Cuban peso was on a par with the dollar, and my earnings went a long way when exchanged for Argentine pesos. I was able to send back the money I had borrowed from Uncle Enrique to buy my airfare from Buenos Aires to Miami. Then, I worked a bit longer to have money to travel to Collegedale, Tennessee. On July 4, 1954, I flew to Miami, Florida, and took a taxi to the bus station. It was about noon, and I had about a half hour before the bus to Chattanooga would leave. Trying to get something to eat before getting on the bus, I went to the lunch counter at the station and looked for the least expensive thing on the menu. It was the soup. With my Spanish way of reading vowels, I ordered. The waitress insisted I needed to go to the drug store across the street, but I could not see why I should. I insisted I wanted soup ("soap"). I tried three times and then boarded the bus totally frustrated by not having been able to eat at all. After thirty hours on the bus, traveling on two lane highways that crossed every little town along the route, I arrived in Chattanooga. After a call on the phone, the transportation department at Southern Missionary College in Collegedale sent a driver to pick me up at the bus station. I was finally at the place I had been envisioning for over a year.

Looking back, I could not quite come to terms with how easy it had been. When I first thought I would go to the United States to study theology, I was aware that most likely it would turn out to be another adolescent dream. Under the influence of movies, especially Los Verdes Prados ("Green Pastures"), I dreamed I would be a farmer who had a model farm with all the conveniences of modern life and the peace and independence of the countryside.

In Puiggari, I had become buddy with Juan Plenc, an idiosyncratic guy with a history of rebellion behind him. We spent hours in an empty classroom designing a catamaran we would build in the forests of Paraguay and then sail down the Paraná River and out into the Atlantic. In our custom-built boat we would be self-supporting missionaries who traveled around the world before settling down in the Amazon basin and doing mission work there, with no ecclesiastical ties. Dreaming those dreams I was acutely aware that more than likely they would never become anything else. Thinking about going to study theology in the Unites States, in the back of my mind I was afraid it was going to be just another dream. Arriving at Collegedale I was amazed that this was actually becoming a reality. The distance from the mud clogged college in Puiggari to the beautiful valley in southern Appalachia had not been so forbidding or long after all. The exhilaration of having escaped the Argentina of Perón almost prevented me from realizing exactly how much of me was still back home. At the time, even though I was keeping myself open to the future, I was thinking that I had come to study for a three or four year period.

5

COLLEGEDALE

Southern Missionary College was nestled in a little valley in the hills east of the Tennessee River just before it made a big loop by Lookout Mountain. From Chattanooga, going north on highway 11, after about ten miles you took a little road that wound around a hill in order to enter into Collegedale. Some of the last curves before reaching the valley were sharp. As the road ran at the edge of the hill, leaving the pastures to the left undisturbed, the college buildings followed one after the other hugging the slope to the right: first the music building, then the women's dormitory, then the science building, the library, the administration building, the men's dormitory and finally the tabernacle where church services were held, along with entertainment programs and gym activities. Most buildings had Georgian columns at their entrances. While the music, science and library buildings were relatively new and made of cement beams and masonry, the rest were old wooden structures. Fire drills were regular occurrences.

My arrival on the fifth of July was uneventful. The campus was, for all practical purposes, empty. I had come early to force myself to practice English before the school year started. Besides, selling religious literature was something I had done out of necessity for five summers, but was not something I enjoyed doing. The Dean at the dorm assigned me a room in the second floor. It was hot, and there were no fans or air conditioning. I was intrigued by this building made of lumber from top to bottom. The grand stairway linking the three floors at the center of the building made a gnawing sound that revealed its age when someone ascended or descended. The scenery was peaceful enough and the people seemed quite friendly. On the sidewalks everyone greeted me with a "Hi".

The morning after my arrival I went to see the Academic Dean, Dr. Richard Hammill. He welcomed me with plenty of good advice, such as, "Go everyday to the library and read the newspapers. That will be the best way to enlarge your vocabulary." He was a little man with a small, round face and a pointed nose. His eyes sparkled as he talked, making you feel that you were the most important person in his life. Hammill had earned a PhD from the Oriental Institute of the University of Chicago. At Southern, he was eager to do something to open up the college constituencies to a wider world, one which was not segregated. I later learned one of the reasons why he encouraged me and other students from South America to enroll was to introduce some diversity to a student body that was until then almost ninety-nine percent Southern white. There were only a few students from north of the Mason-Dixon Line. Hammill had been a teacher in the Religion department for a few years, but now he was Dean and only taught one advanced class. Unfortunately for me, at the end of my first year at Southern, Hammill was called to the Education Department of the General Conference of Seventh-day Adventists in Takoma Park, a suburb of Washington, D.C. This meant that I never had him as a teacher. That first year at Southern, he was always interested to know how I was doing and invited me to his home a couple of times. As it turned out, our relationship extended over a number of years.

On that first day I also made arrangements to work in order to support myself while at Southern. The college had two industries that existed primarily to provide jobs for students. The wood shop built furniture sold by Sears and Roebuck. The factory was next to a track from the Southern Railroad which brought in lumber and took away the finished desks and dressers. Most students who needed work found it at the wood shop. Word of mouth had it that the work was dirty, noisy and done at a hurried pace, with a foreman standing next to you telling you to move faster. I fully expected to be sent there.

I was somewhat disappointed when I was assigned to the broom factory instead. I started the following day. My first job was to take the corn for making brooms from the bales that arrived from Oklahoma and hold it against a spinning wheel with spikes that ripped away all the seeds, leaving clean and straight twigs. I soon discovered broom corn had a dust that irritated the skin. My first two weeks were a real crucible. During my first week the temperature reached 104 F. Sweating was unavoidable, and the corn dust on my wet body made me crazy to scratch myself the whole time. After work, a shower took away the sweat and dust, but my skin kept itching terribly. The dorm was an oven at night. Lying on the sheets almost naked, I continued to sweat heavily, my whole body itching. If I had had the money, I would have gone back home to Buenos Aires. Fortunately my skin slowly adjusted to the corn dust, and stopped itching after about two weeks.

Soon I was promoted to dying the corn. Then, a short time later, I was put on a broom-making machine. We were paid by the broom, so, while I had started at seventy five cents an hour, the minimum wage in 1954, on the broom-making machine I could make about $1.10 an hour. Other workers at the shop were faster and made even better money. One of them made almost $3.00 an hour when he put his mind to it. There was good camaraderie among the workers, and the manager, Mr. Fogg, was a considerate and generous man.

When classes were out, I worked full time. When school was in session, I worked Monday through Thursday from one to five, and Sunday all day, twenty-four hours a week, for the two years I was at Southern. When I graduated, the president handed me my real diploma in a leather cover because my bill was paid in full. Nothing I had earned, however, touched my hands. It passed from my credit to my debit column as charges for room, board, books, and tuition at the business office. I spent months without a cent in my pocket.

73

When classes started in September I enrolled for a full load of sixteen semester hours. The Registrar evaluated my credits from Argentina considering the basic requirements for graduation and it turned out I needed 80 credits, not 128, to earn a BA. I decided to try to do it in two years, taking sixteen hours each semester and eight hours each summer school. At the time it seemed the necessary choice. My plan was to spend three, at the most four, years studying in the States and return to Argentina with a Masters' degree. Looking back I can see that my education suffered from my hurried pace. After several years 1 would look back and think that my undergraduate experience was not all it could have been. Also informing this perception was the academic environment at Southern.

In my first semester I started studying Greek, which Hammill had made a requirement for Religion majors. Most of the majors loudly resented it. For me, however, studying New Testament Greek was one of the reasons I had come to the States. In some of my dreams I saw myself as a missionary in the Amazon rainforest of Perú or Ecuador, translating the New Testament into the language of a native tribe. I did my Greek lessons religiously. Many of my classmates could not understand why I thought studying Greek was relevant. They had no use for it. The other theology classes were somewhat of a disappointment.

The biggest difference between what I had done with Peverini at Puiggari and my studies at Southern was the significance attached to Ellen G. White as a prophet of the church. Soon after the start of my second year, Dean Hammill was called urgently to the General Conference at Takoma Park. In a scramble to find a replacement, the administration chose Pastor Denton Rebok, who had just retired as Dean of the Seminary at Takoma Park, as Interim Dean. He also taught one course for the Religion department, "The Plan of Salvation." It was based entirely on the five volumes of Ellen White Conflict of the Ages series. The students loved it. For me it was really an introduction to Ellen White, because at the college in Puiggari, we had not been using

Ellen White, except for a few quotations here and there. Within Adventism in the States, I soon discovered, Ellen White played a dominant role as the inspired interpreter of Scripture. She had been, undoubtedly, the most influential foundational figure in Adventism. When she was sixteen years old, she had her first vision, soon after those who had been expecting the Second Coming of Christ on October 22, 1844, were severely disappointed. As a prophet who received special messages from God, she became a leading member of the small group of men who in time organized the church on top of the wreckage left by The Great Disappointment. I did not know what to do with the notion that her inspiration was to be taken almost at the same level as that of the Bible. At first, I went along with the crowd, but I was uncomfortable with those who gave her veto power over all other interpretations.

My favorite classes that year were taught by Dr. Kathleen McMurphy, the professor of English literature. Her specialty was John Milton, and I was fortunate to read Milton with her. I was amazed to find how much Ellen White took from Milton. Many students, however, became uncomfortable and complained bitterly. When she had us read Nathaniel Hawthorne's *Scarlet Letter*, things turned into open rebellion. Many students believed they should not be required to read novels in a Christian college. The course had to be suspended for a class period. Pastor Rebok came to the next class and defended reading Hawthorne's novel. I was totally confused, unable to understand what was going on. I was not sure whether the upheaval was due to the fundamentalism of the Bible Belt or student chicanery. My inclination was to attribute it to the former.

As is well known, 1954 was the year the Supreme Court issued Brown vs. Board of Education. When I arrived at Southern, I was unaware of what segregation in the U.S. South really meant. At the bus station in Miami, the day I arrived from Cuba, I had seen drinking fountains labeled "Whites Only". On the bus to Chattanooga I had seen a few black passengers, but had not paid

75

attention to the fact they were seated in the back. I do, however, remember a heated conversation among professors at Southern about the implications of the Supreme Court's decision. The chairman of the music department, Dr. Adrian Lauritzen, who had recently arrived from Minnesota, was talking with two or three others. I was listening, trying to follow along. Their conversation left me wondering whether I had come at an auspicious time. They feared there were going to be violent riots in the South. At least one of the professors was really upset with the decision. The Adventist church also operated Oakwood College, an institution for blacks in Huntsville, Alabama. Both Southern and Oakwood were supported by the Southern Union, but the two had little to do with each other. Their relationship seemed to be limited to a yearly visit by the Oakwood College Choir to present a Saturday evening music program. Southern did not reciprocate in any way. People at Southern thought "the Negroes could sing." The presence of the Oakwood choir on campus, however, created all kinds of logistical maneuvers in order to prevent contact between the students from the two colleges, especially in the dining hall. Other than at this special occasion, Southern's campus was kept lily white.

Hammill's desire to change this was beginning to bear fruit, however. A new contingent from the Caribbean, Central and South America was making a small breakthrough. The Mendoza brothers from Puno, and four other Peruvians, together with Ivan Namihas from Manaos, Brazil, and myself made up the South American contingent. There were enough of us, together with some sons of missionaries who had grown up abroad, to play soccer, which was totally unknown to the rest of the students. There were also students from Central America and the Caribbean: one from Honduras, a couple of Cuban guys and about seven Puerto-Ricans. Sometimes students would join us playing soccer and then teach us baseball. It was very good to have this little island in which to speak Spanish and enjoy the camaraderie of people who understood your culture.

At Southern I discovered dating. Since I didn't have a penny in my pocket, it was almost impossible for me. For special evening programs you were expected to buy a corsage for your date. I was locked out. Besides, going out with a woman, one-on-one, required that you be an extrovert full of entertaining stories to tell. I was a quiet introvert who spoke broken English and felt that the pressure under the circumstances made the costs outweigh the gains. During my two years at Southern I only had three or four dates, and I must confess that they were not very successful. I had been accustomed to socializing in groups, where everyone went out together and contributed whatever they could to the shared enjoyment. This meant that I could go out without the feeling that it was up to me to provide the entertainment. The harshness of the dating system revealed itself better, however, in its devastating effects in the women's dormitory. On Saturday nights it was left full of pretty, eager, young women who spent the evening alone in their rooms, some of them crying, because it was already the fourth or the fifth weekend without a date. I thought that was quite cruel, indeed.

At Southern I developed a special friendship with Donaldo Alfaro, who every one knew as Hondy, since he was from Honduras. Donaldo was a short fellow with a striking physique, curly short hair, an easy smile and picaresque eyes. He was a bit unpredictable, very humorous, and popular. The descendant of English pirates who settled on the islands off the coast of Honduras, he grew up speaking English and Spanish, and was fluent in both. For secondary school he had attended Forest Lake Academy, near Orlando, Florida. Since this was a feeder school to Southern, he had friends as soon as he arrived. Hondy worked at the Creamery, where the milk from the college herd was processed to be sold to the supermarkets as milk, cottage cheese, or ice cream. Usually he worked the night shift. It happened that we took the literature course with Dr. McMurphy together. Many times I would go to the creamery at night when he was working alone, and we would discuss the class assignments. The next day he and I would have some questions to ask in class. We were proud to see Dr.

77

McMurphy's frustration when we, the Latinos, instead of her majors, asked the questions that kept class going. Hondy and I had some serious talks about all the things that disturb young men in a foreign land. Sometimes, on Sabbath afternoons we would take long walks in the wooded hills behind the college, immersed in some issue that had come up in class or disturbed us at the time, like the deep racial prejudices of our surroundings, the lynchings that were not yet a faded memory, capital punishment, and so forth. Our long discussions were therapy. They provided the space in which to make the transitions necessary to take full advantage of the opportunities we were having.

As a group, Adventists were known then for being activists on a few fronts, including temperance. It was natural, therefore, for the General Conference to have a Temperance Department. Temperance, in this case, did not mean practicing the golden mean, not going to extremes; it meant abstaining from alcoholic beverages. Drugs had not yet cut a prominent profile on the horizon. One of the main activities of the Temperance Director was to hold oratorical contests at the twelve Adventist colleges in the United States and Canada. It was one of the biggest events of the year. Students prepared their orations well ahead of time, and there were preliminary rounds to determine who would be a contestant on the big night. On the Saturday night of the contest, the finalists would stand before a packed tabernacle and give a ten minute oration. Hondy had always applied as a contestant and was among the finalists. In my first year at Southern he ended up the winner. A small group of close friends were just ecstatic with this great achievement. The prize was fifty dollars, and with it Hondy immediately invited four of us to go out that night and celebrate. It was my only meal at a restaurant during my two years at Southern.

Dean Hammill had been able to move in this direction because he had the support of the college president, Pastor Wright. He was not an intellectual, but still a broad-minded fellow who delegated authority and took care of public relations, allowing the faculty and students to have a voice in planning activities and managing student life. The Board of Trustees, however, saw these developments as a denial of traditional Adventism and a threat to its authority. After my first year at Southern, the Board fired Wright and brought in Dr. Thomas W. Walters. He was given specific instructions to take control of the situation and bring the college back to its old ways. The poor man suffered terribly trying to please the faculty and the students, now accustomed to participate in the decision making process, and the Board of Trustees, who wanted to use Walters to keep control for itself. In his second year as president he suffered a nervous breakdown.

The religious atmosphere infused every aspect of life at Southern. Every morning and every evening we attended dorm worship services. On Friday nights and Sabbaths, the college emptied into church. Each semester there was a Week of Prayer held by a guest speaker. I think it was Spring of my first year that Pastor Robert Pierson was the preacher at Week of Prayer. He had just returned from mission service in the Caribbean. I was greatly moved by his sermons, and responded positively to his appeals for a greater commitment to God's will. When he invited students to see him privately, I made an appointment and had a session of private prayer with him. It was one of the most calming and beautiful experiences of my years at Collegedale.

As a Religion major I had to go out to churches in the vicinity to help with Sabbath services. Since I did not have a car, I went with another student who usually had the sermon for the day. My part was to tell a story from the mission lands. My English pronunciation at the time was poor, but the listeners were always graceful and kind. These Sabbath trips were a great blessing, not only because they took me out of the little valley and included the enjoyment of a home-cooked meal with the family who invited us to their house, but also because they allowed me to see first-hand what Americans were really like in their homes and at worship.

I had expected Adventists to feel very much a part of the protestant majority in the States. It was obvious, of course, that they enjoyed full religious freedom. I was somewhat surprised to find that they felt marginalized. They had a distinctive sectarian attitude toward all other religions. In a way, I guess, I should have known that much. In her interpretation of the last days, Ellen White makes the point that Adventists, along with those who keep the commandments and in particular the Sabbath commandment, will be persecuted by both Catholics and what she designates as apostate Protestantism. This blending of Catholics and Protestants as the manifestation of those who stand against the redemptive will of God in the last days makes dialogue with the rest of the protestant world in the States strained or impossible. The fact that many southern states had blue laws, prohibiting commerce on Sundays, was taken to be a clear sign of the apostasy of Protestantism, exacerbating the distance between Adventists and Protestants.

According to the Adventist interpretation of the book of Revelation, a law by the United States Congress supporting the observance of Sunday as the Christian day of worship is one day to be established as the Mark of the Beast. Thus, in the large scheme of things, the United States government is to be at that time on the wrong side of the divide between the forces of good and evil. The United States government would renounce the wall of separation between church and state and side with Catholics and Protestants who worship on Sunday, for all practical purposes establishing a state religion.

Before coming to the States, I had heard that Adventists are a North American "cult". Of course, we would defend Adventism from this charge by pointing out that rather than being pro America, Adventism identified the United States as the power described in Revelation as a wolf in sheep's clothing, one that would devour the people of God. Once in the States, however, I found that Adventists here were quite ambivalent about this interpretation. On the one hand, they were constantly looking at local Sunday laws as premonitions of a national Sunday law. On the other, they were full blooded Americans who took for granted that America could do no wrong in God's eyes. In their eyes, the United States are the Promised Land that God has blessed in a special way and given to a special people to live, prosper and multiply in it. I was fully aware that the Protestant ethic was pervasive in the land, and that the religious commitment of the people was obvious everywhere, not just among Adventists. In Catholic Argentina, by contrast, religion was totally absent from the way in which people conducted their lives, except within the Protestant subculture. I soon discovered here that Adventists were theologically quite distinct from the surrounding religious culture, but culturally they were totally assimilated into the larger nationalist culture. I also learned that in the States one of the first rules of etiquette is not to talk about religion with your neighbor. In the States, evangelism consisted of preaching to the choir.

It took me a while to discover that the Adventist fear of the government of the United States as the one who passes the national Sunday Law that serves as the marker that informs "the remnant" that "the time of the end" has arrived, had to be understood within a larger cultural context. It was one of the characteristics of those who opened up the western frontier to distrust all forms of government, especially the national government that exercised real power from away in Washington, D.C. Adventism had prospered in the frontier among rather independent-minded farmers, and took a strong stand against "big government", a powerful political shibboleth. Seeing the national government as the agent of Satan who gives power to those who wish to impose a Sunday Law, thus bringing about the persecution of those who refuse to obey this godless law and by doing so are sealed with the Seal of God as Sabbath-keepers, only reinforced the long-standing suspicion of government. There was, therefore, a significant difference between the government and its power to write and enforce the laws, and the Promised Land where the people of God had been given religious freedom and a prodigal land full of natural resources.

On the Sabbaths I spent on Southern's campus I often joined the "Sunshine bands," organized by a fellow student, Dean Kinsey. Dean was a bit older, already married with children. He was a clean cut, good looking red head with whom I had some classes, and who was also an assistant to the manager at the broom factory. He drove a big De Soto in which he could take several of us quite comfortably. Others also volunteered with their cars. About two o'clock in the afternoon volunteers would get together at an appointed place and organize into bands to go to Chattanooga. One band would go to the state tuberculosis hospital. Another would go to the city jail, and, if there were enough volunteers, another would go to a nursing home. Once at the designated place, we would sing gospel songs and hymns to our captive audiences. In fact, our listeners were mostly glad to see us come, and would beg for us to keep coming back. For some we were their only 'visitors'. The Sunshine Bands were something new to me, and I really enjoyed them. Most Sabbaths I came back to my room feeling that the prisoners, the tuberculosis patients, or the old-folks had done me a favor and given me a blessing.

My worst times at Collegedale were the breaks, when everyone went home to spend time with family, and I stayed to work full time at the broom factory. For my second year, I secured a room on the first floor, next to the main entrance, and Don Wilson became my roommate. He was very athletic, with a sure demeanor and a very outgoing personality. Even though a freshman, he almost immediately became a campus presence. It did help that he was very good both on the tennis and the basketball courts. It also helped that he came from a very well-established Adventist family. His father had been, at different times during the course of his career, the president of five different divisions of the Adventist church. By then he had retired, but continued serving as the pastor of a small church. After a short time, however, he was asked to become fully active again as the president of the Georgia Cumberland Conference, where Southern Missionary College is located. It had been a disappointment for the Wilsons when, at the

General Conference of 1954, Don's father, Nathaniel C. Wilson, had not been elected president of the General Conference. Eventually, Don's brother, Neil Wilson, became General Conference president for several terms. Don's parents were a lovely couple who had lived in almost every corner of the world, except in Central and South America. They took pity on me, and on one occasion took me home to spend a week during Christmas.

At home, Don revealed a side of himself he could not display at Southern. He loved guns. He had a regular armory: several pistols of different calibers and not a few rifles. I was absolutely stunned. I just could not take it in that in an Adventist home, the home of the would-be president of the General Conference, an 18 year old had all these guns with the full approval of his father. A few months later, when Don's father became the Conference president and purchased a large farm with river frontage in Northwest Georgia to build what would become Bass Academy, Don took part of his armory with him to the woods next to the river and invited me to do some target practice with soda cans. I did put out a couple of shots, but I never felt comfortable around loaded weapons. Don, on the other hand, was having the time of his life. It was my introduction to another cultural aspect of the United States: its obsession with guns. I think that while I was dreaming of going to the rain forests of Perú to translate the Bible into a tribal native tongue, Don was dreaming of going to the jungles of Southeast Asia to kill communists.

My second year at Southern, soon after classes began, I received word from home that my father, who would be sixty years old on December 18, had become ill with an infection. I was told not to worry. He was getting good medical attention by Klinton and Arturo, who were looking after him and taking him to the best doctors around. After some weeks, word was that my father was responding to antibiotics and getting better. Things were going to be just fine, and I should not be unduly concerned. Then, a few months later, word came that his situation was becoming chronic and it might take a while for him to get rid of this infection, which now had been localized in his heart. One afternoon during the Spring Break the Dean of men came to my room and said he had bad news. Then he told me that my father had died. He had only lived four months past his sixtieth birthday. By the time the news reached me, my father was already buried.

When I had left home, almost a year and a half before, it had not crossed my mind that something like this could happen. I could not remember one single time when my father had been ill. He was the picture of health and good humor, always ready to be engaged in work or play. My mother, by contrast, had been sick many times as I grew up, but dad had never been sick. How could it be that the first illness that came his way could take him down? One of the things that kept me going when I canvassed in Cuba and while I was earning my way through college was that in my mind I could see him on his knees by the bed he shared with my mother for long periods of prayer. Now I could no longer count on his prayers for me. I knew that he had been very keen to know how I was doing. Was I facing any difficulties that made things extra hard? I was now a few months away from graduating with a B.A., but I was not going to be able to give him the joy of hearing the news. I felt powerless. I just had to accept these circumstances, which instead of paralyzing me gave me one more reason why I had to succeed in my efforts to get an education. My father's many prayers had to be answered.

The South American Division acknowledged my scholarly efforts by offering to sponsor me as a graduate student at the Seventh-day Adventist Theological Seminary in Takoma Park, Maryland, a suburb of Washington, D.C. Of course, I was delighted. Without my asking, this offer had come my way and, of course, I immediately accepted it. Evidently God was opening another door for me.

I must confess that I did not feel very secure with my education at Southern. I was happy with my English courses. Freshmen Composition, was a most effective course for me because I had no experience writing research papers in secondary school. I also had two years of New Testament Greek under my belt, a good foundation. From the religion department, I felt that the best course I had taken was the one I did as an independent study. Due to my tight schedule I had not been able to take Old Testament Prophets when it was offered. So I made arrangements to do the requirement as an independent study during my last summer, before the August graduation. I read a great deal and wrote a long paper contrasting Isaiah and Jeremiah. It was my best college experience. Doing the research, however, I became aware, for the first time, of what biblical scholarship was really all about. I saw the biblical authors as witnesses with messages that were more or less cohesive by themselves, not writers from whom one picked texts to prove doctrines one organized according to modern needs. I also discovered that I had to consider the possibility that not everything found in the book of Jeremiah had been written by Jeremiah. Deuteronomic editors surely left their imprints as they put the oracles together. Isaiah, the eighth century prophet who lived in Jerusalem, may not have written the sixty six chapters of the book with his name. Spiritual descendants of his, most likely, were responsible for chapters forty to sixty six, and some of the material in the first thirty nine chapters could also be from another hand. None of this would have come up had I taken the regular class on the prophets.

Doing my independent research in the library, I realized how to read the Bible with the mind fully engaged in the process. Until then "higher criticism" had been presented to me as the work of those eager to undermine the Bible's authority. My readings taught me that those who used it were eager, to the contrary, to hear what the Bible had to say on its own terms, without preconceptions of the nature of its authority. Reading the prophets to find out what they were interested in, to determine their message as a unified witness to their contemporaries, was the most logical first step toward understanding. I began to think that all the texts I had memorized out of context had not really put me in touch with the Bible and its message after all. It was with these thoughts turning in my head that I left Collegedale for Washington, D.C.

6

TAKOMA PARK

The day after my graduation in August, I left for Takoma Park, a suburb on the Northeast side of Washington, D.C. I had already made arrangements to live with three other Southern graduates who studied at the Seventh-day Adventist Theological Seminary. Ferdinand Wuttke and Richard Shepherd had graduated the year before and had been living in a rented apartment three blocks from the seminary with two other students, but one had married and the other had graduated. So now there was room in the apartment for David Bauer and me. We were half of the singles in a student body of around one hundred. Our apartment was rather large, on the first floor of a U-shaped apartment building with a small formal garden at the front between the two forward wings. I lived in that apartment for the whole year without having a key to the front door. During the day the door was always unlocked. At night the last one in locked the door.

At the apartment we had a common treasury, sharing everything. The rent was one hundred dollars a month, and we spent about twenty five dollars a week on groceries for the four of us. Ferdy and I were responsible for doing the weekly shopping. David was responsible for cleaning the apartment once a week, and Dick kept the kitchen clean on a regular basis. We all did some cooking. This meant that I had a regular expenditure of about fifty dollars a month for room and board. Since my scholarship from the South American Division paid for my tuition and books and gave me one hundred dollars a month for living expenses, I thought

I was rich, especially after having spent two years without a cent in my pocket.

I immediately bought myself a student season ticket for the National Symphony, which allowed me to attend ten concerts at Constitution Hall. The best of the season were the guest artists and guest conductors, since Howard Mitchell was not too impressive. I will never forget hearing Zino Francescatti playing Beethoven's Violin Concerto when a string in his violin broke. As the music continued, he wished to exchange violins with the Concertmaster, but the Concertmaster refused, so he had to switch violins with the second chair. He put a new string on Francescatti's Stradivarius, and then they switched violins again when the soloist had a pause. At Constitution Hall the guest conductors included Eugene Ormandy, Dimitri Mitropoulos and Antal Dorati, whom I had heard in Buenos Aires. I felt I was living again.

I soon became enamored with Washington, its museums, the big avenues and the complex grid of the city streets. I frequented the National Gallery regularly and discovered that there were free Sunday concerts of chamber music on the East Garden once a month during the season. I then became a frequent attendee at these concerts.

At the Seminary I registered for Greek exegesis classes and began to study Hebrew. I was doing an M.A. in Biblical Languages. As a matter of interest, I also took a class in Church History in Art. For it, I eventually wrote a paper on Salvador Dali's Last Supper and Crucifixion. The former, of course, was directly available at the National Gallery. Dr. Charles Weniger, the Seminary Dean, also taught a course in Graduate Research, which required first hand searches at the Library of Congress. I still remember that one of the items we had to document was a marker of the boundary between the District of Columbia and the State of Maryland, found a few yards from the Seminary property.

Dr. Ronald Loasby, the professor of Greek Exegesis, was a delight. I took several courses from him. He was an Englishman who had been a missionary in India for many years before World War II. When he returned he had earned a doctoral degree in History at American University. I think he had studied Greek in high school in England and had taught it at the Adventist College in Puna, India. He just loved the precision of the language and really enjoyed pointing out its nuances, thereby making exegetical points. This close reading of the Greek text often got him in trouble with some students who carried their concerns to the ecclesiastical authorities.

It happened that when the denomination decided to establish a school for advanced studies in theology, the building for it was erected next to the main offices of the General Conference in Takoma Park. On the same city block were housed the General Conference, the Seminary and the Review and Herald Publishing Association, the most important of the three publishing houses the church had in the States. Going from one building to the other was just a matter of a few steps.

Students were taking those steps often in order to complain to some General Conference official about what Dr. Loasby was teaching in his classes. They could not accept that the meaning of a text was not what Ellen White made of it. They would report Loasby's interpretations as heresies to the ecclesiastical authorities next door. It was not difficult for them to find eager listeners who would then call in Dr. Loasby for questioning. A few of us in his classes were eager to know exactly what went on in these inquisitions. Were any of those questioning Loasby up on their Greek? Surely most of them were staunch defenders of the authority of Ellen White. Arthur White, Ellen's grandson, was now the custodian of her legacy. He defended her inspiration on a level with that of the biblical authors. As the last in the long list of inspired prophets, she occupied a commanding position. For many she was the last word. Loasby, for his part, would stand by the Greek text of the biblical authors.

As a result of these complaints, it was not uncommon for Loasby to come to class a bit late because he had been called to a

General Conference office and asked to explain himself. I was always amazed at the good humor with which he took this unmerited persecution. He would come to class and make a joke about his last performance on the carpet next door. Then he would just continue his teaching with the same enthusiasm as always. His passion for what the text actually said was contagious, at least for me. He could question the available translations of the text most effectively, pointing out the force of a preposition here, or a genitive there. Once the translation had gotten straightened out, the meaning of the text, according to Loasby, was obvious. I was really fascinated by what knowledge of the original languages could do. So I became adept at taking notice of the range of meanings in prepositions and genitives, especially. Class discussions were more or less limited to determining whether to read an objective or a subjective genitive. It had to be determined also whether it was a genitive of authorship, of possession, of agency, of origin, of manufacture, of material, etc. Interpretation, thus, was strictly grammatical and syntactical. Often we only covered five to eight verses in a class period as we dissected the sentences and put them together again, phrase by phrase. This was the way to really get into what God had written.

Of course, part of the effectiveness of those exegesis classes was the inimitable style of Dr. Loasby. Those of us who took his classes back then, when we happen to meet, always end up recollecting some of the mannerisms and the jokes he would pull with such success, making one of us look foolish. He could get away with it because he was such a peaceful, decent, fun-loving, sensible human being that no one could take offense from him. After a while we began to detect from where he was getting most of his ideas, which seemed to be his favorite commentaries on Scripture. Coming to terms with the knowledge that his notes were not quite original did not detract from his effectiveness as a teacher. Another element of the fun and effectiveness of his classes was that here all the students were serious students of Greek. He regularly offered both an English and Greek version of the same exegesis class. That meant that these classes had only those who really wanted to work on the Greek!

After two quarters of Hebrew grammar and syntax, I took a class on the Prophet Hosea in Hebrew. It was not the same thing. In part this was due to the Hebrew language, which does not have the nuances the Greeks had given to theirs in their efforts to develop the art of reasoning. Hebrew is more a matter of free association. But it was also a matter of the professor. During the whole quarter we did not quite finish the first chapter because we could not decide whether Gomer bath Diblaim, the prostitute God told Hosea to marry, was a real, historical person, or the whole story of this marriage with the prostitute was a parable that illustrated the relationship of Israel and God. If I remember correctly, most agreed that it could be both, without giving much significance to its historical reference. But some suggested that it could be just a parable and nothing more. That raised all kinds of problems for those who could not allow for fiction in the Bible.

The most scholarly professor at the Seminary was Dr. Siegfried Horn. He was a German who had also been in India as a missionary before World War II. During the War, he was interned in a British concentration camp in India. There he had killed time translating the Bible from the original languages into German. When the war ended he came to the States and went to the Oriental Institute of the University of Chicago, from which he received a PhD in Egyptology. At the Seminary he was supposed to be the professor of Old Testament, but he made it clear that he was the professor of Old Testament history. He would not touch questions of exegesis or theology with a ten foot pole. During the two years I studied at the Seminary, I took every class he taught. His classes were in archaeology, chronology and history, what was called "backgrounds". They were intended to provide the horizon, the topography, and the scenery in which the Old Testament personages lived.

Horn's mastery of his subject was well recognized by his colleagues in the discipline. By the time I took his classes he had participated in the archaeological excavations at Shechem under George Wright of Harvard. Eventually he would distinguish himself as the organizer and the director of the excavations at Madaba, in Jordan. When I was a student of his, he was writing most of the introductory articles for the Seventh-day Adventist Bible Commentary, which, unfortunately, did not specifically acknowledge any of its authors. As it turned out, many of the pieces written by others proved to be quite inadequate and Dr. Horn ended up re-writing them under the pressure of publishing deadlines, without any recognition. Since he was so busy with his scholarly work, it was difficult for me, at least, to establish some kind of personal rapport with him. His having been reared in Germany may also have been a factor. He was a very private person with a different sense of humor.

The one Seminary professor who really made a mark on me, besides Loasby, was Dr. Edward Heppenstall, another Englishman. Before coming to teach at the Seminary he had taught at La Sierra College in Riverside, California. While there he had earned a doctoral degree in Education from the University of Southern California. At the Seminary, he was the professor of Systematic Theology. For this task he was, admittedly, ill equipped. As an intelligent person doing theology, however, he was first rate. He organized biblical passages in a coherent way and presented them to the class with exceptional liveliness. His lectures were marvelous disquisitions that made the biblical text come out as gospel. This however, meant that Heppenstall, like Loasby, also was repeatedly called to defend himself before the ecclesiastical authorities on account of what he was teaching.

The centerpiece of Heppenstall's offerings was a class in Righteousness by Faith. In it he was trying to open up the church to a more Protestant understanding of the gospel. Adventists, as said already, have strong prejudices against Catholics. Their major offense, in Adventist eyes, is to have changed the Christian day of worship from Sabbath to Sunday. But they are also wrong on account of their teaching on confession, penance, indulgences, and the mediating agency of the Virgin Mary and the saints. In this view Adventists are in agreement with most Protestants. The classic expression of the Protestant argument was presented by Adolf von Harnack at the turn of the twentieth century. According to him, as soon as the Church Fathers began to express and defend the Gospel in Greek philosophical terms, Christianity deviated from its original truth and eventually fully apostatized from the pure Gospel of Jesus Christ. What the reformers of the sixteenth century did was to recover the purity of the first century gospel. Adventists see themselves as the ones who carried this enterprise to its culmination by retrieving the Sabbath as the day of worship. Protestants in general, however, accused Adventists of being no different from Catholics, since they also taught salvation by works. The technical way of making this accusation was to say that Adventists were guilty of the Galatian heresy.

In his letter to the Galatians, the apostle Paul accuses the recipients of the letter of seeking "the righteousness of works." One of the specific things they are doing, which Paul finds appalling, is that they "observe days, and months, and seasons and years!" (Gal. 4:10). Reading between the lines, it would appear that the Galatians are doing this because other Christian apostles had come to their towns and told them that the way to salvation is through knowledge of the structure given to the cosmos at its creation, now revealed in the calendar. They were, therefore, to observe the Jewish religious calendar of yearly, seasonal, monthly and weekly feasts. As traditionally interpreted by Protestants, these other apostles insisted that Christianity was a Jewish sect, and in Judaism in order to be right with God the observance of the commandments is of the essence. Now, there is no question that for Adventists the observance of the Ten Commandments is absolutely necessary, especially, of course, the fourth commandment which prescribes abstention from work on the seventh day of the week. The goal of every Adventist, therefore, is to attain to full compliance with the demands of the commandments in order to be found worthy at God's judgment.

93

Heppenstall was at the vanguard of those who wished Adventism to be more of a gospel with good news. No one may take credit for their salvation by keeping the commandments. In fact, those who could succeed in perfectly keeping all Ten Commandments would still not be in the kingdom of God on account of their achievement, apart from faith in Jesus Christ.

The question of Adventism's position within the Protestant spectrum had been an issue for some time already. When at a famous General Conference Session at Minneapolis in 1888 the issue became central, Ellen White gave her support to two mavericks, Pastors Jones and Waggoner, who pointed out that the emphasis on the commandments, characteristic of Adventist preaching, did not give Christ the place he should hold in the Plan of Salvation. Aware of this issue, Ellen White wrote that some Adventist preaching about the law had been as dry as the hills of Gilboa, where it hardly ever rains. The scuffle caused by Jones and Waggoner at Minneapolis, however, was soon squelched and the emphasis on law-keeping became the standard fare of Adventist sermons. Heppenstall was opening up the issue again, and some thought his views on the Gospel were a sell out.

Heppenstall was obviously caught by a profound sense of God's love, and all his classes communicated fully the pervasive possessiveness of God's love, which could only be responded to with love. In his mind, and for this he would have ample evidence from the writings of Ellen White, the whole history of the world was the way of establishing the supremacy of love. The rebellions against God in the universe, first on the part of Lucifer in heaven, and then on the part of Adam and Eve on earth, had been a denial of God's love. Thus what is going to be vindicated for ever when the New Heaven and the New Earth are established is the power of God's love. In order to support this theology, Heppenstall disagreed with the facile and common caricature of the Bible as showing a God of Wrath in the Old Testament and a God of Love in the New. He would spend much time showing how the presentation of a God of Love was to be found with just as much power equally in both testaments. After having done my research at Southern on the prophets, he did not have to convince me.

Heppenstall's troubles with some students and his appearances on the carpet next door were part of something quite significant that was taking place as the culmination of a project that had been going on somewhat underground in the General Conference offices for some time. In the early fifties, one of the most read religious magazines was Eternity, published by the Methodists. The editor of Eternity, Donald G. Barnhouse, also had a very popular radio program, which aired the church service at his church in Philadelphia. When the president of the Pennsylvania Conference of Seventh-day Adventists congratulated him on a sermon on divine grace which he had heard over the radio, Barnhouse wrote back perplexed that an Adventist pastor believed in grace. As far as he knew, Adventists believed in salvation by works. At the time, Barnhouse was contemplating a series of books on the American cults (as then usually classified): Mormons, Jehovah's Witnesses, Christian Scientists and Adventists. The actual writing had been commissioned to a young scholar, Walter Martin. To write the volume on Adventism, Martin and Barnhouse established a dialogue with LeRoy Froom, considered by the ecclesiastical administrators to be the most prominent Adventist scholar. Froom was best known for his four volumes on the history of Christian apocalyptic interpretation, a rather unscholarly accumulation of quotations from Christian sources with no connection to their historical contexts. His objective in this work was to argue that Adventism was to be understood within a well established exegetical tradition, and not as a deviant Christian sect. Martin had decided not to write an exposé of Adventism, but a balanced, scholarly description. In his contacts with Froom he was primarily seeking information. Eventually, he asked Froom to give him in writing the answers to forty questions. Froom formed a small committee which included some Seminary professors, in order to write these answers. The outcome of this effort was the publication of Questions on Doctrine, a book that immediately became quite controversial within the denomination.

Since Froom felt confident that he had established the legitimacy of the Adventist interpretation of the book of Daniel in the Old Testament and the book of Revelation in the New, in his answers to the questions Martin asked, he unabashedly reaffirmed very traditional Adventist positions. On some issues, however, being eager to take advantage of the opportunity to integrate Adventism within the Protestant spectrum, in what some considered an underhanded way, he edited what some Adventist pioneers, including Ellen White, had said. As a result, the book created two distinct camps. One was eager to see Adventism accepted into the family of Protestant denominations; the other thought the eagerness to belong was turning into a denial of distinctive Adventism. For them sectarian exclusivism was non negotiable.

The church found itself at a crossroads. Of course, entangled in the dialogue with the Evangelicals were a host of theological issues. Most prominent among them were: a) the peculiar Adventist interpretation of the image of Christ as High Priest in the book of Hebrews, where he is not only the sacrifice offered for the sins of the world, but also the High Priest who takes the blood of the sacrifice behind the veil into the Holy of Holies in the Heavenly Temple; b) the characteristics of the human nature the Son of God assumed at the incarnation, and c) the inerrancy of Scripture and the nature of its inspiration. Debates about these issues became endemic to any kind of intellectual life within Adventism at the time.

I spent countless hours debating with fellow students, friends, and later colleagues the nuances to be taken into consideration when trying to settle one's views on these questions. They seemed, at times, to be matters of life and death. This was especially the case when one remembers that it was presupposed that salvation depended on holding the right doctrines. It was at this time that I began to see that the real danger for Christians, after twenty centuries, was still the one that first raised its head in the first century: Gnosticism. In the late fifties and early sixties, I became aware that Gnosticism, in its most broad definition, has been a constant companion of Christianity. In antiquity, as it has become well known, Gnosticism took many forms and eventually became a panoply of "systems", using elaborate descriptions of the topography of the space between heaven and earth and its spiritual inhabitants. Knowledge of the cosmos provided the key to escape from the prison of earthly existence. Of course, these offers of salvation succeeded because there were those who agreed that esoteric knowledge, knowledge available to a few select souls, is the one essential ingredient to salvation. Some Christians have fought hard, and sometimes killed, in order to establish that they are the ones in possession of real knowledge of God's plan of salvation. The doctrines they teach are the only true ones. It is only those who hold these doctrines who will enter into Heaven.

Faced with the seriousness and the vigor with which people argued about things human beings are incapable of determining with any degree of certainty made me realize that these kinds of debates really have to do with something else. They are fueled by a Gnostic environment. On the surface, the debates were about whether Christ had accomplished the atonement for sin at the cross, or whether he was now a mediator, a High Priest, in heaven presenting the case of individuals who had attained to perfection before the Father. Only those who could be thus presented before God are worthy of entering the Holy City. Whether the number of the redeemed would be, as Revelation says, one hundred and forty four thousand, or this was a symbolic number. Whether when the Son was incarnated he assumed the nature of Adam and Eve before the Fall, or after the Fall, or of a humanity which four thousand years after the Fall had developed innate propensities to sin (assuming that Creation took place around four thousand B.C.E.). Whether the Bible was verbally inspired and without error of any kind, or the men who wrote it were inspired and wrote under the limitations of their time and culture, thereby making possible the presence of views which later advances in knowledge proved inadequate. Even though at the time I was not able to decide what these debates were really about, I became convinced that at issue was something else which had little to do with the Bible or with salvation. I became, therefore, quite eager to pursue further studies.

The late fifties were heady times for a young student at the Seminary. Most of my classmates were older men, already married and with families, and many had been missionaries, pastors or evangelists for quite a few years. All of them seemed quite certain of what they believed, and some were extremely conservative, a few to the point of fanaticism. This was primarily the case in reference to adherence to the divinely ordained diet as required of those to be counted among the 144,000 who were to receive the Lord at His second coming. The dialogue between Froom and the members of his committee with Barnhouse and Martin, and the appearance of the first volume of the Seventh-day Adventist Bible Commentary, made for a very effervescent atmosphere in which to do theology in the church. Of course, all this was possible because the president of the General Conference at the time was Pastor Reuben Fighur, an enlightened administrator who, even though not a scholar himself, had an open mind and a clear vision of a more open-minded church. Years later I heard a friend describe his reaction when all the complaints on the part of experienced pastors about Seminary professors came to him. According to this story, he would put on his construction-site hat and let the stones fall.

At the Seminary I had gained confidence in my knowledge of New Testament Greek, and some confidence in Biblical Hebrew. I also felt that I had a good grasp of the history of the times surrounding the Old Testament narratives. Still, I felt that my knowledge of the Bible was rather skimpy. I had not moved much beyond the "proof text" method for its understanding. Of course, I was totally taken by the assumption that the Bible has one message that is coherent and specific, and the task at hand is to discover it, the assumption being that only one interpretation of the text could be correct. The task of the exegete is to expose it.

It was becoming clear to me, however, that in order to accomplish this job one had to find the proper method for Bible study. At the Seminary I studied languages and history, but the "historical, critical method" was denounced as a tool of the devil. It was the most recent form of "higher criticism," what those wishing to demonstrate the untrustworthiness of the Bible used to destroy the faith of the innocent. It was important to be wise and not let oneself be deceived by its purveyors.

On the other hand, it was permissible and helpful for good Christians to engage in "lower criticism." This was also called "textual criticism." It is the method used to determine, as far as possible, what the original authors of the Biblical text actually wrote. The earliest full copies of the New Testament available are from the middle of the fourth century. There are some full copies of New Testament letters from the third century. The earliest copy of a New Testament manuscript is just a little scrap of papyrus about an inch and a half in diameter with writing on both sides from the seventeenth and eighteenth chapters of the Gospel of John. It is dated around 125 to 150 C.E. On the other hand, there are several hundred manuscripts of the New Testament, or of the four gospels, or of the letters of Paul, from the seventh to the fourteenth centuries. Not all of them have exactly the same text. Sometimes the variations are quite significant. Textual criticism is the attempt to determine, by carefully studying the available manuscripts, which of the variations has the best claim to being the original text. This is very tedious work, but if you believe that the text is the inspired Word of God, nothing is more important than the recovery of the words the original text actually had.

My first year at the Seminary I took a class in textual criticism of the New Testament, and, before I knew it, I had decided to write a Master's thesis doing a collation of a tenth century manuscript found in one of the monasteries on Mt. Athos in Greece. I was to collate the Gospel of Luke as part of the Greek New Testament project then under way. A microfilm with the Gospel of Luke in manuscript 1076 was sent to me and I had to compare its readings against the standard for all collations, the Textus Receptus. Every difference between my manuscript and the Textus Receptus, whether large or minute, I faithfully recorded. After I had finished that part of my project, I collated a section of about forty verses in 1076 against twelve other ancient manuscripts whose text types were already well known. This was to determine to which family of text types my manuscript belonged. This work, then, served as my thesis, and was incorporated into the files of the Greek New Testament Project, then at Princeton.

Doing textual criticism requires a great deal or attention to details. As I progressed along my manuscript and became familiar with the handwriting of the scribes who had produced it, reading it became easy. I soon discovered that their peculiar readings, at times, expressed their peculiar theological concerns, or attempts to make corrections or improvements on what their exemplar said. This meant that the dogmatic differentiation of "lower" from "higher" criticism turned out to be artificial. In the medieval scriptoria the monks may not have been evaluating the words of Scripture with literary, historical, or psychological tools, but they certainly felt free to adjust the text according to what they thought made better sense. The same is true of the textual critic who today aims at reconstructing the original text. Those using literary and historical methodologies are not doing something different.

At the time when I decided to do this thesis, I was thinking of my dreams of going to the Amazon jungle and translating the New Testament to the language of a native tribe. It turned out that this project served as my ticket to Duke University. One of the best known textual critics in the United States then was Kenneth W. Clark. In 1950, on a grant from the Library of Congress, he had spent a year at Mt. Athos, making microfilm copies of the New Testament manuscripts in the twenty monasteries in that sacred peninsula. Of course, some monasteries have richer libraries than others. Clark had done pioneering work searching and photographing manuscripts. My manuscript, 1076, was one of those he had photographed. When my application for graduate work went out to five or six graduate programs in New Testament, the only one who responded positively was the one in which Clark taught. Thus my efforts to continue my search for knowledge of the Biblical texts were rewarded. Acceptance to the graduate program at Duke, however, was not quite a reward. It turned out to be quite a challenge. Still, there was no doubt that God's hand kept opening doors for me.

My desire to go to Duke was in opposition to some commitments I had made. I had been able to study at the Seminary in the first place on account of the scholarship I had received from the South American Division of the General Conference. About the middle of my first year, working for my Masters in Biblical languages, the South American Division told me that I was scheduled to go to the Adventist College in Chillan, Chile, to be a professor in the theology department. In a way, I was elated. On the other hand, I felt totally inadequate to the task. Besides, I was only twenty three years old. I considered myself too young for a professor of theology. It happened that at the time of these developments, Victor Ampuero Matta, the professor of theology at Puiggari, whom I knew even though I had taken no classes from him, was in Washington for a few days, and I confided my dilemma to him. I explained that I felt totally inadequate, especially on account of my total lack of experience. To this he responded with words which have stayed with me. "Don't be fooled;" he said. "Experience many times only means that one has become hardened in one's mistakes."

When I decided to stay at the Seminary beyond the Masters for a Bachelor of Divinity, I asked the South American Division to allow me to continue studying without a scholarship from them. By then I had obtained two jobs. At night I did the cleaning of an office building. This gave me quite a bit of flexibility. Some nights I only spent half an hour emptying all the waste baskets. Other nights I also dusted every thing and passed the vacuum cleaner. On weekends I would at times wax the entryway and the corridors. My other job was as a receptionist at the Takoma Funeral Home, located half way between the Seminary and my apartment building. Mr. and Mrs. Walters, the owners, took me in as if I were their own son. Most times there was no activity in the house. I spent time in the office doing my studying, waiting for the phone to ring and being paid.

My social life expanded considerably in Takoma Park. For one thing, I had a little money in my pockets. For another, living in a city made it possible to go places, even without a car. Collegedale was an island where I had been marooned for two years. My three roommates were actively engaged in finding a wife. They were quite aware that church officials were reluctant to hire single men as pastors, or to teach or be administrators in the church's academies. They had been interviewing for jobs with Conference presidents who cut the interviews short the moment they realized they were interviewing a single man. I was being sponsored by the South American Division and was committed to returning to work there. Therefore, I was not looking for a lasting relationship. I was quite aware that it would be unrealistic for me to ask a young woman accustomed to the American standard of living to go with me to live on my meager ecclesiastical salary without any hope of visiting her family in the United States. At one time I had a few dates with the receptionist of the Statistical Department of the General Conference. Louise was a serious young woman with a lovely singing voice. She had started working at the G.C straight out of one the church's academies. Before I knew it, Louise and I were asked to meet with Pastor Paul Bradley, the Vice-President who was the liaison person for the South American Division. Pastor Bradley, a very likable fellow, thought it was his responsibility to inform Louise that she was making a big mistake dating a man who would return to South America as a native worker.

At the time the church had a very elaborate, quite prejudicial, pay scale. American missionaries who went overseas were paid salaries that allowed them to live comfortably in the country where they served. A supplemental salary was deposited in a bank account at home for them to be able to establish themselves comfortably

102

at their return. The normal tour of duty was five years and they were able to ship furniture and electrical appliances to their destinations. They also received paid trips home every two years to visit family. As a native Uruguayan returning to the Austral Union, I would be under a totally different pay scale and enjoy none of the other benefits. Were I to have an American wife, she would have to say good by to her family. Louise and I had had a few dates. We were not even near getting engaged. I thought it was quite revealing that Pastor Bradley had thought it necessary to establish the rules of the road even though we were not on that road.

When I contemplated going to Duke, I had to get the South American Division to give its consent. Of course, it was not known exactly how long it would take me to complete my degree. Under the circumstances, the Division opted to make me sign a contract for the money they had given me while I worked on my Masters. They figured that between books and stipends they had given me fifteen hundred dollars. The contract read that this debt could be paid in one of three ways: 1) working for the South American Division for five years; 2) being hired by any other Division, which would pay South America the debt, or 3) paying this debt myself if I did not work for the church. It turned out after all that, instead of a scholarship, I had been given a student loan. This realization allowed me to sign the contract and leave for Duke with a clear conscience.

7

Durham

The trip from Tacoma Park to Durham, North Carolina, was the most exciting up to then. I was venturing out into the unknown. I was leaving the shelter of institutional Adventism behind and entering the world of theology in the Christian West. I was eager to find out how real scholarship was done in the trenches and to get to know the people who did it. Once classes got under way, it did not take me long to realize that I was laboring at a great disadvantage in comparison with my classmates. My major weakness was the total lack of knowledge of what theology in the twentieth century had been about. I knew the names of the famous theologians, but neither in college nor at seminary had I been asked to read any of their writings. I am quite certain that if a professor had actually asked students to do so, there would have been a major upheaval at the school. Since I had specialized in Biblical Languages at the Seminary, and had done a thesis in textual criticism, I had not done much theology there. The crucial deficiency in my education, I thought, had been at Southern. Several factors had conspired to prevent me from receiving a formal liberal education. Even if my heavy work schedule was responsible for distracting me from my studies, I did not think the classes had been as demanding or as broadening as they should have been.

Students in the graduate program in Religion at Duke had to chose among three concentrations: Biblical Studies, Historical Studies, and Theological Studies. As a student in the Biblical Studies program one took classes in both Old and New Testament. During my first semester I took a class on the Habakkuk Commentary with

William Brownlee, the editor of the printed text of the scroll found at Qumran. Brownlee happened to be one of the two American graduate students spending a year at the American Schools of Oriental Research at Jerusalem when a dealer in antiquities brought the first scrolls of the Dead Sea caves to the attention of scholars. Since then he had been at the forefront in the study of the new materials. Reading the Habakkuk Scroll with him was a privilege. It was my first experience with a Hebrew text that did not include vowel pointing. I must confess that it was tough going.

Another one of my classes was on the Gospel of John with James Price, who had recently defended with distinction his dissertation under C.H. Dodd at Cambridge. His course blew my mind. Step by step I learned to read a Biblical book as a literary unit with its own integrity. For the first time I could see that the author is a significant force who employs his literary skills in the production of a book trying to open up the spiritual world to its readers by means of irony, double entendre, symbolisms, allusions to the Old Testament scriptures, etc. Finally I was getting what I had been looking for. This meant, of course, that the question of history was not uppermost in the mind of the author. It should not have taken me that long to realize this, but the religious culture to which I belonged had assigned to history the power to confirm the truth of the Bible. The Gospel of John was showing me that the truth of the Gospel was bigger, much bigger than what history could confirm. This gospel, as is well known, is explicitly concerned with the question of truth. It has Pilate asking Jesus, What is truth? It has Jesus affirming that the truth is what gives human beings freedom. But then it links truth to the way and the life, neither of which are exclusively intellectual properties. My eyes were not being opened by Professor Price, or by my reading of Dodd and of the very recent commentaries by C.K. Barrett and Rudolf Bultmann. The Gospel of John was making me see that transcendent truth was not in a book, but in the life, death, and resurrection of the Incarnate Word. By definition, no human being should pretend to have it safely folded and stored in her/his pocket or purse.

In 1958, when I began my work at Duke, New Testament studies were done under the shadow of the imposing scholarship of Rudolph Bultmann. Whether one wished to learn from him and follow his lead or to argue against him, no one could just ignore him. Price made clear that the course he was teaching was not on Jesus, but on the Gospel of John. One of my fellow students, a convinced radical, took the position that whether Jesus had actually lived was irrelevant to the Gospel. He may have lived, and his name may have been Jesus or some other name, but the significant point was the Lord proclaimed by the disciples after Easter. The link between the life of Jesus of Nazareth and the life of the community of disciples who worshiped a Risen Lord, for many, had been broken. At this time the New Quest of the Historical Jesus was just getting the attention of students in the field and many were declaring it either irrelevant or misguided.

Much was made of the words of the apostle Paul in 2 Cor. 5:16, "From now on, therefore, we regard no one from a human point of view; even though we once regarded Christ from a human point of view, we regard him thus no longer." The debate centered on the phrase "from a human point of view" which in a literal translation would read "according to the flesh." The question is: To what is this phrase attached? Does it modify the verb "to regard," "to view," or the noun "Christ"? In other words, is the apostle saying that, while in the past he had thought of Christ in human ways, he now thinks of him only in spiritual terms? In this case what has changed between the past and the present is Paul's way of thinking about Christ. Or, is the apostle saying that, while in the past he had regarded Christ as a human being in history, he now thinks of him only as the Risen Lord. In this case what has changed between the past and the present is the object of Paul's contemplation. In technical terms, is this a subjective or an objective relative clause? Arguments on this clause in the late fifties and early sixties were quite heated. Evidence could be brought in from the rest of Paul's writings to defend either reading. Of course, the first time the phrase is used in the verse, "From now on, therefore, we regard no one from a human point of view," Paul seems to use it in an objective sense. It seems more likely that Paul is saying that in the past he had been looking at his fellow human beings with the natural prejudices that normally inform our opinion of others. Now, taking into account that Christ had died for all, as the previous verse says, he saw everyone as the beneficiary of Christ's death on the cross.

I refer to the reading of this passage of Paul, because it had become the pivot on which the debate between faith and history, the most important debate at the time, took its ups and downs. This was the time when Van Harvey's book *The Historian and the Believer: The Morality of Historical Knowledge* was the most talked about theological book. The Barthian theology which ignored historical realities and proclaimed a totally transcendent God who thunders from beyond, before whom human beings must bow in obedience, was being challenged by a theology of the Word of God that was based on serious research into Christian origins and, on account of it, reacted in diametrically different ways. Conservative Christians listened to Barth and supplied the historical underpinning in order to maintain the authority of the Word, which they understood to be the written Word. Bultmann took history seriously to show that the preaching of Jesus was not tied to the historical circumstances of his life, or to the cultural mores and beliefs of the first century. His life had been the presupposition but not the foundation for the proclamation of the Risen Lord on the part of the disciples of Jesus after the resurrection. The power of the resurrection, however, must be proclaimed today in terms that can compel commitment on the part of "modern man" (sic). Bultmann showed that the proclamation of Jesus as the One whom God had raised from the dead was based on an existential experience on the part of his disciples. The life of Jesus that ended with a crucifixion was the presupposition of that proclamation. The Christian gospel is not based on the teachings of Jesus but on the act of God at the resurrection. Proclaiming this event, the disciples expressed their faith with the cultural tools at their disposal, but their language is not essential to the message. The event being proclaimed, the resurrection of Christ as an act by which God introduced new life in the Spirit into the world, is independent of the cultural tools employed by the believers who proclaim it.

Before coming to terms with Bultmann I had thought that preaching the Gospel required a good translation of the original Greek to our modern languages. Bultmann showed me that the culturally-conditioned world view (Weltanschauung) prevalent among the writers of the New Testament needed to be translated to a world view recognizable by our contemporaries. I thought that Bultmann's analysis of the problem was correct. The solution he offered, however, was another matter. His solution was based on a weak detail of his analysis of the problem.

According to him when God's being is revealed to human beings, what is received is not knowledge but life. In other words revelation is a direct subjective empowerment by a transcendent God. The reception of the divine gift of revelation, or life, is then proclaimed from one person to another. What had been received subjectively now is passed to others objectively as language. To speak objectively of the God who reveals Him/Herself is, according to Bultmann, to mythologize. Any description of God's person or of God's activity is, by definition, mythological. Myth is to speak of that which is transcendent in terms of our knowledge of the immanent world. This is, of course, a specialized definition of myth. On its terms, it is not just the story of the Garden of Eden, the tower of Babel and the Flood that are to be understood as sagas, legends or myths. Saying that God punished Israel's idolatry at the groves and the high places by bringing about the destruction of Jerusalem and the temple and the exile of the people to Babylon is mythological language since it is making God, a transcendent being, act objectively on the historical plane. In terms of the New Testament, Bultmann would affirm that Jesus was raised from the dead. Faith can and must affirm that life has triumphed in the world, and that God's life now empowers not

109

only the life of the Risen Christ but also the life of all believers in the Risen Lord. To talk about the resurrection objectively, describing the when, how and where of its happening, making it a historical event, is to mythologize it.

Bultmann's analysis of the problem was on target. The problem was created by the spirit of modern times and its scientific frame of reference. Many things which in antiquity could be explained mythologically need now to be explained historically or scientifically. In Biblical times it was affirmed that the movement of the sun was the work of a god. For the Romans it was Apollo riding his chariot. For the Jews, if Jehova had not caused the sun to rise above the horizon today, today would not have come into being. When Newton discovered that the movement of the earth around the sun on its own axis could be explained without reference to God, it became more difficult to affirm that God was directly involved in what goes on in the universe. To do so required appeals to miracles, to breaks in the cause and effect connections in nature. These appeals to capricious interruptions in the cause and effect connection, however, became problematic to a majority of moderns. Here is where Bultmann saw the problem confronting those who wished to preach the Gospel. The problem is that the Bible speaks mythologically, describing God's activity as breaches in what modern scientists would consider the unbreakable cause and effect continuum. Scientists presuppose this connection. Their work is to find the real cause of an observable effect from among the possible candidates.

The obvious solution would seem to be to stop talking about God's actions or God's personal qualities and just have a private, subjective relationship with God. Indeed, this has been the way out for many people in our time. It is a modern form of traditional theism. With Newton's new physics and the embrace of "laissez faire" in economics, it was thought that the sun and the earth keep their orbits without God's intervention, and commerce between nations should go on without government interferences. It is advantageous to know that God is in heaven, but on earth we may take care of things without God's help. To posit that God interferes with the law of cause and effect and acts in human affairs is to deny the rule of evidence that informs modern life in society. Miracles are against reason, a refusal to live in the present, a primitive superstitious crutch needed by the uneducated. To modernize the gospel by giving it a more technologically up-to-date description of God's activity, having Christ ride a rocket rather than a cloud, is no less mythological.

Bultmann strongly rejected the theist way out from the challenge of modernity. He insisted that it was absolutely necessary for Christians to talk about God's activity on earth. As is well known, his was a kerygmatic theology, that is, a theology that proclaimed God's redemption of humankind. More precisely, then, this was the problem: God's saving activity on earth must be proclaimed, but to proclaim it signaling historical events back in the first century, or now in the twentieth, as miracles, makes the proclamation unbelievable to our contemporaries.

The most mythological language in the Bible is found in the apocalyptic descriptions of the second coming of Christ, the last judgment, the resurrection of the faithful and the life of the saints in the New Jerusalem. The flowering of apocalyptic language in the Old Testament book of Daniel, scholars have long recognized, was based on a revival of the language of ancient Near Eastern myths, understood as stories in which gods are the principal protagonists. The writing of the books that eventually became the canonical Old Testament took several centuries, many hands, and countless retellings of the stories. The evidence for this is on the surface, and anyone who reads the text without presuppositions as to its origin and contents has no difficulty seeing it. In the process of rewriting little by little, the polytheistic beliefs and the pantheons of the ancestors were purged so that the Old Testament came to embody the triumph of monotheism. In the poetic passages in particular, however, references to the council of the gods, the evil dragon Leviathan, Gog and Magog, the deep waters where Jehovah's reach is sometimes affirmed and sometimes questioned,

111

all these leftovers from classic mythologies by their very suffused presence argue for the effectiveness with which the editors of the Old Testament purged the tradition. The rise of apocalypticism, beginning in the Babylonian exile and flowering in the Maccabean war, found in the old mythological monsters of the sea the means to give expression to faith and hope in most troubled times.

Apocalypticism became popular because it made it possible to maintain that, even though lived experience on earth does not support the notion that God governs the universe justly, in fact God's power is in control. According to retributive justice theory, good people prosper and evildoers suffer. In the Old Testament book of Deuteronomy, and in the writings of the Deuteronomic school, this is in fact the way in which Jehovah governs the universe. As long as historical experience confirms this theory, one may live secure in the universe. But when historical experience disconfirms the theory, one's faith in God faces a serious challenge, and theological efforts to adjust theory to experience get under way. In the apocalyptic view, there is no question that God's retributive justice works. One must understand, however, that it is not working at the moment, in this life. The wicked will suffer and the good will prosper, not in this world, but in the world to come. It could affirm the traditional concept of retributive justice, central to orthodox Hebraic thought, on account of two innovations: the doctrine of the two ages: this age and the age to come, and the doctrine of the resurrection of the dead.

When I came to terms with the historical roots of apocalypticism, I realized that the Adventist approach to apocalyptic interpretation was based on a misunderstanding of the character of these books. As a testament of faith, apocalyptic literature makes perfect sense. As prophetic foretellings of what would happen in the future, at the end of time, the books have been a source of much confusion and hubris of the worst kind, spiritual pride.

Establishment Christianity, on the other hand, has never known what to do with the apocalyptic books of the Bible. They were written by Christians who felt marginalized not only in the world but also by their fellow Christians who were bent on making the Gospel respectable in good society. Once characterized as the literature of those suffering from a persecution complex, who are economically, socially and politically challenged, it was normal to dismiss these books as not relevant to a healthy Christian faith. From the second to the nineteenth century, the Christian apocalyptic literature was felt to be meaningful only by Christians who were in the periphery, and sometimes were persecuted as heretics.

All this was changed by Johannes Weiss and Albert Schweitzer at the beginning of the twentieth century. They argued that Jesus himself had been an apocalyptic Jew. Schweitzer's doctoral dissertation in theology (the explanation is necessary because he earned doctoral degrees also in philosophy, musicology and medicine) became a landmark in New Testament studies both because it effectively did an autopsy of the search for the historical Jesus and concluded that the Romantic optimism of the nineteenth century had missed what the Gospels themselves make obvious. Jesus had been an apocalyptic Jew. If he were around today, among modern men and women he would be "a stranger and an enigma." Weiss and Schweitzer effectively placed apocalypticism at the center of theological discourse in the twentieth century.

Of course, the development of nuclear weapons of mass destruction and their proliferation among nations have also contributed most significantly to the modern and post-modern imagination. One of the things that made apocalyptic prognostications quite dismissible was their dependence on a traumatic divine intervention in human affairs. This would be the miracle of miracles, and educated modern women and men do not believe in miracles. We live in a world in which the absolute and total destruction of the world is quite imaginable without a divine intervention. Humans now can do it by themselves. Thank you for your willingness to help, God, but no, thank you. Cosmic scenarios for the battle between good and evil are offered by the hundreds

113

at the movies, and American presidents can refer to their work in its context without setting off major alarms.

In 1958-60, during the presidency of General Eisenhower, America was still enjoying the blessings earned by having been victorious in World War II. The GIs who came home from that war and the Korean War had gone to college in numbers well beyond expectations, and those who had not were working contentedly for high wages guaranteed by union contracts. Having two cars in the garage of a suburban home and eating chicken every day was making everyone think about many things except an apocalyptic denouement of history. That is, until the Cuban missile crisis changed everything and for a couple of days everyone thought that World War III, with the possible deployment of nuclear weapons, was about to get unleashed. It was not long before Civil Defense took a life of its own and everyone was encouraged to build a shelter and stack it with goods in order to survive a nuclear attack. In the middle sixties I was deputized as a Civil Defense official with authority to organize and command civilians in case of a nuclear emergency.

All this gave apocalypticism a totally different connotation. Rather than being something that gave unwarranted hope to marginalized members of society, in its religious or its secular form, it became the dominant thought of a majority of the population. What is really interesting about this is that even though Adventism was in a most enviable position to have something significant to say in those troubled times, on account of its cultural isolationism, it was totally ignored by an American culture that became wedded to apocalypticism. Whereas in the past, as their name proclaims, they were at the forefront in the expectation of the Glorious Advent of Christ triumphant, now they felt that others were taking the wind out of their sails. Now apocalypticism is at the core of evangelical fundamentalism. It would seem that the view that human efforts can produce a global community at peace with itself is becoming a minority opinion. Only a miraculous divine intervention is considered by many as the viable solution to the pervasive power of evil in the world. This had been the popular view in the third world, but now is embraced by large numbers in the United States. Popular Christianity is emptying the traditional denominations of their memberships by taking a sharp turn to the right and giving new vitality to "literal" readings of the apocalyptic literature in the Bible.

As an affirmation of faith in the God who created the world and who, in spite of all the evidence to the contrary, takes care of it and guides it to a good end, apocalypticism provides a usable vocabulary. The power of this language resides in its ancient roots at the very core of the first attempts to conceive the world as God's creation. The ancient myths of creation, which the editors of the Old Testament took good care to eradicate from its pages with very few exceptions, were given a new lease on life by the apocalyptic authors who opened up the heavens, or received direct messages from heaven, in order to speak confidently of the magnificence of God's power and dominion. Their concern is God's justice, which manifests itself both as salvation and as wrath. Their appeal is to loyalty to God in the face of persecution and death, and their promise is that those who display faithful obedience to God's commandments in trying circumstances shall receive life as their eternal reward. If justice is conceived as retributive, the ethic of rewards is unproblematic.

The ethic of Jesus in the gospels is unashamedly an ethic of rewards. Some ethicists have challenged this as a disqualifying blemish in his teachings. If one is doing the good for the reward, then one is doing it for the wrong motive and for most ethicists motives are the determining factor in ethical judgments. From their perspective, one should do the good because it is good. Only then it may be said that the good action is pure. Apocalypticists do the good for selfish ends, we are told. Martin Luther, appealing to another metaphor used by Jesus, famously insisted that it was impossible to make a good apple tree by hanging good apples on it. On the other hand, a good apple tree naturally produces good apples. Here motives and rewards are totally bypassed and an appeal is made to the constitution of the person doing the good. In other words, what determines the nature of the deed is the nature of the actor, not her/his intentions. With this apocalypticism also agrees, because in the apocalyptic literature trust in the faithfulness and power of God against all odds, is of the essence.

When first confronted, as a graduate student at Duke, by the reading of apocalyptic literature as theology rather than as predictive of the sequence of tragic events preceding the coming of Christ, I was guided by Rudolf Bultmann, who considered apocalyptic literature the most mythological in the Bible and therefore the most in need of being defoliated of its myth. Bultmann thought Paul was the one who took the first steps toward demythologizing by refraining from giving descriptions of the end and placing eschatological significance on the cross and the resurrection. Then, the evangelist of the Gospel of John had been, in his view, the first Christian to have thoroughly demythologized the Gospel by transforming the message of Jesus which in the synoptic gospels is centered on his preaching of the kingdom of God, a clear apocalyptic motif, into the preaching of eternal life which all those who believe have now, thus eliminating the need for a cosmic second coming in the future. Taking his cue from the Fourth Evangelist, Bultmann also transferred the eschatological denouement which apocalypticism places in the future to the existential present, thus dispensing with apocalypticism altogether.

Reading Bultmann, and the other Form critics who were intent on interpreting the language of the kingdom in the message of Jesus, made of my days at Duke a time of great inner turmoil and much soul searching in order to find my way in the new topography I was traversing. Preparing to take the comprehensive examinations I had to do a great deal of reading, and the classes by Professor Hugh Anderson, the gentle Scot who graced the Duke campus at the time, had given me a compelling demonstration of what the new Biblical theology, which in those days was coming to the forefront, was really about. Anderson himself was struggling with

116

the challenge of Bultmann. His classes were quite disorganized, but most effective ruminations of his struggle to bridge the gap between the historical Jesus (on whom the disciples placed their hopes for an earthly kingdom) who died on a Roman cross, and the Risen Lord who sits at the right hand of God (on whom the disciples placed their faith after Easter). His efforts came out soon after in his influential book *Jesus and Christian Origins*.

I was being torn apart by the need to resolve in my own mind the tensions created by my traditional understanding of the apocalyptic literature and the reasonableness of Bultmann's analysis. The struggle within me was quite intense. I had become convinced that the apocalyptic literature had to be interpreted theologically, taking into consideration the cultural constraints within which it had been written. The apocalyptic authors were courageously affirming their faith in the creator God, and their confidence that the future of creation was still in the hand of God. Doing this, I had to admit, they had used the language that had become standard in the surrounding cultures. Certainly my struggles were neither unique nor original, but in the most profound sense they were mine, and I was very much aware that I needed to go through them quite aware of their significance. I also was aware that I needed to find closure for them. It was not something I wanted to keep unresolved for the rest of my life, constantly reviewing the terrain I had already traveled. Finding some kind of solution to this tension would not mean, however, that I would not be willing to look for better solutions in the future. I knew that admitting to my agreement with Bultmann's analysis of the prevalence of mythological language in the Bible would not be looked at favorably by the ecclesiastical authorities in Adventism. I also feared that my own family would have difficulties understanding me.

These internal debates benefited greatly from the support the Adventist community gave me from the time of my arrival at Durham. The local church was small, and it had a rather strong lay leader who was also its major financial supporter. The pastor had three churches to take care of; thus he was not there every Sabbath for the services. This meant that I was asked to preach with some regularity. I have always remembered the advice he gave me the first time he asked me. He said, "You are a graduate student, but remember that your audience is not. Keep in mind sister Bennett and preach to her." Sister Mabel Bennett was a lovely old maid about sixty five years old, the salt of the earth, the very picture of resignation, inner peace and good manners. I have tried to remember sister Bennett every time I have been called to preach ever since, at least to think of the recipients of my words as distinct individuals, not an amorphous congregation. At the Durham church, however, the person who really became a beacon of light to guide me and give me confidence was sister Dorothy Thompson. She instinctively saw a lonely soul and adopted me as her son, in the most generous, kind and considerate way. It was clear that she did not wish to intrude in my affairs, run my life, use me for her emotional needs. It was that she and her husband opened their home and let me know that I was always welcome. I was very conscious also that I did not wish to abuse their hospitality. I did, however, on one occasion, when school was out, spend four days at their place just relaxing, reading and working on some paper for a class. Dot and Virgil Thompson lived in a lovely home on a little knoll about six miles out of Durham. Virgil had built the house himself. He worked as a carpenter building houses as his regular job. Most Sabbaths I would have lunch with them and enjoy a walk in the country afterwards. They were good old fashioned Adventists, but Virgil was not a member of the church because as a youth he became a smoker. Now as an adult he was unable to quit, or so he said. This disqualified him for membership. But I could not think of anyone who was more of an Adventist than he was. In terms of honesty, sincerity, kindness and generosity, he was as good as most, as far as I could judge.

Virgil Thompson was a true Southerner, quite conscious of race and yet as courteous and kind with a black person as he was with any white. Still, I remember his telling of his grandfather escaping from Bennett Place, where the Confederate General Joseph Johnston surrendered to General Sherman on April 26, 1865, not too far away. Then he would remind me with a strong voice that enunciated every syllable with extra care, "Young man, the South knows what invasion means."

On a couple of occasions my roommate at the graduate dormitory at Duke visited the Thompsons with me. My first roommate was Dewayne Dutton, who studied history. He was an extremely talented fellow who not only was doing excellent work in history but was also a great pianist. Some time before he had had a difficult time deciding whether to go to graduate school to study history or go to a conservatory to pursue a career in piano performance. Sometimes he would practice at the piano in the dorm's lounge, much to my delight. When we went to the Thompson's home, Dewayne would relax at their piano. He also had a marvelous state of the art disc player with wonderful speakers and a good record collection. With him I began to get some classical records myself. Among the records Dewayne had acquired were the first that had come out of Russia with performances by Sviatoslav Richter. When we learned that Richter would make an American tour and play in Washington, D.C., Dewayne and I made the five hours one way ride to the capital just to listen to him. I remember the trip back to Durham after the concert as one of the most lively I ever took. We could not stop going over and over what we had just heard. Listening to Richter play Ravel's Pictures at an Exhibition was the necessary evidence to conclude that it was meant to be a piano, not an orchestral piece.

These wonderful friends made it possible for me to live with the internal tensions created by my serious engagement with theological research. Still, the demand to come to terms with what New Testament studies were revealing about the nature of the text and the best way to study it would not go away.

In time it became impossible not to admit that the way to proceed was by means of the historical critical method which took the text seriously and analyzed it in terms of what it said in its most

119

probable historical and grammatical form. Having taken this position, I did not consider it necessary to proclaim it to the four winds. I still wished to make a contribution within my church, opening windows and letting some fresh air come in. I also decided that I could not write a dissertation on a discrete Biblical topic since it would raise red flags with my fellow believers if they saw me using critical methodologies. I did not want, however, to do another thesis in textual criticism, even if one of the most prominent textual critics alive was to be my dissertation advisor. I decided to do a dissertation on the religious world of the Hellenistic age.

I had taken a two semester seminar on Hellenistic civilization with Professor Samuel Rogers, a classicist, and a seminar on Hellenistic religions with Professor Clark. I proposed a thesis on the traditional religion of the Romans at the time of Jesus and the apostles. I explicitly wanted to avoid the mystery cults and other Oriental religions which had become prominent in Roman society at the time. In this way, quite consciously, I was following the path of the religious conservatives who specialize in archaeology, language studies of Hebrew, Aramaic, other Semitic languages, even Egyptian hieroglyphic, and Greek or Latin, or the political, social and economic history of Egypt, Babylon, Assyria, Syria, Greece and Macedonia or Rome, but avoid as the plague the critical reading of the Bible itself in their dissertations. Some, of course, do their critical study of a Biblical theme or passage as an academic exercise, and then return to their denominational home to teach theology using the Bible uncritically as the resource of choice for proof texts. I could not see myself following that path.

By the end of my second year I had successfully passed the comprehensive exams and had chosen my dissertation topic. I then spent the third year researching and writing my dissertation. I had to do a lot of reading and eventually I determined that I would write an introductory chapter on what the traditional Roman religion was essentially about before looking at how four Latin authors who were contemporaries of the apostles viewed religion. My authors were Petronius, Pliny the Elder, Lucan and Juvenal.

This short list was arrived at after I had read all the Latin authors now available who had been active in the first century. Some of them had some very interesting things to say, but had not said enough about religion to justify my writing a chapter on them. Thus, I included a chapter which treated them in a more general way, as evidence that my findings were not based on a very limited sample. The main argument of my dissertation was that what most books said about Roman religion in the first century was off the mark.

Books on the origins of Christianity usually began with a chapter titled "The fullness of time", or something to that effect. The idea was to say that God had sent his Son to the world at the most propitious time. Accordingly, appeals were made to a number of factors: the bankruptcy of Jewish legalism, the unifying power of the Greek language as a lingua franca, the extensive network of Roman roads, the benefits of the pax romana, the thirst for a true religion to fill the place left empty by the collapse of traditional Roman religion, the confusion created by the many mystery cults being imported to Rome, etc. My dissertation argued that as a matter of fact the traditional Roman religion of the countryside altars at the boundary lines, which sought to maintain the ius divinum (divine justice or law) by means of pietas, was healthy and doing just fine among the Roman people. In the process of investigating the evidence and coming to the articulation of this argument, I learned something else that influenced my thinking since. I learned that the basic need supplied by religion is the need for security, both in its practical, mundane aspects and its spiritual, eternal ones. The many other human needs satisfied by religion, comfort, authority, guidance, communion with higher beings (or a higher reality), etc., are secondary to the need for security in a world were life is very fragile and rather ephemeral. The passage of time has only underlined this point of view for me. It should not be at all surprising that a reactionary revival in different religious traditions has been gaining in strength when we live quite conscious that the power to end all life on this planet is in human hands, and possibly in irresponsible ones. Security is what we need most, and that is what religion is about. I had been seeing it from a sectarian perspective as a way to reach heaven. Within a larger horizon, I came to see that it had a more proximate role.

It soon became apparent that it would be impossible for me to finish the dissertation before the beginning of the following school year. Matters got complicated when I learned that Professor Clark would be on sabbatical leave in Greece for the following school year. I had to decide whether to finish the dissertation with another professor as my advisor, or to wait until Professor Clark returned from his sabbatical. I decided for the latter course.

This gave a totally new perspective to my life during the rest of my third year at Duke. I worked more relaxed. I was not being challenged by the use of critical methodologies in the Biblical text, and my work on the dissertation progressed at a sure pace, determined by the knowledge that I would not be defending it until the Fall of 1962. This made it possible for me to plan a trip to Washington, D.C., in the spring of 1961, for the cherry blossom festival at the tidal basin next to the Jefferson Memorial. At the time, my cousin Eduardo, who had lived with us in Paraná in the late forties while studying at the Teacher's College, was in D.C. trying to finish a doctorate in history at American University. I would visit with him during the weekend.

While at Duke my social life was quite limited. Between working weekends to pay for room and board and the demands of graduate studies on one who entered them with a less-than-excellent foundation there was not much time left for socializing. I often wondered how my fellow students who were married and had families could do the work. Besides, the Adventist community in Durham did not include young ladies who caught my attention. I was still quite committed to return to work in South America; therefore, I took it in stride. My thinking on this question was so clear that when William Stinespring, the professor of Old Testament, advised me that he wished to nominate me for a Rockefeller Fellowship, I told him not to do it because the fellowship was for students committed to college teaching in the United States, and I was returning to South America upon graduation. Thinking seriously about marriage had to wait until my return.

It happened, however, that my trip to D.C. turned out to be most eventful. On Sabbath morning, I went to Sligo SDA Church in Takoma Park. It is the campus church for Columbia Union College and the Adventist Hospital next door. Of course, other Adventist institutions are also found in the immediate vicinity, making Sligo one of the best known Adventist churches in the world. After the service, Eduardo, his wife and daughter went home and I stayed greeting old friends. By the time I was leaving there were very few people still around. As I entered the parking lot where I had left my car, I noticed that there were only two cars left in it, and they were close to each other. Just a few steps behind me two young women were walking, as it turned out, toward the other car. They were having a lively conversation which, even though I could not quite tell what they were saying, I thought was in Spanish. When I looked directly at them, they were laughing, so I could not resist the impulse to talk to them. It turned out that they were cousins, and had come from New York City to see the cherry blossoms. Naturally, I suggested that, since I had come from North Carolina for the same reason and I had already arranged to go that afternoon with my cousin and his family, they were more than welcome to join us. It became evident that while one was a bit reticent and shy, the other was eager for her shy cousin to go with me to see the blossoms that afternoon. After some more talk, it was agreed that I would go by their place at three o'clock.

That is how I met Aida Almira Acosta, who a little more than a year later I married in New York City. Aida was at the time doing work on a Masters in Nutrition at the Institute of Nutrition of the College of Physicians and Surgeons of Columbia University. That wonderful afternoon spent admiring the lovely trees around the tidal basin passed by rapidly. I then invited her for just the two of us to go canoeing on the Potomac the next day and listen to the concert of the Navy band playing on a shell just a bit up river from the Lincoln Memorial. When on Monday I traveled back to Durham, I knew that I was in love. I still am forty eight years later.

Somehow after that weekend in Washington, all my determination that plans for married life would have to wait until I returned to South America had gone out the window. For the first time since I had come to the States I was seriously thinking that a commitment to a woman I loved would take precedence over my commitment to return to South America.

In a few months after our Springtime meeting, Aida was going to leave to spend the summer in Guatemala, where she was to conduct clinical studies on the effect of high doses of crystalline cholesterol on the low blood level in children as well as the effectiveness of Incaparina, a nutrition supplement being developed by INCAP (Instituto de Nutrición de Centro America y Panamá), where her professors at Columbia were also heavily involved. This formula was intended to combat malnutrition among children in the third world. Without a doubt, Aida was very intelligent. More importantly, she had a lively demeanor, very distinctive easy manners, a big smile, black hair and hazel eyes. When she talked her hands also conveyed meaning to what she was saying. I was enchanted. We soon discovered that, without knowing it, we had been playing cat and mouse with each other. She had studied at Southern her Sophomore year, in 1953-54, but had stayed at the University of Puerto Rico from 54 to 56. I had been at Southern during those two years, and gone to the Seminary in 56-58. She had been back at Southern during those two years. Thus we had the same *alma mater*. We were bound to meet.

Sometime before my fateful trip to see the cherry blossoms, I had received a letter from an old friend from Seminary days, Ivan Blazen. After finishing his B.D. he had become a professor at Andrews University in Michigan. His letter informed me that one of his colleagues would be on sabbatical leave during the 1961-62 school year. Would I be interested in teaching for one year as a sabbatical replacement at Andrews? Since Professor Clark was going to be in Greece during that year, it seemed to me that this opportunity was another door being opened for me by the hand of Providence. Indeed, I would be interested in teaching for one year. I thought that this would allow me to finish my dissertation while teaching at Andrews and waiting for Clark's return. I was aware, however, that events were taking a life of their own, and my plans for South America were being modified as new doors were opening with enticing opportunities.

I had already been in the United States for almost seven years on a student visa. Every year I needed to apply for an extension with proof that I was registered for at least twelve hours of credit. How could I go to teach at Andrews? When I went to see the advisor for foreign students at Duke, he immediately knew what to do. Duke would vouch that my teaching was part of my training for becoming a college professor. To my surprise and relief, the Immigration Service agreed with him. Thus everything was set for still yet another adventurous move, this time to Berrien Springs, Michigan.

8

NEW YORK

My wedding with Aida took place on July 8, 1962. We asked uncle Andrés, with whom I had spent five months in La Habana, to officiate. The ceremony took place at the New York Center, the Seventh-day Adventist bastion for evangelistic outreach in the heart of Manhattan, on West 46th Street between Sixth and Seventh Avenues. Aida's father had come from Puerto Rico to be the coordinator of the Spanish Seventh-day Adventist churches in the greater New York area. At the time there were twelve Spanish churches, with their own pastors, for which he was responsible. He arranged with the president of the Conference to hire me as the assistant to the pastor of the largest of these churches, in the heart of Spanish Harlem, on 123rd Street just off Second Avenue.

The pastor of the Manhattan Spanish SDA church was Eugenio Valencia, a diminutive Dominican with a large heart and a good mind. His congregation was known for having members with strong personalities who had come from different Caribbean and Central American countries with inflated ideas of their own importance. Pastor Valencia was often challenged by these aspiring caudillos, but his easy manners and wisdom usually were able to smooth the rough feathers of those who looked for confrontations. One of the reasons for my being hired as his assistant was that the Manhattan church had established a branch Sabbath School on the West side of Manhattan on Broadway just north of 100th Street. This Sabbath School had now been organized as a new church with thirty nine members.

When I reported for duty to Pastor Valencia, he told me his plan of action: He would pastor the Manhattan church and I would pastor the Broadway church. He was not going to be organizing my schedule as his assistant. I would be responsible for my church and would devise the plans for it by myself. Thus, before I could really understand what was happening, I found myself the pastor of a church, something which I had not really been planning for. As it turned out, this was another one of those wonderful doors that the Almighty opened for me without my asking for it.

The members of the Broadway Spanish SDA church were just the people I would have wished for a flock. There were Cubans, Puerto Ricans, Dominicans, one Nicaraguan, one Haitian, a few Colombians. The largest group was made up of Dominicans. Many of them had entered the country as tourists and stayed without papers. Most of the ladies worked in the garment district for minimum wages. The men earned just as little as janitors and restaurant help. The lucky ones worked in construction as laborers. They lived in run down apartment buildings without elevators, where the rent was a bit more than a person's weekly salary.

The church had its meetings at a hall on the second floor of a store front building. There was a social club on the third floor and an antique shop on the first. Fortunately, the stairs leading up were wide enough for two people. The hall itself was rather long and not too narrow. On the street end there was a wall of glass. On it, in golden English gothic letters, was written the name of the church. At the back end there was a small room which served as the staging area for organizing what was to be done on the pulpit, just in front. There I conducted services on Sunday nights, Wednesday nights and Sabbath mornings.

I soon learned that one of my biggest blessings was that this was a church without a history. It had been organized just three months before I became its pastor. Being a pastor in New York City was both exhilarating and challenging. I had a hard time preparing for the services and taking care of all kinds of other responsibilities. Visiting the members in their homes, I learned first hand of the struggles of poorly educated migrants with minimal skills in a major metropolis. For many I became the translator at immigration proceedings and labor problems. I advised them about the education of their children. I got involved in making peace among gangs. Many times at the transient hotels, where some recent arrivals would be staying and where privacy was almost unknown, I was taken for an immigration officer or a detective, and shunned like the plague.

The most memorable and scary of my experiences as a pastor of the Spanish Broadway church involved a recent arrival from the Dominican Republic. Brother Martinez had two daughters and a son. The oldest was a beautiful blond about eighteen years old. The son of one of the most prominent ladies of the Adventist community in the Dominican Republic, who now lived with his mother in New York, became engaged to this girl. He had ceased being an Adventist but still was well known in the community. For the wedding both families had gone to Santo Domingo. The ceremony was a big success, and the new couple left happily for their honeymoon. Brother Martinez and his family had returned to New York thinking everything was fine. Much to their surprise, their son-in-law returned to New York and repudiated his bride, accusing her of not being a virgin. A few days later, at a gathering at the Martinez home, there was a loud exchange of words, and brother Martinez pulled out a knife and attacked his son-in-law, causing a minor cut.

Now the young bridegroom had sworn that he would kill the man who had cut him with a knife. It was when things had developed to this point that I was asked to intervene. Of course, the would-be assassin was not alone. He was a member of a gang in Queens, and one of its members had been posted by the Martinez home in the upper West Side of Manhattan, around 207th street, waiting for him to come out. With the help of the mother of this young man, I made an appointment to see him.

I was told to meet him at the basement of an apartment building in Queens, where his gang had a small gym with weight lifting equipment and a boxing ring. I must confess that I was not sure exactly what I would face at such a place, or what I could hope to accomplish with this stranger. When I arrived, there were only two people. While the other guy was punching a light bag with short, rapid punches, Luis and I talked. The conversation ranged over many topics of interest to him before I tried to learn his side of the story. My idea was to give Luis a basis for placing his trust on me. I knew very little about boxing and had hardly any interest in the sport. Still, I asked about the kind of training he did at this club, learning in the process a few things about the gang he belonged to. My main message to him was that even though I was Brother Martinez' pastor, I was not his lawyer. I also had the interests of his mother at heart, and intended to be an honest mediator. I don't think he believed me that day. After a few more meetings with him, he came to see that I was being true to my intentions. He needed to admit, however, that his accusations had been provocative and his way of solving the problem was wrongheaded. In all, I had several private sessions with both parties before I felt the situation had been defused. Of all my pastoral activities in New York, sometimes I feel that this intervention was my most successful. The sworn enemies did not become friends, but the threats were withdrawn and the families went on living their lives in peace.

I have always remembered this experience as a most important lesson. The gospel is not so much concerned with doctrines, theology, a truth to be extracted from a book, but with the business of living in God's world as God's creatures in peace with each other, loving and supporting each other in the emergencies of practical living. I don't remember at all any of the many sermons I preached at the second story hall on Broadway. I only remember the celebrations of the Lord's Supper which, in the Adventist tradition, for reasons that are obscure to me, is celebrated at the end of every quarter of the year. They were occasions when I felt that, as Jesus promised, there He was in the midst of us. We struggled together to be a functional body that accomplished works of love and sustained its members in health and happiness. I think that, by the grace of God, we became that. I spent three years as pastor of the Broadway church and always had a sense that as a community we were rather remarkable on account of the Spirit that had developed a real bond among us.

The fact that Aida is Puerto Rican certainly helped me a lot. Sometimes she had to translate for me idioms peculiar to Caribbean Spanish. Sometimes she had to explain to me the mores of this region. In spite of my shortcomings, however, the members of my church took me in and made me one of them, and by doing so opened before me a whole new dimension of the love of God. I never cease to be amazed at their understanding of the meaning of the gospel. According to them, it is the power that gives life to those who are dead. I hope my sermons helped them to think about this power, so as to better internalize their experience. The beauty of the bond that kept that congregation together and made my being the pastor such an easy task is a blessing I continue to contemplate to this day.

In the fall of 1963, after I had spent a whole year in New York without having looked at my still unfinished dissertation, I received a letter from the director of graduate studies at Duke telling me that by next spring it would be four years since I had taken the comprehensive exams. At that time I was expected to have defended my dissertation. I could petition the school for a year's extension, but if I did not present the dissertation by the deadline, I would have to take a new set of comprehensive exams before I could defend my dissertation. That letter was one of the best motivators I have ever had. From October of that year till February of the next I concentrated my efforts on finishing the two chapters and the conclusion I still had to write.

Both Dr. Clark and Dr Rogers read the chapters as I finished them and offered suggestions, thus helping me to get everything finished on time. Dr. Clark was a very reserved person who did not laugh or rejoice forcefully. I was somewhat taken when the Librarian at the Divinity School at Duke, before I defended the dissertation, one day stopped me and asked what I had done to Dr. Clark. I pleaded total innocence. Then he told me that he had never seen him going about so happy about a dissertation before. Apparently, he had not directed dissertations in a field other than textual criticism, and my dissertation showed his expertise in another field. Knowing that I had Clark on my side, I went to the defense with some confidence. For the actual graduation and granting of the degree, Aida and her parents came with me to Duke for a rather pleasant weekend. I was very glad to have Aida's parents with us at Duke. I could not ignore during that weekend, or at any time thereafter, a void that I felt most strongly, but I could not fill. By the time I graduated from Duke both of my parents were dead. Neither of them learned that their sacrifices on behalf of the education of their child actually bore fruit. My father had died after I had been at Southern for just a year. He never learned that I had received a BA. My mother died in April of 1963. Even though already suffering from advanced heart disease, she had been able to spend a year with me while I taught at Andrews, and had attended my wedding in New York. But a few months after her return to Argentina, while visiting with her own mother, who was now 83 and somewhat ill, she died one morning while still asleep. Her mother died a couple of weeks later. My father was seven years older than my mother and my mother died seven years after my father's death. Both of them were exactly sixty years old at death. Too young.

Back in New York, I continued my work as a pastor as if nothing had happened. Taking care of the needs of my parishioners forced me to keep my feet on the ground. Still, things were beginning to change. Richard Hammill, the Dean who had welcomed me to Southern in 1954, was now the president of Andrews University in Berrien Springs, Michigan, and the Seminary where I had studied was now part of Andrews. Dr. Hammill came to see me in New York and invited me to join the faculty of the Seminary. I was somewhat reluctant because I did not feel that I was up to it. Besides, Aida was doing graduate work at Columbia

University, and it would keep her there for a while. Hammill and I finally came to an agreement. I would be appointed an Assistant Professor beginning in the fall of 1964, but I would not actually start working at the Seminary until the fall of 1965. As a seminary professor on leave, I now applied to become a visiting scholar at Union Theological Seminary in New York, at Broadway and 120th street. This allowed me to register as an auditor at several classes and have use of the library. At Union I audited a class on Heidegger with John Macquarie, the translator of *Being and Time* into English. I also sat in classes on the relationship of theology and philosophy with Prof. Martin and one on Neoplatonism with Prof. Horn. I was trying to use this opportunity to broaden my horizon, and, indeed, it turned out to be a most helpful experience.

While I was pastor of the Broadway church, Aida was continuing her graduate work in biochemical nutrition research at the Institute of Nutrition and Public Health of the College of Physicians and Surgeons of Columbia University. There she was working with doctors from all parts of the world. Thus, she became friends with Habiba Hassan and her husband Wassef. Both were Egyptian copts, who had been doing research in Paris and now had come to New York. Wassef had been studying with Maurice Merleau Ponty and was very much taken by his kind of existentialism. He was somewhat of a dilettante who dabbled in philosophy, was doing experiments in animal psychology and was also an artist. To this day we have at home two of his paintings on plaster, one abstract, the other on an Egyptian motif from the tomb of Amenhotep II. He was also a wonderful art photographer. I spent many long hours talking with him about religion and philosophy. Even though I was not attracted to the radical freedom of his thinking, which I found undisciplined and at times capricious, I did find the challenges he posed to some of my positions rather helpful. These conversations with Wassef were going on while I was reading Heidegger for the class at Union. Thus while MacQuarrie expounded on Heidegger, Wassef would take him on from the perspective of Merleau Ponty, one that was

133

more aesthetic and dynamic. I was finding this debate fascinating, even though I felt very much as one barely being initiated into the field and, therefore, not in a position to contribute much to the debate directly. I could only make tangential observations from where I felt I had some expertise. Still, the exercise was very stimulating and enlightening. It forced me to learn to listen to what the powerful voices shaping the culture were saying. Living in the cultural capital of the world at that time, I could no longer remain content viewing the gospel as an escape from the challenges of modernity. For one who before going to Duke had lived in a rather sheltered environment, becoming fully alert to the intellectual currents of the time was rather liberating. I consider it a tragedy when intelligent believers return to a denominational ghetto to deny what they learned while in graduate school.

During my second year at Duke, a new Dean of the Graduate School had been appointed. He arranged a meeting with the students of the different graduate programs to exchange impressions. Something he said on that occasion has stayed with me. His advice was: "Don't think that your dissertation is your magnum opus. It is an academic exercise to prove that you can do the kind of work that is expected of a PhD. It is the springboard for really good things in the future." After receiving my degree, I knew that I had just been certified for an academic future. Now I had to spend the rest of my life in dialogue with other members of the academic community. As far as I was concerned, being a faithful believer alive to the intellectual conversation taking place in the culture was not a desirable goal, but a must. This did not mean at all that one tailored one's faith to the culture. It meant that one is supposed to be able to express the faith in that enchanting and oppressive metropolis intelligently. My three years in New York City forced me to look at the world in all its complexity. They gave me a new confidence in my ability to participate in the large intellectual conversation carried on by all those who care about the future of humanity. New York is a wonderful teacher of the high price to be paid by human labor for the attainments of civilization.

Being at the same time the pastor of a small congregation of recent immigrants from Latin America, a graduate student writing a dissertation, and later a visiting scholar at Union Theological Seminary who enjoyed the cultural benefits of the city opened before me a spectrum of experiences that I could not have had, probably, anywhere else. It was at this time that I came to terms with the fact that I had become an ecclesiastical employee after all. I resigned myself to it, thinking that I was, maybe, doing something worthwhile for the congregation I served. The members of my congregation, of course, are the only qualified judges of my attempts to serve them.

9

BERRIEN SPINGS

In August of 1965, Aida and I moved our household to Berrien Springs, Michigan, home to Andrews University. When I had lived there for ten months during the school year 1961-62, I had been a sabbatical replacement at the undergraduate college. Now I was coming as an assistant professor of New Testament at the Seminary. The village of Berrien Springs is a rather sleepy farmers' town with hardly any manufacturing. Michigan is dotted with little shops that produce parts for the automotive industry, some of them one man affairs in a garage. The farmers who had manufacturing jobs worked at Clark, the producer of heavy road construction equipment at Buchanan, just a few miles south. The farms were mostly fruit farms, mostly of apples, blueberries and strawberries. Some vineyards produced grapes that were sold to Welch for grape juice.

In its early days, Berrien Springs had been the county seat, and steamboats that crossed Lake Michigan from Chicago came upstream on the Saint Joseph River to Berrien Springs. When the railroads were built, they bypassed Berrien Springs, and fostered the development of Niles upstream on the river, and Saint Joseph and Benton Harbor at the mouth of the river on the lake. The original Berrien County court house, county jail, and log cabin home of the sheriff are now part of a nice historical museum, the most significant attraction in town.

Adventism had moved from its origins in up-state New York and New Hampshire to Battle Creek, Michigan, in 1855. There Adventists had established a publishing house, a college, a

137

sanitarium, and the denominational administrative offices. A great fire on those premises created a crisis and the dispersion of these institutions. Battle Creek College was moved to Berrien Springs in 1901 and became Emmanuel Missionary College. Then in 1960, the Seminary, which had been in Takoma Park, Maryland, was incorporated with Emmanuel Missionary College to create Andrews University.

I now became an assistant professor at the seminary where I had studied and, therefore, a colleague of some of my former professors, most significantly Edward Heppenstall and Siegfried Horn. Dr. Murdoch, the grand old Scottish gentleman who had taken six weeks to decide whether Gomer bath Diblaim was an actual lady or a metaphorical image, was now the Seminary Dean.

The transfer of the Seminary from Takoma Park to Berrien Springs coincided with a denominational restructuring of the requirements for future ministers. Up to that time those wishing to enter the profession were required to hold an M.A., but many Conference presidents were hiring them with B.A.s in theology from an Adventist college. Those attending the Seminary to earn an M.A. came for one year, sponsored by a Conference which had already hired them to become future pastors in one of their districts, or churches.

Lately the denomination had been engaged in a major push to integrate itself into the mainstream of American Protestantism, aided by the new relationship with the Evangelicals in the persons of Barnhouse and Martin. As part of this effort, it was felt necessary to upgrade the educational level of the Adventist ministry. This meant that ministers would be required to obtain a Bachelor of Divinity degree, which was the standard in the mainstream denominations. This meant, of course, that Conferences would now have to sponsor candidates to the ministry for three school years, rather than one. It also meant that the curriculum for the B.D. would have to be restructured as training for ministers, rather than training for future college professors, as it had been up to then.

I was hired in order to supply the needs created by the expansion of the ministerial program from one to three years. Behind these developments was Richard Hammill, who had been in the Education Department of the General Conference and was now the president of Andrews University. The change had given Hammill the idea that, in order to train college professors of theology, Andrews needed to develop a PhD program. Thus, when he talked to me about coming to Andrews, he mentioned that Andrews would be offering doctoral programs in the future and he needed people with PhDs in the specialties which they taught.

It was my great fortune when I arrived at Andrews to have Earle Hilgert as my chairperson in the New Testament department. Without a doubt, Earle was the most sensible, compassionate and intellectually alive human being in the Adventist denomination at the time. He had studied in Basel and written a ground breaking dissertation using redaction criticism to interpret the stories about Jesus on a ship in the gospels. With him, one could talk freely and openly about any problem in New Testament interpretation knowing that he knew more about the text, its context and the history of its interpretation than one could ever hope to know. He is that rare combination of a true scholar who has his feet firmly grounded in the human predicaments of every day life. The other member of the department was Sakae Kubo, a Hawaiian Japanese American who had just finished his doctorate at the University of Chicago. Like me, he had avoided the tensions of writing a dissertation on the interpretation of the biblical text. On the other hand, he had done what I had avoided. He did textual criticism of manuscripts of the First Epistle of Peter. The three of us formed a very congenial and united team that planned courses together and team taught the course in Introduction to the New Testament, which all students were required to take.

In this course we required the students to face the problem of the literary relationship among the synoptic gospels, the marked tensions between the synoptics and the Gospel of John, the stylistic and theological dissimilarities between the Paul of the letters and the Paul of Acts of the Apostles, the integrity of the Pauline canon, the trustworthiness of the traditional authorship given to the general epistles, etc. A few students found the investigation of the evidence in these matters fascinating. The majority found it deeply disturbing. It soon became evident that their reactions to our presentations of the critical questions to be asked of the New Testament writings were conditioned by the professors they had had in their undergraduate colleges. All the students came from Adventist colleges. Unfortunately only in two of them they had been trained to develop an open mind.

When students matriculated at the Seminary they were required to have two years of Greek under their belt. Upon arrival they were given a Greek exam designed to determine their actual proficiency in the language. Those who scored high could take a course in the exegesis of the Epistle to the Hebrews with Kubo. Those who scored well could take exegesis of the Epistle to the Romans with Hilgert. Those who scored the lowest took exegesis of the Gospel of John with me. Of course a student with a high score could also register for John, but a student with a low score could not register for Romans or Hebrews. I was delighted with the arrangement. Of the three professors, I was certainly the weakest in the handling of the language, and at Duke I had read John with James Price. Thus, I felt that I had a good start in my preparation for teaching John. With either Romans or Hebrews, I would have had to work much harder to prepare my classes.

I had found John to be a wonderful text on account of its deceptively simple language, carrying several levels of meaning. I really enjoyed preparing and teaching the course. Some of the students found it most interesting and saw new avenues for advancing their own theological development. Others saw in the course a great threat to their faith. It only served to compound the problems they were facing in the course on the Introduction to the New Testament.

To make matters worse, I was naive enough to accept the invitation to teach a course in Old Testament theology. Until then,

140

such a course had not been offered at the Seminary. Hilgert was teaching a course in New Testament theology, but no professor in the Old Testament department was willing to teach a course in theology. They were doing archaeology, historical backgrounds, and languages, including Akkadian, Summerian and Egyptian hieroglyphics. At Duke I had done some biblical theology with Hugh Anderson, and as a visiting scholar at Union in New York I had audited lectures by James Muhlenberg in Old Testament theology. At least I had some understanding of the debates in this area. I was also somewhat taken by Ernest Wright's theology of the God Who Acts and its roots in von Rad's descriptions of salvation history. At the time the field was alive with major contributions from von Rad, Eichrodt and Edmund Jacob, now available in English. Thus, I almost welcomed the opportunity to teach Old Testament theology, and Hilgert thanked me warmly for filling such a glaring vacuum in the offerings.

With such an array of courses, I soon found out I was classified by a vocal minority in the student body as a dangerous liberal. Thus, for four years, I suffered continuous tension between what I sensed to be the parameters allowed by some members of the faculty and some students and what I honestly thought I needed to discuss in my classes if I was going to be faithful to my discipline and its academic standards. I was quite aware that my agenda as a professor was, as Loasby liked to insist about his, "to disturb their pure minds." Those who hired me, I thought, wanted me "to fortify their made-up minds." The fortifications they expected me to provide were supposed to confirm "the truth" they already possessed. In my estimation, to do that would only provide them with false security. Therefore, the tensions between me and the defenders of "the truth" already possessed were, I well understood, both inevitable and not to be avoided. I wanted to give the students a better understanding of what the Bible was about, one which was open to sincere dialogue with the views of others. To most of the students and the ecclesiastical hierarchs, I was, therefore, a dangerous destroyer of their faith. If you grant their vision of what

141

makes for a healthy church, they were right. But a church guided by unquestioning parrots or fundamentalist reactionaries is not a healthy boon to the well being of its members. I thought that if they were to be effective exponents of the gospel to the modern world, my students needed to be able to face crucial questions being asked by their contemporaries in the ever expanding cultural horizon, not able exponents of what the conservative, sectarian world wanted to hear.

Professors of biblical studies do not take a Hypocratic oath at their PhD graduation, like medical doctors do. Like medical practitioners, however, professors are given license to use their skills freely, but in accordance to the standards of their science. They are also professionals, that is, they supervise themselves in the performance of their duties. Thus professors are expected to have academic integrity. They are expected to be up to date in their discipline. They are expected not to settle with mediocrity, not only in the work of their students but, more importantly, in their own work. They are given academic freedom in order to deal with subject matters in terms of a critical understanding of the subject, and not according to understandings preferred by someone in power.

At Andrews the problem always ended up being a matter of authority. To me it was always a matter of honesty, of integrity. Some students were not willing to listen to a review of the evidence before making up their mind. They had it on undisputed authority that this or that was the case. There was no need, therefore, to review the evidence in order to determine which might be the most probable case. Of course, many times what they claimed to be the clear statement of Scripture was in truth the nineteenth century conservative understanding of Scripture.

The real problem, however, I soon found out, was not with the authority of Scripture. The real problem was the authority of Mrs. White, the prophet of the church who had interpreted the Scriptures, according to some Adventists, definitively. I would be exploring a double entendre in John's Gospel, suggesting its

142

implications about the experience of those Christians for whom it was obvious, only to be told by some student that the meaning of the text was already clear from what Mrs. White had said about it. It was impossible to say that the Gospel of John was the result of several re-writings in a Christian community that was not close to early mainstream Christianity. Mrs. White clearly states that the Gospel was written by John the son of Zebedee, the disciple of Jesus. According to them the text also identifies him as the beloved disciple. These frequent confrontations in the classroom were not just annoying; they were taking away the sense that I was actually accomplishing my mission.

The new dialogue with the Evangelicals had sparked an internal dialogue about the doctrine of inspiration. Within the Evangelical movement in the early sixties, there was some tension about those who insisted on verbal inspiration and those who wished to allow the authors of the biblical text more input into the final product. Some Evangelicals made room by saying that inspiration had brought about the original text in the original language. Of course, we do not have access to any original text of any book of Scripture. On the one hand this gave room for the introduction of problems into the text in its transmission from its original manuscript to the manuscripts now available. In some cases this means the copying of the text by several hands over hundreds of years. On the other, it gave great importance to the science of textual criticism and its efforts to establish as best possible what the original text may have actually said. Thus, conservative evangelical scholarship concentrated on having good command of the original languages and of the rules of textual criticism in order to be sure to read what inspiration actually produced.

Adventists have repeatedly claimed not to subscribe to a doctrine of verbal inspiration. This was in the sixties a matter of some concern to some of the Evangelicals with whom Adventists were trying to engage in dialogue. The reason for this is that there are statements of Mrs. White in which she specifically says that the Holy Spirit "did not inspire the words, but the men who were free to use their own vocabulary and stylistic preferences in the actual writing of the text of Scripture." Discussing this issue, therefore, Adventists openly rejected any doctrine of verbal inspiration. In practice, however, they are the most slavish adherers to the view that equates the written text with the Word of God.

Students repeatedly demanded that I make clear my understanding of inspiration. Consistently I would explain that I adhered to the views of Martin Luther. His view, in a nutshell, was that the same Holy Spirit who had inspired the author of Scripture to write had to inspire the hearer (reader) of Scripture for the word of Scripture to be Word of God. Thus the word written on ink on a piece of paper was not per se Word of God. It became Word of God when read by faith. I would also remind my students of what Papias, a second century Christian leader who wrote *The Oracles of the Lord*, says. He reports having made a concerted effort to learn about what the Lord had taught. Seeking sources of information, he says, if he could talk to someone who had been a disciple of one of the disciples of Jesus, he would give much more weight to what they had to say than to what he could find written in a book. In other words, in his estimation, the oral tradition was more trustworthy than the written one. Of course he lived in an oral culture.

We, of course, live in a culture of written signatures. Anything important has to be in writing, signed and notarized. Thus, the written Bible must be signed with the names of recognizable disciples or apostles and notarized by the seal of the Spirit. Churches have through the centuries tried consistently to make sure that the Holy Spirit works through ecclesiastical channels. A seminary professor who does not support the traditional interpretations which ecclesiastical authorities approve is working against the Holy Spirit. This is not something peculiar to any one religious denomination. At the same time that these problems were becoming apparent at Andrews the Seminary faculty at Concordia Theological Seminary in Saint Louis was facing even greater

144

turmoil. As it happened, most of them ended up creating a Seminary in Exile, which did not last long.

Probably the point at which the literal inspiration of the biblical text is most seriously affirmed by those espousing verbal inspiration is the first three chapters of the book of Genesis. Adventists have been at the forefront of Creationism ever since the debates spawned by the Scopes trial. Of course, Adventists feel that they have an extra burden to defend Creationism. They fear that, if they were to allow for an interpretation of creation that does not read the story of Genesis literally, there would not be a rationale for the Sabbath commandment. This, of course, is based on the version of the commandment found in Exodus 20. It is rare to find an Adventist publication that admits that there is another version of the commandments in Deuteronomy 5. In Exodus 20, the rationale given for Sabbath observance is the fact that God observed a Sabbath rest as the culmination of creation week. Deuteronomy 5, however, bases Sabbath observance on the Exodus from Egypt. The Jews had been slaves who had been abused by a malevolent taskmaster. From there God had liberated them and given them rest. Now they were to observe the Sabbath as a memorial of their liberation from heavy labors. Within Judaism the two rationales for the Sabbath have been given equal billing. The balance between the two has made it possible to insist that the Sabbath is not a negative commandment which requires one not to work. As a memorial of liberation it is a commandment that facilitates those other activities which are not related to the labors required to gain material sustenance. The Sabbath is to be dedicated to the pursuit of wisdom, peace, joy and purity, those things that allow humans to enrich their souls. By tying the Sabbath to the version of the commandment in Exodus 20, Adventism has tied the commandment to creation week and has felt that defending the veracity of the Genesis story is essential to its identity.

As the new professor of Old Testament theology, I was really in a bind. I knew I could not openly challenge the "historicity" of the Genesis account of creation, but conscientiously I could not

145

affirm it. Thus, in my classes I tried to expand the theology of creation in the Old Testament by looking at other views of the matter, especially in the Psalms and Job. But most of all, I tried to move on to other important themes. I am sure that the rumor mills were working on campus. Some students were very appreciative; others complained to their Conference presidents and other professors on campus. In a chance meeting with president Hammill on a campus sidewalk, he asked me how my Old Testament theology class was going. I said that it was going well. He suggested that it would be good for me to attend the seminars that were taking place at the Geoscience Institute on campus.

The Geoscience Institute had been established by the General Conference some years back with the specific mission of defending creationism scientifically. Hammill, I think, had been somewhat influential in its creation. Originally it had been housed at the General Conference building in Takoma Park, but with the creation of Andrews University it had moved to new quarters on campus. The scientists at the Institute were good people with impeccable scientific credentials. Some of them, however, were rather reactionary fundamentalists. Others were quite open-minded. I remembered very well that during my first full summer at Southern Missionary College in Tennessee there had been a long weekend workshop on the question of creation. The featured speaker was the Adventist icon on the subject, George MacReady Price, who by that time was already in semi-retirement. I attended some of the sessions and got the distinct impression that the presentations were efforts at treading water in order not to sink. Now I began to attend some of the seminars at the Institute at Andrews, and I got, again, the same distinct impression. The presentations insisted on pointing out that at this or at that point of the evolutionary theory the evidence was not yet in, or the evidence was not quite consistent, or there were serious difficulties in the interpretations being made of the evidence. The fact that there were these little gaps here and there meant that evolution was not quite proven; therefore, one could hold to an alternative account of how the

146

world we now live in came about. To this day, with consistent regularity, the General Conference organizes rather expensive field trips in the American West. Adventist scientists and theologians spend a week to ten days traveling to important geological deposits where the scientists explain the evidence and punch holes into its traditional interpretations and offer alternative interpretations. Usually these appeal to a cataclysmic event that accounts for the evidence, or at least a significant proportion of it. It is to be remembered, they insist, that the evolutionary theory cannot give a full account of all the evidence either. The cataclysm referred to, of course, is the biblical story of the flood.

I must confess that I am not a scientist, and that, therefore, I cannot evaluate critically the presentations made by Adventist scientists. Still, from my first exposure to the workshop at Southern in the summer of 1955, through my seminars at the Geoscience Institute at Andrews in 1967-68, to my reading of the reports that come out after the current Summer Conferences on Geoscience, they have all impressed me as examples of special pleading. On the other hand, as a biblical scholar, I have always found them to be motivated by a myopic reading of the Scriptures and theological naivete. To demand from Scripture scientific or historical seriousness is to force the Scriptures into an anachronistic straight jacket that can only prevent it from being the channel for the liberating power of the Spirit.

One of the most liberating moments in my spiritual journey was when I realized that what the Bible was really about could not be demonstrated by archaeological excavations that recovered evidence from the ancient biblical world, or by scientific arguments about the evidence in geological columns. I had taken quite a few classes in archaeology in which the unspoken message was "the spade proves the truth of the Bible." Geology, paleontology, anthropology, archaeology or history may illustrate that the circumstances surrounding biblical narratives correspond to what these sciences say concerning them. Sometimes, however, they may demonstrate the presence of anachronisms in the biblical accounts as, for example, with the availability of domesticated camels at the time of Abraham. The question, however, is: To what were the authors of the Bible witnessing? And witnessing they certainly were. In their telling of the stories of the ancient past, they availed themselves of the narrative elements that were within reach, and sometimes they were, from a modern historical or scientific point of view, inaccurate. Still, as means for the witnessing of their faith in the God of Abraham, Isaac and Jacob, they were quite effective. Today, we can identify with their faith even if we do not share their historical and scientific limitations. To be noticed in this connection is that, without a doubt, sometime in the future our historical and scientific understandings may very well come to be considered also no longer up to date. Those who think that they are establishing the authority of the Bible by proving that its account of creation or its descriptions of the end times are to be defended as scientifically or historically correct are totally misguided as to what is at stake. Even if science were to prove that the world came to be in seven days of 24 hours about 6,000 years ago, and history were to record that after a series of devastating plagues the Pharaoh of Egypt allowed Hebrew slaves to leave and establish themselves in the frontier between the Egyptian and the Hittite empires, this would not authenticate at all the theological claim that in these events God was directly involved.

One of the amazing things about my teaching at the Seminary was that while I was feeling extremely unhappy on account of the constant challenges brought about by ultra conservative students, I was doing rather well over all. After the very turbulent 1965-66 school year, when first year students taking Introduction to the New Testament did not have upper class students who could calm their fears about what they were being forced to look at because they were the first ones in the new curriculum, Earle Hilgert became the Vice-President for Academic Affairs of the university. Walter Specht, a seasoned teacher from La Sierra College in Riverside, California, became my new chairperson. He was a quiet man, a serious scholar, and a very decent human being. In time I came to love and respect him immensely because, even though on some crucial issues he did not see things as I did, he stood by me and defended me as his colleague with an integrity and honor that I could only wish I could some day fully attain.

One morning in the spring of 1968, I received a phone call from Earle asking me whether I would be interested in teaching a course at Saint Mary's College, a Catholic women's college just twenty miles south of Andrews in Notre Dame, Indiana. The administration of Saint Mary's was interested in a possible exchange of teachers. They would like to have a course in Protestant Theology taught by a Protestant. This was just an initial inquiry and Earle thought that I might be interested in participating in such an exchange. I said that the idea was appealing but that he had caught me by surprise. I would certainly give this proposal serious consideration.

Not many weeks after, I got another phone call from Earle. Was I free to go to his office that very minute? The president and the dean of Saint Mary's College were there, and they would like to meet the prospective professor of Protestant Theology. It happened that at the moment I was free, so I walked the few yards from the Seminary building to the administration building wondering what was going on. When I arrived at Earle's office I was introduced to Father John McGrath, the president, and Dr. Jack Detzler, the dean. At the Second Vatican Council, Protestants had ceased being heretics in the eyes of the Catholic Church and had become "separated brethren." After the council, at Saint Mary's it had been decided that they needed to know these sisters and brothers better. Thus, a priest had begun to teach a course in Protestant Theology. Now Father McGrath had become president, and he thought that it was not enough to have a Catholic priest teaching Protestant theology from a Catholic perspective. For the course to fulfill its purpose, it had to be taught by a Protestant. With this in mind, he had approached several Protestant colleges in the vicinity of Notre Dame trying to establish a friendly exchange. This way the professors involved would just remain faculty members at their respective institutions, with no money involved. It turned out that while they were talking with me at Earle's office, right there and then it was decided that I would be the one teaching Protestant Theology at Saint Mary's College, and they would work out which professor from Saint Mary's would come to teach a course at Andrews. The likely possibility discussed was a course in Russian history taught by a Saint Mary's professor who was a specialist in the area.

In view of this arrangement, my teaching load for the 1968 fall semester was adjusted so as to make room for a course in Protestant theology at Saint Mary's. This was totally out of my area of research, but I prepared myself gladly for this new adventure. In any case, I would have the whole summer to prepare.

Not long afterwards, Andrews decided that they could not have a non-Adventist teaching a course in Russian history. So the arrangement was that I would get my regular salary from Andrews and Saint Mary's would pay Andrews for my teaching and pay me mileage for the travel. I was not at all surprised that Andrews had not been open enough to have an exchange with a Catholic institution. The longstanding practice of Catholic bashing could not be discontinued at the drop of a hat. As a matter of fact, at the Seminary the chairman of the Systematic Theology department, Raoul Dederen, taught a very popular course on Catholic theology, in which all the errors of their ways were exposed so as to reinforce the prejudices the students already had.

That school year I was also taken by surprise when I was asked to spend the summer of 1968 teaching in an extension of the Seminary in Jamaica. For that extension program the Inter American Division had selected about fifty pastors from all its Unions. Since most of the pastors came from Spanish or English speaking countries, the classes were given in both languages separately. Those coming from French speaking countries knew one of these two languages. I was going with Wilbur Alexander, a member of the Systematic Theology Department who taught a class in Righteousness by Faith. I taught a course in New Testament

Theology twice, once in English and then in Spanish. Then I served as the translator for Alexander in his class with the Spanish students. I was somewhat surprised when Alexander said that since I was hearing him giving his class, he would sit and listen to my class in English. I was not sure if he had been asked to do that by someone higher up or he was doing it on his own initiative, but I was quite sure that he was coming to check on me. As it turned out, some time after we were back on campus, in a conversation in which I was one more in a small group, Alexander inadvertently revealed that he had attended my class in Jamaica to find out what went on in my classes, because all sorts of things were being said. I am sure that Alexander gave Dean Murdock a good report. Thus when I returned I was given a very warm welcome by the Dean.

Still, I was very uncomfortable with my situation. Secretly, I had initiated a job search two years before going to Jamaica. A job agency in Chicago was informing me of all job openings in my field, and I had been doing my best applying to them. I was not getting any letters of interest in reply. Only short letters informing me that my application had been given due consideration, but I was not the applicant they were looking for. At the annual meetings of the Society of Biblical Literature I had been seeing my old classmates at Duke. Among them was James Zink. He had specialized in Old Testament. After his second year at Duke he had applied for a scholarship at the American Schools of Oriental Research in Jerusalem. Every year, only two are given. James had received the scholarship and spent 1961-62 in Jerusalem doing research. Most graduate students in Old Testament in American universities would give an arm and a leg to be able to do that. Those who get the scholarship, for the rest of their careers have a special badge of honor on their curriculum vitae. After graduation James went to teach at his denominational seminary in Memphis. After a year or two he found himself applying for every job available anywhere. At the SBL annual meetings we would compare notes. James would tell me that most of his letters of application were not even acknowledged. The silence he was getting from his applications spoke volumes. We were both coming from the wrong denominations. Our academic credentials meant nothing. Eventually James went back to graduate school in library science and found employment at the Library of the University of Oklahoma. After a few years he became the head librarian of the university's library system. It was a tragic loss to the field of Old Testament studies.

In the fall of 1968, with my very discouraging prospects for finding a job in New Testament teaching and my new good standing with the Dean, I was beginning to resign myself to life at the Seminary. Then two unexpected things happened, more or less concurrently.

One had its roots in the General Conference session that appointed Robert Pierson, the Week of Prayer speaker I had met at Southern, as president of the General Conference. He proved to be very different from Reuben Figuhr. While Figuhr, a conservative, had a rather broad vision of the place of the church in the world and had encouraged the dialogue with the Evangelicals and the raising of the educational standards of the ministry, Pierson was a narrow minded reactionary who wished to bring about a reaffirmation of the church's nineteenth century roots. For some time he had been hearing complaints about some Seminary professors, and he would talk with Hammill about the need to clean the Seminary of them. Apparently his pleas to Hammill had been repeated a few times. Now Pierson threatened Hammill that if he did not have the stamina to purge the Seminary faculty, he would assume the job himself. Within a denominational structure in which everyone works at the pleasure of the one above, incursions from above are not rare. Hammill now knew that he had to do something that would allow him to report to Pierson. The last thing he wanted was for Pierson to interfere with the university's internal procedures.

Hammill, therefore, invited the whole Seminary faculty to meet with him for an open session. We all filed in to a conference room in the administration building wondering what was up, and as is to be expected, fearing the worst. Hammill then very diplomatically, but with a definite sense of urgency, communicated to us his predicament and his sincere desire to be a mediator between the faculty and the General Conference president. He also said that the complaints that worried Pierson had to do with the inspiration of the Bible and the doctrine of creation. Immediately faculty members began to defend themselves and assure the president that one had to admit problems in both areas, but that the faculty was committed to upholding these truths. It was obvious to some of us, however, that we could not really speak our minds in that forum. Some among the faculty said that one of the problems was that we did not communicate enough with each other as a faculty. Meetings such as the one we were having were to be had more often so that we could teach more as a team, knowing the minds of our colleagues better. With that in mind they suggested that we should have a series of faculty retreats in order to talk about these matters among ourselves.

Others felt that the last thing we needed were faculty dialogues, because the moment some of us would speak openly about these topics, there would be an immediate split in the faculty between those who were the inquisitors and those who were required to make an auto de fe. Thus, we voted against having a retreat for a long weekend in the near future. After about three hours, Hammill suggested that we meet again in a week in order to finish our conversation.

At our next meeting, things got a bit more specific. Hammill insisted that we should all uphold a short chronology for the age of the earth. At this Siegfried Horn spoke out. If he was being required to say that the earth was about six thousand years old, he would offer his resignation immediately. I was amazed. I wanted to hail him a hero and sing a song in his praise. At this, Hammill backed off a bit. Well, it was not necessary to hold to six thousand years. There was room for some movement, but certainly one could not affirm the geologic ages held by evolution. Some suggested a round figure of ten to twelve thousand years as the age of the earth. Some of us knew that Horn had written scientific articles in which he had dated evidence of human habitation at thirty thousand B.C.E. But we kept our peace. Again the meeting was not coming to whatever Hammill was looking for. Thus, he said that if any one felt that he would like to discuss some of these questions, he would appreciate it if he or she would see him at his office.

After thinking about it over the weekend, I decided that I had to see Hammill, so I made an appointment. I knew that I was daring my fate. Unlike Horn who had challenged Hammill and made him back off a bit, I was just beginning my career. This was my fourth year as a professor. Horn was within retirement age.

At our meeting, I began by assuring Hammill that I had no particular burden to teach something in opposition to what the church taught. I did not feel that I had a truth that needed to be taught. I was coming to see him because I wanted to know whether one could expect a bit more space to investigate some of these issues in an open manner in class. I was aware that right now things were difficult. I did not say so, but I was thinking that things were not going to improve while Pierson was president of the General Conference. I just wanted to know whether Hammill, as the president of the university, envisioned a day in which at the university there would be room for a free discussion of ideas, and not just indoctrination. Hammill's answer to me was, "Not in your lifetime." Those words of president Hammill have kept ringing loudly in my ears since: "Not in your lifetime."

I had approached president Hammill with a question: Was the administration aiming at making it possible in the future to open some doors and windows and letting some fresh air in? Was the Adventist leadership willing, like the leadership of the Catholic Church had been, to courageously bring about an aggiornamento, a cultural catching-up? Hammill had given me a clear answer. But in the process, in his eyes, my position in the faculty had become suspect. I was not the only Seminary faculty member in trouble. Jim Cox, a PhD candidate in New Testament at Harvard who had recently joined the faculty, Roy Branson, a recent Harvard PhD in ethics, Gottfried Oostervald, a Dutch anthropologist who taught missions, were also being questioned. Probably, and most tragically, the one who was in deepest trouble without his knowing it, was Edward H. W. (Ted) Vick. He had been teaching systematic theology at Andrews for a few years, the first Adventist with the necessary credentials to do so. He had written his doctoral dissertation with Walter Kaufmann at Vanderbilt. As a good Englishman, however, he thought he had to have a British degree, so he had asked for a sabbatical to study at Oxford. We thought that being in England he was safely avoiding the turmoil going on at Berrien Springs. During the summer Earle Hilgert, now the vice-president, had visited him at Oxford and let him know that the university was looking forward to his return.

During my first initial meeting with Hammill, he had asked me to explain to him how I viewed the story of creation in Genesis. I took it that I was talking with a PhD graduate of the Oriental Institute of the University of Chicago. So I explained that I thought there were two stories which did not jibe with each other, reflecting different points of view and different theological agendas. He then proceeded to tell me that he thought the two stories actually dovetailed into each other, the second being a complement to the first. As our conversation proceeded along the lines of professional integrity and academic freedom, Hammill, to my surprise, began to cry. It was clear that our conversation had touched a rather profound emotional nerve in his soul. I did not know, exactly what was going on. Under the circumstances, I volunteered to continue our conversation at some other time, and we agreed to it. Afterwards I considered possible causes for Hammill's emotional reaction to what I had said. I thought that it might be related to the fact that his only son Roger, now in graduate school, a brilliant intellect and great human being whom I had known as an adolescent at Southern, had openly left the church on account of its narrow vision of the world. I thought that maybe, since I had approached him in times of need when I was at the

155

Seminary in Takoma Park and he was at the General Conference next door, with requests for help in matters that one would normally take to a father or a mentor, he may have been considering me his protégée. I also considered the possibility that being one who converted to Adventism as a young man, he may have been having extra tensions with the convert syndrome. I, by contrast, was a fourth generation Adventist.

At the convened time we had our second meeting, and it went badly. After a while I was the one who was totally overwhelmed emotionally and broke down crying. This only confirmed, I think, the impression in Hammill that my position was one which the university could not support, but I am not really certain of what he was thinking at the time, just as I am not quite sure what made him break down emotionally at our first meeting.

In the meantime, I was now traveling 20 miles twice a week down to Notre Dame, Indiana, to teach Protestant theology to the young ladies at Saint Mary's College. From the beginning things had been going well, from my perspective amazingly well. The chairman of the Theology department, Sister Maria Assunta Werner, received me with open arms, invited me to faculty functions, and went out of her way to make me feel at home. The students were excited about what was going on in their church after Vatican II. They were eager to discuss the new point of view that was being presented to them as something that was part of the Christian tradition. Soon after I had started teaching there, I learned that four of the faculty members in the department had been given terminal contracts. They were graduate students at the new theology graduate program at Notre Dame who were teaching at Saint Mary's and not advancing toward graduation. Father MacGrath had decided to make a clean sweep and build a new department.

When I heard that, I approached Sister Assunta and told her that if she was looking for a person in Scripture I would like to apply. She very politely told me that she could not allow that because she did not want Andrews to think that they were stealing a member of their faculty. I then said, no one can think so because I am the one initiating this conversation. She thought for a moment and agreed to take the matter of my application to the rest of the faculty. Just before Christmas, Sister Assunta informed me that they had unanimously agreed to offer me the job. To this I immediately responded that I was gladly accepting their offer. Not long afterwards I signed a one year contract to teach full time at Saint Mary's beginning in the fall of 1969. The contract also specified that the position was tenure track and that I was given three years of credit toward tenure for my four years of teaching at Andrews.

A few weeks after my second meeting with Hammill, Jim Cox called me to say that it was imperative that I meet with Hammill and make an effort to clear up things with him before he left for Washington D.C. on Sabbath evening. He informed me that Oostervall, Branson and he himself had had meetings with him and he had agreed to give them a clean bill of health. In Washington, Hammill would be giving his report on the investigation of the faculty to a General Conference committee overseeing the matter. Before I knew it, someone had scheduled a meeting of Hammill, the president, Earle Hilgert, the vice-president, William Murdock, the Dean of the Seminary, Walter Specht, the chairman of the New Testament department, with me at Hammill's office, for Sabbath morning at eight o'clock, before people had commitments at different Sabbath services on campus. This was an emergency which overruled all the rules for Sabbath observance, or so, apparently, all those involved in the matter thought.

Going to the meeting I knew that Earle Hilgert was a friend on whom I could count. I did not know exactly what was in Hammill's mind even though I had had two meetings with him. They had been so emotionally draining that after the meetings I had a headache and not much understanding of what had transpired. I knew that Murdoch and Specht were gentlemen, but also quite conservative.

It turned out to be a memorable occasion, one of those when one remembers the disposition of the chairs, the room atmospherics, and the participants quite distinctly. Hammill opened up saying that I had approached him with some questions which had left him a bit confused about my position as a Seminary faculty. He did not wish, however, to act on his own; therefore, he was asking those present to participate in an enlarged conversation. Immediately Hilgert picked it up and began to vouch for my commitment to the faith, my commitment to the church, my commitment to the students, etc. Murdoch also spoke mentioning the great report that had come back from my teaching in Jamaica the past summer. As the conversation continued without reaching a conclusion and time was running out, Walter Specht asked for a decision. He said: "I need to go to meet other appointments, but before I go I need to know whether Herold can stay teaching at the New Testament department or not. I, for one, want him to stay." At this, Murdock said, "I also want him to stay." Hilgert, of course, wanted me to stay. Finally, Hammill also agreed that I would stay, and he would report so in his trip to the General Conference.

After this vote of confidence from the four of them, I could do no other but let them know that I had already made other plans for myself. I had already signed a contract for a tenure track position at Saint Mary's. They were all stunned. Hilgert recovered immediately with a question, and I had to admit that it was a one year contract. Immediately it was agreed that they would grant me a one year leave of absence for me to fulfill my contract and then the following year I would come back to Andrews. I thanked them all for their vote of confidence and for their offer of a year's leave of absence. And we all left the meeting feeling good. I cannot fail to mention that the following spring Walter Specht wrote me a letter telling me that the position at the New Testament department was there for me to come back and occupy. In my heart of hearts, however, I knew that I could not return to Andrews to be under constant questioning concerning matters which did not deserve all the emotional and psychological energy that they were continually sapping from the open-minded faculty.

158

This story deserves two codas full of irony. Before that year was over I learned that I had been promoted to Associate Professor at Andrews. In my letter of resignation to Hammill, I told him exactly why I was resigning. Maybe I should not have done it. My promotion, however, served me well. When the administration at Saint Mary's learned about it, I was hired at the rank I had at Andrews.

Hammill remained president of Andrews until his retirement several years later. A few years after he retired, he surprised everyone by announcing that now that he had more time at his disposal he had been studying the question of creation and he could no longer hold to a short chronology or the historical value of the Genesis account. So he spent the last few years of his life trying to enlighten others with his new perspectives on the subject. To those of us who had spent months in emotional and psychological distress on account of the tensions created by his desire to please the chairman of the board, his belated conversion seemed more than just ironic. On the other hand, no one questioned his desire to be honest about it.

The really tragic note of that whole episode was that Ted Vick, the best systematic theologian in the church, fully committed to her service, and in many ways quite conservative theologically, became the lamb that was sacrificed by Hammill, much to the embarrassment of Hilgert, at the altar of the General Conference. Two days before Christmas, without any warning, he received a letter at Oxford informing him that he had been fired. When he asked, in several letters to Hammill, for an explanation, none was given. I was and still am a good friend of Ted, and I know how deeply this mistreatment hurt him. It was a tragic mistake that resulted in a great loss to the church. It is a wonderful testimony to his faithfulness that he still publishes wonderful little pieces for her benefit. I tend to think that the difference between what happened to Ted, who desperately wished to stay teaching at the Seminary, and to me, who for some time had been searching desperately for a way out, was the difference between my chairman,

Walter Specht, and his chairman. My chairman was a person of honor and goodwill who always dealt with things above board and with integrity. The one who happened to be his chairman was not cut of the same cloth.

Even though I felt strongly that I needed to find a different environment in which to pursue my desire to continue doing scholarly work on the New Testament, my inner self was torn by the prospect of severing my professional ties with the denomination. Many of my colleagues could not quite see how I could find fulfillment not 'serving' the needs of Adventist youth. Moreover, I was not just leaving denominational employment. I was going to a Catholic institution. How could it be possible for an Adventist to teach theology in a Catholic college? I was leaving home and getting lost in the world. Most actually thought I had been fired. An Argentine student at the Seminary who had taken a class with me went back to Argentina and left no doubt in anyone's mind that I had abandoned the faith. Members of my family who heard of my being lost became quite alarmed. I was quite aware, of course, that my actions impacted not only members of my family but also members of Aida's family.

Those were confusing days. For some months I had a recurrent dream. I am not much of a dreamer, and most of my dreams I no longer remember once I wake up. This one I can still recall. In my dream I would get up from bed and go outside naked or in briefs and, without any difficulty, start flying with very little movement of my arms or legs. The space in which I flew, however, was full of obstacles: towers, tall buildings, and innumerable electric cables. I had to be very alert navigating through this jungle. The charged electric wires could electrocute me in an instant. Somehow I managed to stay away from the wires, and land in a crowded place where I would walk away quite comfortable in my state of unclothing. In any event, I felt somehow better, thinking that, after all, I was keeping my adolescent vow not to work for the denomination.

The real victim of my decision to talk to President Hammill as to whether he saw a more open theological atmosphere in the future for the Seminary was Aida. In the fall of 1968 she was teaching Biochemistry to pre-med students at Andrews. The Chairperson of the Chemistry Department was an ultra conservative Adventist with political ambitions. Of course, what was happening at the Seminary was immediately known by all the faculty. Everyone knew that Hammill had to report on the orthodoxy of the Seminary faculty to the President of the General Conference. They also knew that I was one of those about whom some students had lodged complaints. The Monday after I announced to the administrators that I had signed a contract with Saint Mary's College, the chair of the Chemistry Department talked to Aida just before an impromptu departmental faculty meeting suggesting that since she had recently given birth to our first son it would be best to stay home and take care of the baby. Then he went into the faculty meeting and reported that Aida had resigned to take care of her new born son.

Fortunately for us the birth of Herold Eduardo provided a totally different perspective to the tumultuous days of my resignation and Aida's dismissal from Andrews. Heroldito (the Spanish diminutive of endearment) was a healthy, happy child who made us forget the ups and downs of life within denominational politics. In fact, life was beginning on a new plane and the wonders it had in store were promised prodigally in the person of our son.

10

NOTRE DAME

When Father McGrath interviewed me as a prospective professor of theology at Saint Mary's College in Notre Dame, IN, after some general pleasantries, he said he expected of me two things: 1) that I be up-to-date and engaged with my discipline, and 2) that when I did not agree with the Catholic position on something, I would present the Catholic position fairly. I left that meeting realizing I had been given freedom to teach, to guide students in the exploration of important issues without worrying that a student would accuse me of deviating from the current orthodoxy and find that the administration would take the side of the student. In those days the Saint Mary's faculty was in the process of creating a chapter of the American Association of University Professors (AAUP). Academic freedom and the rights and responsibilities of the faculty were discussed daily. For me a new day had dawned. Professionally, I was now breathing the atmosphere of American culture at a Catholic institution that had for years intentionally been fully engaged in that culture.

Since its beginnings in 1843, Saint Mary's has been sponsored by the Sisters of the Holy Cross. Many of the faculty and the administration were members of the Congregation. The mother house was on campus. At the time, the Sisters had two other women's colleges, several high schools, and three hospitals in the United States. The Sisters were teachers and nurses. As nurses they had participated in military operations since the Civil War, when they nursed soldiers from both the North and the South. As teachers they had run, besides Saint Mary's, Cardinal Cushing

College outside Boston, and Dumbarton Oaks College in Washington, D.C. The sexual revolution changing the culture of America at the time and the new outlook of the Catholic Church after the Vatican II Council forced the Sisters, for financial reasons, to close both Cardinal Cushing and Dumbarton Oaks. Saint Mary's was also facing serious financial problems.

When the faculty had consisted of nuns who had taken vows of obedience, chastity and poverty, the faculty budget was minimal. Even before Vatican II, however, the number of women entering the Order had been decreasing. After the council, not only did the number of postulants decrease dramatically, many who were professed decided to become laicized. Lay faculty with family responsibilities demanding competitive salaries were hired to fill the positions. The applicant pool which had sustained the college was also becoming smaller due to several factors. Many formerly male Catholic colleges and universities admitted women for the first time. The Catholic elementary and secondary school system began to break down as the nuns who kept them going left religious life. In addition, Catholic families began sending their sons and daughters to secular universities (which also became co-ed during these years). Thus, finances were stretched significantly. Besides, the sexual revolution unleashed by "the pill" placed all women's colleges on the endangered species list.

Saint Mary's had several things going for it. Foremost was its excellent academic reputation in Catholic circles. In this, the Sisters of the Holy Cross could and did take much pride. I was in awe at what the Sisters with their sweat and tears had accomplished over the years. The physical plant was a little jewel by the Saint Joseph River. But the academic tradition and the intellectual climate of the place was in marked contrast to Andrews. For a period of over twenty years, the college had had a visionary president, Sister Madeleva Wolff, a woman of intellect, social consciousness, and indomitable will. Among her many accomplishments was the establishment of a graduate program in theology that granted PhD degrees. This was her answer to the denial of admission to women and lay men at catholic graduate programs in theology. To teach in this program, she had brought to campus distinguished Dominican priests. After Vatican II, Catholic women who wished to study theology were no longer barred from admission to graduate programs at Catholic institutions. The University of Notre Dame, across Highway 31 from Saint Mary's, opened a graduate program in theology that admitted women. By the early 1970s, the program at Saint Mary's was no longer necessary. Still, the tradition of high level theological discourse on campus was well-established, and the Sisters of the Holy Cross, I think, were the most open and progressive of all the religious orders for women in the United States. Across the highway, the Fathers of the Holy Cross, who ran the University of Notre Dame, resented that in the estimation of most Catholics the Jesuits enjoyed that distinction.

From my early days at Saint Mary's I retain two vivid anecdotes. The first has to do with the promulgation of *Humanae vitae*, the papal encyclical proscribing the use of "artificial" means of contraception, leaving the rhythm method as the only acceptable choice for Catholics. Debate about the encyclical was rampant on campus. The New York Times published a full page ad in which many distinguished Catholics signed a protest against the encyclical. At the college, most were opposed to it, and said so loudly and clearly. Particularly striking to me was a conversation with a priest who was a visiting professor of sociology. He referred to the pope in almost vulgar language while describing what he considered a piece of nonsense dealing with methods of contraception rather than with contraception itself. My naive conception of all Catholics as most reverential toward the pope and his authority suffered a fatal blow that day. Later, when Pope John Paul II revealed his very conservative and culturally conditioned biases by promulgating *Ex corde ecclesiae*, the animated negative reactions of American Catholic academics did not surprise me. Through the years I learned to appreciate deeply this healthy tension between the curia and the academics among Catholics in the United States. I only wished just a small proportion of it could find its way among conservative Protestants.

165

The other anecdote from those early days involves a discussion among a small group one late afternoon in the faculty lounge. At the time, the administrations of Saint Mary's and Notre Dame were beginning to entertain the possibility of merging the two institutions into one. Most of Saint Mary's faculty was opposed to a merger. I was new, not quite aware of the history behind the move and, therefore, did not have a strong opinion on the matter. Still, I thought that the merger offered good possibilities to both institutions and had good chances of success. Anthony Black, an ultra conservative lay Catholic professor of history with a Notre Dame PhD, was strongly opposed. As we were talking, he presented different reasons for his opposition. His final argument was that the merger would bring about the moral bankruptcy of Saint Mary's. According to him, if the merger were to take place, before long there would be mixed gender dorms. With both genders in one dorm, it would not be long before there would be men and women taking showers together. To this, I replied that if a Saint Mary's woman and a Notre Dame man wanted to take a shower together they could do it at any time. They did not have to wait for the two institutions to merge. There were many motels down the road on Highway 31. To this, in a rather heated mood, Tony responded, "You say that because you are a Protestant." Those words hit me like a revelation from heaven.

I then realized that the way I had been taught to look at Catholics was the way Catholics had been taught to look at Protestants like me. I had always heard that Catholics lacked morals. In Latin America, particularly, it was "obvious" that we Protestants were moral people who observed the Ten Commandments. Catholics by contrast did not even know what the Ten Commandments said. How could they obey the commandments they did not know? Of course, I had always been taught that immorality in the United States was to be found in cities where Catholics were the majority. The good counties in this country were those where Protestants made sure no bars and saloons could open and no alcoholic beverages could be sold. Catholics opposed

166

temperance, and alcohol was, unquestionably, the root of all manner of evil.

Considering Tony's words made me realize that Catholics in the United States and I had something very important in common. We had grown up as a religious minority in our respective countries. Many times in conversations in the faculty lounge, others would explain that they were talking about matters having to do with American Catholic culture which was foreign to me. I would explain to them that, actually, I knew first hand what they were talking about. The feeling that you had to proselytize, you had to uphold your reputation in a hostile environment, the convert syndrome, the need to establish one's identity by whether or not one attended parochial schools, etc., were all very familiar. On one matter, however, I found my new Catholic friends at a great advantage. They could openly disagree with catholic teachings and search for better alternatives. I soon became aware that this was not true among all Catholics. It was certainly true at Saint Mary's and Notre Dame.

During my first full year at Saint Mary's, Sister Assunta, the chair of the Religious Studies department, decided to ask for a sabbatical for the following year. Her request was granted, and before I knew it, I was appointed Chairperson of Religious Studies. I could not believe how things could be moving so fast without my moving a finger. As it turned out, after her year as a resident scholar, Sister Assunta decided to stay at Catholic University for the next six years. As a result, I remained chairperson for five of those years. After this time, I myself took a sabbatical, and insisted that the person who assumed the position should be appointed permanently, not as "acting chair" during my absence. While I was Chairperson, most of my colleagues at Saint Mary's thought it was just wonderful to have a Protestant in that position. None of my former colleagues at Andrews could quite understand how it was possible for me to occupy the Chair.

As already mentioned, when I went to Saint Mary's a merger with Notre Dame was in the air. The board of trustees of both institutions had hired Professors Elizabeth Park and William Mayhew to study the institutions and offer their recommendations for the most effective road forward. For a year everyone waited impatiently for the Park-Mayhew report. In due time the consultants recommended that the best future for these institutions would be to merge into one and offered a road map as to how to proceed toward this goal. Not long afterwards both boards approved the report and authorized the implementation of the steps toward merger. Not everyone was happy with the move. Some faculty at Saint Mary's resigned and secured employment elsewhere. Many were insecure about their chances of achieving tenure at the new institution.

The Park-Mayhew report recommended that the merger proceed from the bottom up. In other words, the first step was for departments to merge, then academic sections, then schools, then administrations, and ultimately the boards of trustees. At the end of the process both institutions would have ceased to be, and a new one would have emerged.

As Chair of Religious Studies it fell on me to merge my department with the Department of Theology at Notre Dame. My dealings first with Father James Burtchael and afterwards with Father David Burrell turned out to be extremely collegial, cordial, and quite successful. Our courses became fully integrated into one curriculum, our faculty participated meaningfully in the teaching of courses for undergraduate majors, and I became associate chair of the joint Theology Department. From my perspective, the merger was nothing if not a resounding success. Personally, I found myself in an advantageous position. When I had been hired I was given three years of credit toward tenure. This meant that I could apply for tenure after three years, in 1972. By the time the merger was finished I would already be tenured, if my application was successful.

Then, the unimaginable happened. In the spring of 1973, the Saint Mary's board of trustees announced, just as the school year was coming to an end, that they were pulling out of the merger agreement. Apparently, it felt that the merger was turning into the absorption of the weak by the strong. The only way to visualize this is to imagine a wedding celebration. The pastor and the bridegroom have come to the front of the church and are standing facing the entrance. The wedding party has marched down the main aisle, much to the audience's delight. The Bible boy and the flower girl have followed, self-consciously doing what they are supposed to do in front of a happy crowd. They have reached the altar and the Bible is in the pastor's hands. Everyone turns around and sees that the bride and her father are standing at the door. The organist begins to play the wedding march. At that moment a scream is heard. The bride shouts: "I can't go on with this," turns around and runs away, seeking someone who will drive her home. Everyone is confused, wondering what's going on, what's next. Some members of the family are totally frustrated, some are delighted. The relationship between the families is going to be tense for years to come, even if everyone tries hard to be as civil and cordial as possible. The situation is bound to get complicated if the bridegroom soon afterwards finds another bride and gets married. Notre Dame did that the following fall, admitting its first class including female undergraduates.

Saint Mary's board of trustees, I think, was fully justified. The administration of Saint Mary's had been following the guidelines for the merger, but the administration of Notre Dame was ignoring them. It was treating the sisters as it had always treated them, with the condescension of those who feel superior. Notre Dame saw itself taking over Saint Mary's as a trophy of conquest. Now, in order to make sure that it would get what it wanted anyway, Notre Dame announced that it would open its doors to female students, thus siphoning a significant proportion of Saint Mary's traditional applicant pool to itself. The future of Saint Mary's became uncertain.

First and second year students decided not to return once they realized they were not going to receive the degree they had been led to expect. The incoming class for the following year was relatively small. All hiring was cancelled, and tenures and promotions were postponed. Saint Mary's had hit bottom. Ever since the presidency of Sister Madeleva, the school had been on a slow but steady decline because of several factors. In the first place the pool of candidates from the Congregation of the Sisters of the Holy Cross for the presidency of the college was very limited, and no one among them had lived up to the standard set by Sister Madeleva. In fact, those who became president proved totally inadequate and were replaced after rather short tenures. With the new appeal and accessibility of co-educational institutions the student applicant pool shrank while costs increased. The college's endowment at the time was less than a million dollars. The school was surviving on the capital of its reputation. Father McGrath, the first president who was not a sister of Holy Cross, died of a heart attack after two years in office. A sister became acting president while a search for a president was conducted. The person brought in was the first president who was not only not a sister but a layman who resigned after three frustrating years. It must be recognized in his favor that the board of trustees, consisting of Sisters of the Holy Cross, was not up to its job either. Those were trying times, and the future was bleak.

In the midst of all this, I was actually doing quite well. God kept opening doors for me. As chairperson I had major influence over the shape of things to come, and I steered the department toward serious inquiry of important issues. Since the department was small and needed more personnel, I was able to hire faculty with a vision toward the future. Then when the merger with the Theology Department at Notre Dame was being implemented, I was asked to teach the basic course in New Testament for the majors. When the merger at the institutional level collapsed, the gains achieved at the departmental level were kept on foot. Thus, for many years afterwards I continued to teach the New Testament course for the majors. Notre Dame also had a special summer program that granted an MA in Theology to students who worked as teachers in Catholic high schools during the school year. I was asked to offer

170

courses in this program also. This meant that the sense of collegiality with professors at Notre Dame gave my experience at Saint Mary's a positive quality.

As I said already, the year I applied for tenure, Saint Mary's placed the granting of tenure on hold. Those who were being denied tenure were told. Those who were supposed to receive tenure were not told anything. Silence in this case meant that the rank and tenure committee and the president had voted that the applicant merited tenure. Whether it was actually granted would have to wait until the following spring, when the college would have a better sense of its future. I waited patiently until the following spring. To my surprise, when the long-expected letter finally arrived, I learned that I had been granted not only tenure but also a promotion to the rank of professor. I just could not believe it. I had not applied for a promotion. Of course, I did not have to believe it. It was a fact staring me in the face. It meant that for the rest of my life in the academy I did not have to be anxious about my future. It seemed to me I had been led to the right place.

Knowing that I had a future as a professor at Saint Mary's College forced me to reconsider the location of our home. By this time Aida had given birth to two boys. We still lived in the house we had purchased when I became a professor at the Seminary in Berrien Springs. Driving to work at Saint Mary's was not a hardship, but it was not absolutely necessary. Berrien Springs was a sleepy little village with no source of employment other than Andrews University. In fact it was a bedroom community for people who worked in Saint Joseph, Benton Harbor or Buchanan. After many long conversations, Aida and I came to the conclusion that we had to decide whether to move to South Bend or to go to live in the country. For several months we looked at properties in both areas. There were many reasons that made staying in Michigan attractive, among them the proximity to Lake Michigan and the marvelous northern woods. In our deliberations we were, as hindsight makes obvious, children of the sixties. The flower generation was in revolt against the urban or suburban conformist society that tried to keep-up with the Joneses. It was our great fortune to find 20 acres for sale four miles west of Berrien Springs, just fifteen minutes from Weko Beach. We bought them in December, when ten inches of snow covered the ground. After seven years our home had built enough equity to pay for those twenty acres. Since I owned the land, a bank was willing to lend me the money for the construction of the house.

Our property was a rectangle on a north south axis with a rather nice incline toward the north. The top four acres was a wood of large sugar maples, beaches, elms, cherries, oaks and ironwoods more than 70 feet tall. The rest of the land had been many years before a very productive peach orchard, but the trees had been uprooted and the land had been left unattended for some time. Tall grasses made for an abundance of wild life. We were particularly enamored of two large flocks of wild pheasants who roamed the place. In the spring of 1973 I bought a chain saw and began to clear the place where the house would be built, a bit inside the woods. When spring came I realized that the large trees I had left standing at the edge of the woods were elms dead from Dutch elm disease. Eventually they became wonderful fuel for our wood burning stove.

Looking back I have always wondered how I came about deciding to embark on such a big project. I had not done much physical labor since I had left the broom shop at Collegedale, and I had very little experience driving a nail with a hammer. For a couple of months Aida and I studied books with floor plans and eventually decided that none met our needs. I began, then, to draw plans myself, asking Aida for criticism. Eventually we arrived at a very simple floor design with living quarters on the first floor and bedrooms and two baths upstairs. The family room was to be two stories high with a balcony on the second floor. Its southern wall was two stories of mostly glass. To actually build the house, a friend put me in touch with LaVerne Jewell, a teacher of English at a nearby High School who had already built several houses during summers. So, even though I had no credentials and no experience,

172

I functioned as the contractor for the building of my house. My budget did not afford the services of a professional. The rather primitive plans I drew proved good enough to secure a bank loan and a building permit. I would not be able to do that under today's regulations at our township, but in 1973 the building inspector was a neighbor with a rather large apple orchard. I sub-contracted the pouring of the cement for the foundations and the basement walls, the brick and stone work, the plumbing and heating, and the drywall. LaVerne, one of his students, and I, did the framing, the roofing and the installation of the windows and doors. Two friends helped me with the electric wiring, and by the beginning of October, with most of the finishing and the installation of appliances still to be done, we moved in.

I must confess that never in my life, not even when I was cycling in Mendoza with the onset of typhoid fever, did I spend so much time in a constant state of physical exhaustion. I still find myself wondering where I found the courage to launch such a project. I am certain, however, that the discipline and endurance required contributed significantly to making me who I am. Thirty-seven years later, Aida and I still live in our house. Our boys could not have had a better place in which to grow up than the woods with plenty of wild life and the pond where in winter they skated to their heart's content. Building the house in which to raise our family turned out to be something that, through the years, has given me immense satisfaction. Even though some of the finishing touches reveal my poor craftsmanship, I have absolute knowledge of every detail in its construction and feel confident and secure in it. In spite of all the planning, however, it did not take us long to discover that at night the woods were dark and you could be forced in winter to leave the car stuck in the snow and walk up to three hundred yards hardly able to push yourself forward toward home in a freezing night.

By the time I built our home our two sons were already little boys. Heroldito was becoming an independent little fellow who decided that his name was Dito (the last four letters of the way he was being called). Carlos Orval, who was born in 1971, was already able to walk, but somebody had to be with him protecting him from the hazards that abound in a construction site. Life in the country made it possible for Dito and Carlitos to enjoy contact with all sorts of animals. We always had several dogs and at least one cat, the former outside and the latter inside the house. At times, moreover, we had doves, finches, love birds, parrots, two ponies and an Arabian white colt that became a beautiful gelding. It was always their responsibility to take care of all the animals. They spent long hours wondering in the woods, building look outs in strategic places and developing resourcefulness and curiosity. Eventually Dito graduated from the University of Notre Dame, explored options with internships in the United Nations Headquarters in New York City and in the Washington office of Senator Carl Levin of Michigan, and then decided to come back and develop a nursery that produced ground covers for landscapers. Carlos graduated from the Residential College and the Medical School of the University of Michigan in Ann Arbor and is a clinical assistant professor of geriatric medicine at Johns Hopkins in Baltimore.

Another unexpected opportunity opened up before me in 1974. Portia Prebys, a recent Saint Mary's graduate, had married a pilot from Alitalia Airlines and was living in Rome. She had also begun studies toward a doctoral degree in history at an Italian university. After completing a Master's degree, she approached the administration of Saint Mary's with the idea of establishing a sophomore year of study in Rome. Sister Alma, then the president, saw light in the idea and established the Rome Program. The courses offered at the Rome campus, naturally, took advantage of the opportunities offered by the city and the country. But students at Rome also took courses in the general curriculum, so as not to jeopardize their graduation in four years. In order to integrate the Rome and the Notre Dame programs, faculty from the home campus were encouraged to apply to teach in Rome. I immediately applied to spend a sabbatical year at Rome teaching a half load. Thus Aida, our two boys aged 4 and 6, and I spent the 1975-6 school year at Rome.

As a young man in Argentina I had dreamed of going to Europe to study, but I knew well it was not to be. Financially, it was impossible. I could not do there what I could do in the United States: study and pay for my studies with my own work, requiring minimal extra help. Traveling in Europe as a student tourist had also been beyond my means. Now, I had the opportunity to spend ten months in Europe doing what, until a short time before, I thought was an impossible dream.

The year abroad made me a different person intellectually, culturally and religiously. It is difficult to be original describing the benefits of immersion into another culture, taking a serious interest in its many manifestations in language, the arts, the life of the streets, and the general way of conducting the business of living. Italy makes alive the history of Western civilization from the Etruscans in the ninth century BCE till today with important material artifacts from every century in between. For the ten months we were abroad I had a rented car that made it possible to travel not only in Italy, including Sicily, but also in Greece, Yugoslavia, Austria, Southern Germany, France, Spain and Portugal.

The year in Europe gave me a new appreciation for the importance of the cultural achievements of the human race. As a religious person formed in conservative Christianity, I had been molded to think human beings are essentially fallen creatures totally dependent on God's grace. Any human achievement is not to be trusted, since it is essentially a deceit, a demonstration of the first and last of all sins: pride. Human beings are by nature bad; therefore, they are incapable of doing good things. Plato had been distrustful of art on account of its manifestation in matter: metals, clay, marble, canvas, paint. American Christianity, shaped by the puritan tradition, developed a negative attitude toward art on religious grounds that drew on the Platonic tradition. The only Christian art allowed did not reflect on the artist but aimed to illustrate biblical themes, or was considered devotional and uplifting. My eight months in Rome with excursions here and there,

175

inside and outside Italy, and my two months in Spain and Portugal, made me realize that the human story is not just the story of sin. It is also the story of grace and the grandeur of the human spirit. The Biblical description of human beings as made in the image of God is not exhausted after one brief reference, or canceled by sin. The material culture left in Europe by successive peoples, beginning with the Minoans and the Etruscans, is an irrefutable testimony to the creativity and the beauty that abides in the human soul and can be expressed powerfully and eloquently by people imbued by the Spirit.

Christianity came to be by the power of the Holy Spirit that raised Jesus from the dead. Paul refers to the Spirit as a constant refrain in his letters. Reading them, one is not always sure whether he is referring to the Spirit of God, the Spirit of Christ, the Holy Spirit or the spirit of human beings. As Yeats wrote, How can you tell the dancer from the dance? At times it would seem that it does not matter which it is. The Spirit is the Spirit, and its work among humans is not to be denied. I learned to affirm, like Paul, that we are saved by hope, and that faith is only effective as love. This, however, does not require me to think humans are by nature a rotten bunch whose pride renders them incapable of goodness, beauty, justice or peace. Much of the material remains we now admire in Europe were produced at a heavy price of slavery, mistreatment, injustice or perfidy. And yet, one cannot but admire the imagination, the creativity, the vision of the beautiful, the need to lift one's existence to the realm of the spiritual, inspired by the very spirit of God.

In the conservative Christian tradition the only place for artistic expression was in music, and I had been attracted to it since childhood. Unfortunately, poor hearing and poor muscular coordination made my attempts at singing and playing an instrument unpleasant to others. When I was eleven years old my mother enrolled me at the school of fine arts. I copied reproductions from the masters and drew still lives with pencil and charcoal. After three years, I got bored and dropped out. But the fact of the matter was that I recognized my limitations. Comparing mine to the work of my fellow students, I knew that I did not have the talent required to be good at it. Now in Europe, seeing first hand the works of the great masters made me realize that God is extremely prodigal with gifts. I had been conditioned to think of Rafael, Michelangelo, Leonardo as pagans who served a morally bankrupt papacy, whose work was, therefore, another expression of the corruption of sin. My year in Europe allowed me the realization of the grandeur of their work at a totally new level. I must admit, though, when I went to Europe I had already benefited from the classes by Adventist professors who had transcended the denominational prejudices in these matters. As a student at Southern I had taken an introductory course in art appreciation/history and at the Adventist Seminary in Washington I had taken a course in Church History in Art. Both Dr Lauritzen at Southern and Dr. Walther at the Seminary had been people who had not fitted the traditional Adventist mold and were citizens of the world. The seeds they scattered on me now were grown plants in full bloom.

Something somewhat similar happened during our two months in Spain. In Uruguay and Argentina, Spain, la madre patria, is revered in almost sacred undertones. Of course, Spain's most exalted element is its role as the defender and propagator of the Catholic faith. The Inquisition also made inroads in Spanish Latin America, and to this day, in most of Latin America, Catholicism is a major cultural force. The history of Spain, however, is virtually never told without the invasion of the Arabs in the eighth century and the "re-conquest" of the country that culminated in the expulsion of the Arab rulers in 1492, the same year Columbus discovered America. But at the time when I was a student in Argentina, history classes hardly mentioned the presence of Moslems and Jews in Spain. I was not quite prepared, therefore, to find that the influence of Arab culture was deep and pervasive, even as far north as Saragossa and beyond.

177

In Spain I discovered the beauty of multiculturalism. Spain enjoyed its cultural zenith as the most advanced culture in Europe when Jews, Arabs and Christians lived together in daily social intercourse. When the Arabs were expelled and the Jews and the few Calvinists expurgated by the Inquisition, Spain ceased to be the intellectual light of Europe. The history of Spain reinforced in me the benefits to be gained when peoples with different religious and cultural characteristics find a way to live in peace, as well as the danger of becoming enamored with a vision of one's own purity. Cordoba in the eleventh and twelfth centuries is a model to be imitated on a global scale.

Upon my return from my sabbatical in Europe, I discovered that the new president at Saint Mary's had had a very successful year while I was away. After many false starts and searches in the dark, finally, it seemed, Saint Mary's had a leader with a vision and the skills to make his vision a reality. He was John Duggan, a Yale PhD who had been Dean of Students at the newly co-ed Vassar and had worked for the Academic Testing Service at Princeton. Duggan came in with a plan. Saint Mary's needed to reconfigure its board of trustees and create a new working policy spelling out the principle of community governance. In the meantime he also took as his first priority to bolster faculty morale, which, after the failure of the merger, was very low. He worked at this indefatigably. He also restructured the scale of faculty salaries to make them competitive. This resulted in the hiring of a new class of junior faculty with outstanding credentials and real promise. Teaching at Saint Mary's became a real joy. The place began to percolate with academic excitement. When the accrediting association sent a team of inspectors for a three-day visit, they could not believe the place was real. They were frustrated because they could not find one faculty member with serious charges against the administration. Faculty morale was in the clouds. I had not been a believer in the "hero" theory of history. I was more inclined to think that real changes in the affairs of institutions were very slow and driven by mysterious forces at work in history. John Duggan showed me

178

otherwise. He changed Saint Mary's for the better in a way no one could deny through a combination of wisdom, vision, empathy and energy, and all those who benefited from his leadership remain in his debt. Most important in his success was that he did not just talk about community governance; he practiced it. He actually listened to the faculty, and when he disagreed, he did so openly and logically. When after ten years he resigned, having accomplished all the goals he had set for himself, the dismal days preceding the merger and then the fiasco of the non-merger, seemed a faint memory of a very distant past.

My association with the theological faculty at The University of Notre Dame during the merger negotiations resulted in two very distinct by-products for the enrichment of my personal life. The first came as a result of my getting to know Father John Dunne, a Holy Cross priest who was doing original theology in a personal, luminous, and engaging style. I soon discovered that Father Dunne was without question the most well-liked professor on the Notre Dame campus. His courses were always crowded with seniors, who had priority at registration. The rest of the student body had to wait their turn to be able to sit at his feet. At the time he was preoccupied with a theology of death. His books were theological best sellers. He then studied the Sufi movement within Islam and emerged with a new approach to doing theology. He argued that in order to fully understand one's own religion one needed to "cross over" to another culture, to another religion, and understand it. That allows one to come back and, using newly gained perspectives and insights, ask new questions and gain a clearer understanding of one's own religion. In this he was a forerunner of the new wave of cultural awareness sweeping academia now.

One of the most famous anecdotes among theologians is an apocryphal dialogue between Adolph von Harnack, the famous church historian, and Max Weber, the sociologist of religion, which supposedly took place at the beginning of the twentieth century. Von Harnack is reported to have said: "If one knows one religion well, one knows all." To this Weber is said to have replied: "He who knows only one religion, knows none." Dunne, obviously, had taken Weber's argument and developed a method for improving one's knowledge of one's own religion.

I found his suggestion most helpful. Of course, I had been engaged in the study of the religions of antiquity, particularly those alive during the time of Christ. I had written my dissertation on the concept of pietas in Roman religion. I was quite aware of the contributions many religions made to the development of Christianity. At first, I had looked at those contributions as illegitimate accretions which needed to be expurgated. In fact, that was the argument developed by von Harnack. According to him, Christianity had gone wrong as soon as it began to speak the language of Greek metaphysics, rather than the simple language of the gospels. True Christianity, therefore, needed to recover the pristine purity of the apostolic age. This, of course, has been the basic posture of most reform, or sectarian, movements within Christianity. It was also the position I had been inculcated as a youth. Dunne's argument was firmly based on the Catholic understanding of the value of tradition, the recognition that twenty centuries of Christian theological development, of a constant struggle to understand what one actually believes, cannot be cavalierly dismissed as wrongheaded or pernicious. Understanding the way our predecessors came to understand their faith as they confronted the challenges posed by their times can help us in our own times with a faith that has something meaningful to say to the issues we need to address. If we really wish to understand our faith we cannot ignore how our ancestors understood it and then transmitted it to us. Dunne, a poet and visionary, was pushing for a methodological dialogue with non-Christian traditions. After a while, he won me over to his point of view. This theological step, unquestionably, made me a better informed Christian. The desire to understand and do God's will would no longer be a private, or a parochial, matter, even if I had to come to terms with it in the solitude of my own soul. How to understand God's will can not be the projection of an internal tradition. One's understanding

180

must be open to the light of a universal sun that, as the gospels remind us, shines both on the just and the unjust.

Of course, to see those who do not share one's faith as dialogue partners on religious matters, rather than as candidates for conversion, does not happen at once. I had long cherished what is considered the basic Protestant Principle. It was the issue at the heart of Luther's stand against the theology informing church life in his times. According to him, theology can only be based on the Scriptures and the Scriptures alone. The theologians defending the selling of indulgences argued that theology was based on Scripture and tradition. Of course, my studies of the Scriptures had convinced me that the matter is not that simple. As a matter of fact, tradition played a role in the writing of both the Hebrew and the Christian Scriptures since in them we have the compilation of oral traditions. The four canonical gospels are based on oral traditions which, within different early Christian communities, developed in different directions, with different emphases and different agendas. One cannot, therefore, dismiss tradition out of hand, as if by doing so one preserves the authentic, pure gospel preached by the disciples in the first century. In the first century, when the only Scripture available was the Hebrew Bible, all Christians depended on tradition for their knowledge of what Jesus had done and said. When I came to see this, it became obvious that the battle over Scripture and tradition fought at the time of the Protestant Reformation can no longer be fought intelligently today. Those who insist on the principle of Scripture and Scripture alone often fail to realize that their reading of the Scripture has been shaped by traditions from the eighteenth and the nineteenth centuries. Therefore, their claim to the pure gospel of the first century is based on a failure to recognize what they are reading and how the way they read is shaped by culture.

The second result of my friendships with the Notre Dame faculty was that, in the fall of 1979, Joseph Blenkinsopp, the professor of Old Testament, asked me to be his assistant, as director of volunteers, at an archaeological excavation he was planning with Vassilios Tzaferis of the Department of Antiquities of the State of Israel. They were planning an expedition to Capernaum on the shores of the Lake of Tiberias, known in the Gospels as the Sea of Galilee. Another door was opened by the grace of God. While inviting me, Joe informed me that all my expenses would be covered. Of course, I had no difficulty in deciding what to do. Thus, in the summer of 1980, I found myself in Israel doing archaeological work. I had been an avid student of Siegfried Horn, the professor of Old Testament at the Seminary, who had been an armchair archaeologist until then. Soon after I graduated, Horn went to Jordan as director of the excavations at Tell Hesbon. I had taken all his classes in archaeology and ancient near eastern history and eventually came to believe that doing archaeology was more or less a requirement for anyone who dealt with the Biblical materials in a scholarly way because published reports are already interpretations of the data accumulated by the excavators. Actually digging in the ground and then participating in the interpretation of the data being exposed, I thought, was necessary in order to be an intelligent reader of archaeological reports.

Slow-digging in a desert is not a joy ride. Temperatures in the summer in Israel reach an abominable height by noon, and the early afternoons are suffocating. Thus, work at the dig begins at six a.m. and ends at noon. This means being up by five, and I am not a morning person. Our dig was conducted on the Greek Orthodox property, east of the Roman Catholic (Franciscan) part of what was once the city of Capernaum. Excavations in the Franciscan property had uncovered the magnificent synagogue now visited by most tourists who go to Israel. This synagogue was originally identified as the one Jesus had visited according to the Gospels, but later proved to have been built in the third century. The same was true of the housing units found nearby. Tzaferis and Blenkinsopp worked on the hunch that the first century synagogue could be found in another section of the city.

As soon as we began digging we found remains from the

eleventh century, but not long afterwards we were recovering remains from the ninth and eighth centuries. By and large, the digging was routine work with little excitement. For me it was a great learning experience since I was assigned to supervise a small group of three in a particular square. We had to be careful looking for, preserving, and recording the location of anything of interest. We learned to distinguish stones that had fallen from walls from stones that constituted a floor or the remains of a wall still in place.

The best part of the summer were the weekend excursions Vassilios Tzaferis conducted for the benefit of the volunteers at the dig. Unfortunately, Blenkinsopp had to leave for the States on the second day of the dig for personal reasons and did not get back for a while. Tzaferis had been an Orthodox monk in his youth. Now he was married, had a PhD in archaeology from the University of Haifa, and was on the staff of the Israeli Department of Antiquities. His first brush with fame had been the discovery of the bones of a crucified man in a burial chamber in the outskirts of Jerusalem. That discovery had made news because it proved that all depictions of the crucifixion in the history of Christian art were incorrect. The nails did not pierce the palms of the hands and the front of the feet. Rather, they pierced the fore arm just above the wrist and the heels turned sideways against the cross, leaving the body in a splayed position. In order to prevent the hands and the heels from coming loose, a piece of wood was placed between them and the head of the nails. The ossuary discovered by Tzaferis at Talpioth contained the bones (with nail scrapings), the nails and the pieces of wood holding the body, as well as a knot from the wood of the cross with a bent nail in it.

Tzaferis had used good connections with the Greek Orthodox Patriarchate of Jerusalem to obtain permission for the dig. He also brought two Greek Orthodox monks with Masters in archaeology to the dig: Father Kyprianos and Father Cyrillos. They were a great addition to the dig and became my good friends. While in Jerusalem Kyprianos took me to the patriarchate and gave me a guided tour of the treasury, containing ancient relics and icons. Then, at the request of the American volunteers, Vassilios, Kyprianos and Cyrillos agreed to sing the liturgy of John Chrysostom for us. One early evening we all went to the small chapel at the Greek Orthodox property at Capernaum and listened with joy to the sung liturgy. It was a memorable experience.

As it happened, Blenkinsopp asked me to help him again in 1982. I was to go for the first four weeks of the dig, when other commitments would prevent him from being in Capernaum. I happily fulfilled my obligations with the volunteers for four weeks and then stayed in Israel for another week of independent travel. As it turned out, the second summer proved even more blessed. The volunteers in my square discovered the largest hoard of gold coins ever found in Israel, consisting of 286 gold drachmas coined in eighth century Damascus. More exciting, however, were journeys to two ancient Greek monasteries. From Jericho I walked up the Wadi Quelt to the monastery of Saint George following the path used in Jesus' time. Some of its stones reveal the ruts left by the wheels of roman chariots and wagons. If you want to walk where Jesus certainly walked, there is no more authentic place than the old Jericho road, which Jesus took from Jericho to Jerusalem, according to the three synoptic gospels. The laconic way Mark describes the ascent is one of the most graphic scenes in the gospels. They were on the road, Jesus leading the way alone, the disciples following somewhat behind because they were afraid. I shall always carry with me memories of that afternoon on the Jericho road up to Jerusalem.

Thanks to the good offices of my new friend Father Kyprianos, I was taken to the monastery of Mar Saba a few miles east of Bethlehem, in one of the wadis that cut the Judean high mesa as it breaks down toward the Dead Sea. The buildings are in inhospitable surroundings and walking to them is out of the question. A truck takes weekly supplies to the monks at Mar Saba from the Patriarchate in Jerusalem. I was delighted to get a ride on it. Like Saint George, Mar Saba also clings to the cliffs of the wadi and contains wonderful wall murals and other icons. The trip, however, also turned out to be memorable. The monk who drove the truck was an American from New York who had converted to Greek Orthodoxy as a young adult. In our conversation he told me that he had come to monasteries in the Judean desert trying to escape the many temptations and distractions of life in urban civilization. Then he confessed rather sheepishly that his motivation had been illusory. With the passage of time, he had come to realize that the world he had tried to escape had come to the desert with him in his mind.

My year in Europe and my two summers in Israel made a marked impact on my teaching. They allowed me to do a better informed and more confident evaluation of the importance of historical and cultural considerations when studying religion. Reading and the imagination can expand one's horizons. Still, nothing compares to first hand experience when it comes to explaining situations and conditions. It is possible to travel the world and remain the person who never left home, and some people I know prove it. I was glad to see that I had become a quite different person and believer on account of my travels. Of course, the road from Montevideo to Notre Dame had already been rich in experiences. The further expansion of my horizons by sojourns in Europe and Israel allowed me to return home a wiser person.

By 1975, Earle Hilgert had also left Andrews. Like my Duke friend, James Zink, he opted for studying for a degree in library science. He then found work as a reference librarian at McCormick Theological Seminary in Chicago, in the Hyde Park district. It was not long before his colleagues discovered his extraordinary talents. Eventually he became the Chair of the New Testament Department, and on occasions Acting Dean. When McCormick started a Hispanic Program, Earle recommended me to Ruben Almendariz, its first director. Thus, I became a visiting professor of New Testament at McCormick. When Northern Seminary in Lombard, a Chicago western suburb, opened its Hispanic Program, I became an affiliate professor of New Testament there. For twenty years during ten weeks, I traveled to either Hyde Park or Lombard

185

to teach an evening class once a week. Since both seminaries are members of the Chicago Cluster of Theological Schools, students from other seminaries also registered for my classes.

Teaching courses on the New Testament in Spanish to students from different countries turned out to be a particular delight. I never looked upon it as work. My students came from different Christian denominations. Some were professionals, lawyers or engineers with degrees from their home countries, who had decided in middle age to become pastors. With them I developed lasting friendships. I encouraged several to pursue further studies, and some of them are now teaching at seminaries or colleges both in the United States and in Latin America.

The Hispanic Program was established on the insight that every presentation of the Gospel is culturally conditioned and capable of being presented in every cultural setting. The difficult task for me was to remain faithful both to my conviction that the methodologies developed by European biblical scholarship were the most helpful scientific tools available and to my attachment to the mores and cultural insights of Hispanic Latin Americans. Said differently, I had to demonstrate that one could keep one's Hispanic ways of being, which included a particular spirituality, and use critical methodologies to understand the text at its most basic level. Most importantly, I had to demonstrate that, contrary to what fundamentalists claim, accepting critical methods for reading the text with historical and literary tools, did not necessarily destroy your faith. Doing so allowed faith to become mature in the face of experience. Doubts are not the killers of faith but allow faith to strengthen and extend itself to all aspects of life. After all, faith is not a mental exercise that makes possible the holding of peculiar doctrines, but what calls upon all the faculties to integrate you in a way of life. My task in the classroom was to show Hispanic future pastors, most of whom came from fundamentalist denominations, that I was a devoted believer who used conscientiously all the critical methods for understanding what the Bible said.

Teaching at Saint Mary's I had a different agenda. I was teaching in a liberal arts curriculum to students who were, for the most part, taking my courses to satisfy a degree requirement. I had to have for them something that would catch their attention. When the Cold War was raging and the doctrine of assured response was promoted as the way of achieving nuclear deterrence, I designed a course titled "Thinking the Future." It studied the eschatological and apocalyptic biblical texts and then explored nineteenth and twentieth century interpretations of these texts as guides for life in the world today. The material was divided into individualistic visions, communal visions, and cosmic visions. We considered both what meaning immortality may have in the twentieth century as well as the prospects for the survival of the nation state and the cosmos. Apocalypticism was in the air everywhere. Hollywood could not produce enough movies patterned after *Star Wars*. The massive nuclear arsenals that were supposed to assure deterrence of a first strike by an enemy were a sword of Damocles hanging over humankind. The new awareness of the environmental peril also brought to the fore apocalyptic visions. Whether the future was to be cancelled by World War III or by global warming and the depletion of water resources, the end result would not be dissimilar.

At the heart of the doctrine of nuclear deterrence there was, of course, a logical flaw. On one hand, it was imperative to convince the enemy that a first strike would provoke a massive response that would bring about his annihilation. At the same time, in the back of your mind you knew that if your enemy actually launched a first strike and you responded as you were promising to do, every living thing on earth would die. This meant that while you were convincing the enemy of your unflinching determination to counterattack, you were already convinced that to actually carry this out was suicidal madness. The ability to sustain such a contradiction was without question the most important contribution of this doctrine to our understanding of the vagaries of human nature.

From my perspective, the realization on the part of every

187

thinking person that the apocalypse was no longer an exclusively divine prerogative but something that was within the human realm of possibilities brought about the need to rethink how we are to conceive the relationship of God and the world in which we live as God's creatures. Until the middle of the twentieth century, believers agreed that only God could bring about the end of history. Since then, we have been able to do it by ourselves. Thank you very much, God. This shift of cosmic power from God to humankind had been a major factor in the shift from theology to anthropology in religious discourse. Dietrich Bonhoeffer, already before World War II, worked on an ethic for "man [sic] come of age." Christianity, some theologians were admitting, had been treating adults as if they were children in need of protection and constant supervision. With the production of large stockpiles of nuclear weapons, it became obvious that the survival of all living creatures rested on the non-use of these weapons. There was no question that these developments weakened God's image and established the need for seriousness and a deep sense of responsibility on the part of humans. As a reaction to this perceived weakening, fundamentalism has resurged in all religions. The need to proclaim God's omnipotence is strongest when God's power is hardest to envision.

These developments also had an effect on the apocalyptic mind-set. The ability of humans to obliterate life in this planet has been seen by many as a fulfillment of one of the signs announcing the imminent Second Coming. In the Second Letter of Peter, a pseudonymous writing from the second century, the author condemns Christian preachers who take advantage of new converts and teach them a Christianity that the author rejects. As he says, "It would have been better for them never to have known the way of righteousness than after knowing it to turn back from the holy commandment" (2 Pet. 2:21). The author then launches an apology for the delay of the Second Coming. "The Lord," he assures his readers, "is not slow about his promise" (3:9). To substantiate this claim he offers two arguments. One is that time is relative. It would seem that a long time has passed since the destruction of the temple of Jerusalem, when the early Christians thought the Parousia would take place. Time is relative. "With the Lord, one day is as a thousand years, and a thousand years as one day" (3:8). Thus, in the heavenly calendar, a delay of fifty or so years is a wink. Besides, the delay makes the preaching of the gospel and the conversion of more people possible. God's desire is "that all should reach repentance" (3:9). Then comes a detailed description with an admonition,

> *But the day of the Lord will come like a thief, and then the*
> *heavens will pass away with a loud noise, and the elements*
> *will be dissolved with fire, and the earth and the works that*
> *are upon it will be burned up. Since all these things are thus*
> *to be dissolved, what sort of person ought you to be in lives of*
> *holiness and godliness, waiting for and hastening the coming*
> *of the day of God, because of which the heavens will be*
> *kindled and dissolved, and the elements will melt with fire!*
> *(3:10-12).*

Many modern apocalypticists see in the final words a perfect description of what a massive nuclear attack will do. Of particular importance for them is the fact that the text describes the melting of the elements. What better description of the splitting of the atom and the dissolution of matter by fire in an atomic conflagration?

Apocalyptic interpretations read the whole Bible, not just the explicitly apocalyptic literature in it, guided by two basic hermeneutical principles. The first is that everything written was meant to describe "the time of the end." The second is that this generation, the one to which the reader belongs, is living in "the time of the end." In other words, the Bible was written with us in mind. This may be very comforting to some, but as a method for reading it is arbitrary and ignores the historical and cultural conditioning of the biblical authors. Students of first century cosmology are aware that the author of Second Peter is operating in a universe where the space between heaven and earth is occupied

189

by "the elements." He is not referring to the elements found in a periodic table in an introductory chemistry textbook. He is referring to the spheres, or aeons, or heavens, occupied by spiritual beings who mediate between the human and the divine spheres for good and for evil. Descriptions of ascents into heaven make reference to them. The author is, therefore, emphasizing the complete destruction of the cosmos in terms of a cosmology that is no longer considered helpful to understand the universe in which we live. Modern means of visualizing and exploring space have rendered the cosmology in first century apocalyptic descriptions so obsolete as to be unimaginable. However, even if one takes the description of the day of God with a grain of salt, one can and should affirm the author's main concern. In view of the fact that we live in God's world (something that only faith can affirm, and affirms no matter how conceived), we must consider seriously "what sort of person ought [we] to be in lives of holiness and godliness." This eschatological admonition is relevant at all times. Especially, the author of the epistle insists, when people use the gospel to abuse unsuspecting neophytes guided by their own greed. Apocalyptic reading of the Bible has taken evangelical Christianity by storm, and made best sellers of bad novels, sparking the proliferation of "Christian" entrepreneurs with something to sell. But the way to take the apocalyptic texts in the Bible seriously is not by using them as coded messages for our times. It is to take them as theological messages for their original readers, and then taking seriously their theological insights for the construction of our own theologies.

Apocalyptic scenarios of the end were appealing to those who were at the margins of the Roman empire providing the labor that made the life of the few extremely satisfying, and have been very appealing to the masses of the third world. But in the decade of the seventies these masses also responded with faith and hope to the theology of liberation that was first sketched in Peru by Gustavo Gutierrez and soon found exponents throughout Latin America and the world. One of the few hierarchs of the Catholic

190

Church in South America who identified himself with liberation theology was Bishop Helder Camera of Recife, Brazil. In 1998 Saint Mary's College awarded Bishop Camera an honorary degree. Thus, he was on campus at graduation exercises. The administration had asked Jerome McElroy, a professor of economics, to be the bishop's host while he was in town. The evening after graduation Jerry planned a small reception at his home with Bishop Camera as the guest of honor. It was our good fortune that Aida and I were invited. We had been good friends with Jerry and his wife Birdie ever since they came to Saint Mary's after living in Belize and the Virgin Islands. At the little gathering that evening, Jerry asked me for a favor. He was supposed to take Bishop Camera to breakfast the next morning, but now he had another matter of some importance he needed to attend. Would I do that for him? He also explained to me that before going to breakfast the Bishop wanted to go to the chapel and say mass. I immediately agreed to take the Bishop to the chapel and then breakfast. Early the next morning Aida and I went to the dormitory where Bishop Camera was staying, and the three of us went to the chapel of the Holy Spirit. I expected to sit in a pew and wait for the Bishop to say mass. Instead, he insisted that I assist him in the service. I did some of the Scripture readings and, when the time came, the three of us had communion together. From the time I first went to teach at Saint Mary's I was always welcomed to take the elements of communion at any time I felt inclined to do so. I had, therefore, been at mass on more than one occasion. This time, however, the Bishop made such a marvelous, simple extraordinarily beautiful and personal ceremony that it was indelibly engraved in my memory: Just Aida, the Bishop and I confessing our commitment to the Christian way of life.

When the celebration at the chapel ended, I was eager to take the Bishop for a hearty American breakfast. We drove to a nearby restaurant that offered a magnificent array of options. Since the Bishop was not very fluent in English, I described in half-Spanish half-Portuguese some of the most attractive dishes. He insisted, however, that all he wanted was black coffee and one piece of toast, no butter, no jelly, no jam nor preserve. I was more than a bit disappointed, as I wanted to be a good and gracious host by providing a bountiful breakfast. He then said to me with the same plainness with which he had said mass, "How can I have a big breakfast when my people in Recife are hungry?" I have personally known some of the most distinguished exponents of liberation theology, but I saw this kind of identification with the people they claimed to represent in no one else. There was such integrity, humbleness, and transparency that I thought I was really in the presence of a man of God. After that, I did not have to wonder any more how it was possible that he was still doing his work in Brazil under a hard dictatorship. That morning with Helder Camera stands in my mind as one of the most vivid moments in my spiritual journey.

The morning Aida and I spent with Bishop Camera reaffirmed in me the importance of recognizing that Christianity has to do, at its core, with the living of life and the integrity with which liturgical action echoes the routines of daily life. In this way it takes up the constant refrain of the Old Testament prophets. I was left reflecting on the need to find the people with whom you wish to identify and to determine the boundaries within which you and those with whom you belong live in peace. In a way, I was envious of the Bishop's total identification with the people of Recife. I was thinking of this at the same time I started to prepare a course on the various ways in which the Christ figure has functioned in and out of Christianity. In the process, I came across an essay by Raimundo Pannikkar, the Hindu-Catholic priest and theologian, published in 1988. In it he develops a "potamic " typology using different rivers of the world to illustrate periods in the history of Christianity. The essay made an argument which I thought was worth serious consideration by my students. I must confess, as an aside, that the fact that he mentions the Paraná, even if only in passing, made a positive impression on me.

Pannikkar's argument is that we need to move now to a new

phase represented by the Ganges. It is the stage of pluralism, when relations among religions must be characterized by fruitful dialogue. The traditional exclusivism that has characterized Christian history must not be replaced by an inclusivism that is patronizing or imperialistic. Pluralism is a way of escaping the horns of the dilemma posed by exclusivism and inclusivism. According to exclusivism, Christ is the only savior, and those who do not confess his name will not participate in life. According to inclusivism, all those who are saved, and there may be among them many who have never heard of Christ, are saved by Christ. One of the notable contributions to theological discourse by Karl Rahner was the designation of those who are saved by Christ without their knowing as "anonymous Christians." This notion was received, at the time of its first appearance, as a great step away from exclusivism. It was not long before several voices objected to it as condescending and imperialistic. Pluralism provides a way of escaping the pomposity of exclusivistic claims and the paternalism of inclusivistic "generosity." It admits that in other cultures and religious traditions there are also savior figures who work effectively on behalf of the members of those cultures and traditions.

Looking for materials for my course I also came across a much earlier essay by J. Peter Schineller, S.J., published in Theological Studies in 1976, which drew a typology for understanding Christ's and the church's roles as agents of salvation. According to him, one may take one of five positions, and all of them have Biblical support. Whereas some Christians insist that the only way to be a Bible believing Christian is by holding Christ to be the only Savior and my denomination the only agent of salvation now on earth, it is also possible, at the other end of the spectrum, to find support in the Bible for granting to the savior figures of all religions legitimacy and think that no institution is a bona fide agency of salvation The world, and all its cultures and traditions, were created by God and have developed under God's providential care for centuries. It is well to remember the astonishing words of the prophet Amos, addressing the Israelites who considered themselves the elect of God. Amos explicitly places his indictment of Israel in the context of God's indictment of the surrounding nations. Then he points out that on account of her election, Israel will be punished even more severely (Amos 3:2). He insists that on account of sin, Israel has fallen no more to rise (Amos 5:2). The book closes with a series of disturbing questions: "Are you not like the Ethiopians to me, O people of Israel?" says the Lord. "Did I not bring up Israel from the land of Egypt, and the Philistines from Caphtor and the Syrians from Kir? (Amos 9:7). To compare as of equal significance the exodus of the Israelites from Egypt with the arrival of the Philistines to the West and the Syrians to the North, must have been the height of treason and apostasy to most worshippers of Yahweh in Amos' time. Everyone knows that the Philistines were Israel's worst enemy and constant threat. The Syrians, of course, were the ones about to destroy the kingdom of Israel with its capital in Samaria. Neither one of these peoples were worshipers of Yahweh. How could the prophet dare to say that their history was just as important to God as that of the chosen people? We can certainly transpose this tune to our own times and say that God is also active in the cultural and religious developments of the Chinese, the Hindus, the Japanese and the tribes of Polynesia who do not confess Jesus Christ as their savior. Of course, Islam worships the God of Abraham, Isaac and Jacob, who is also the God of Jesus. My work at Saint Mary's College gave to my spiritual journey a marked turn. The needs of my students and the generosity of thoughtful colleagues, strangers who had entered my life accidentally, were the facilitators of my progress.

My satisfying academic life at Saint Mary's was paralleled by active participation in my local church. In 1973, under the leadership of the chairperson of the Department of Modern Languages at Andrews, a small Spanish congregation was organized as a church in Berrien Springs. Aida and I were invited to become charter members, and we were happy to join. The congregation consisted of a few families who resided permanently in the area

194

and students, primarily graduate students, from Latin America who were at Andrews for a few years. During the thirty seven years since, I served the congregation in different capacities, from first elder to building manager. Lately, however, I have been more on the sidelines. It has been my home for worship and the life of faith. It has been very important that this is a Spanish congregation, even if it also means that its members are rather conservative socially and theologically. I have felt at home in it because I know perfectly well where they come from, where they are. Its culture, of course, is my own, even if Latin America is not at all a cultural monolith.

Migrant workers, with and without proper documents, have been coming to southwestern Michigan to harvest fruit, tomatoes, and cucumbers since the beginning of the twentieth century. By the early seventies some of them were staying in the area year round, branching off to more permanent jobs. At the church, they have been contributing with their profound religious devotion, their musical talents and their enthusiasm with life and family. I have always felt that church should be as diverse as possible, with as much ethnic, national and cultural variety as possible. The Adventist Spanish Church in Berrien Springs is to this day my congregational home and the fulcrum where the spiritual energies of people are integrated to form a Christian body. My friendships with graduate students who study with some of my former colleagues, as well as with farm workers who found at the church a place where they could feel respected and valued have provided for me a window through which to reflect on the purpose of the local congregation. It is not "to prepare you for heaven," as the often repeated cliché has it. It is to inform your participation in humanity and energize your efforts for the well-being of others here one earth.

Recognizing the need to live with our non-Christian neighbors as children of the God of creation is not just an expedient way of temporalizing a bad situation while sacrificing "principle." It is a command at the core of the gospel of Jesus Christ. We live in confusing times. The twentieth century has been full of marvelous scientific and technological advances. Some have improved the quality of our lives most significantly, both in terms of the easing of human labor and the length of human life. Others have provided weapons of mass destruction and serious threats to the environment. Human folly brought about two world wars, the cold war, the Vietnam war, genocides in Europe, the Middle East and Africa, failed states ruled by despots, etc. On one hand, a new respect for human rights has been informing most societies. On the other, materialism and opportunism have made the acquisition of wealth the value on whose behalf all others can be sacrificed. The truism that power corrupts and that absolute power corrupts absolutely has been demonstrated to the satisfaction of anyone paying attention.

While our strong commitment to the gospel calls Christians to open our arms to our neighbors wider than ever, instead many insist on making our homes armed garrisons to repel any one who is not just like us. At a time when Christians in developed countries know and discover more than ever about the grandeur of the universe under God's grace, many feel threatened instead of blessed and close their eyes and hearts to defend cosmologies that do not reflect what we have learned. Here today's Christians need to listen to Job, who insisted that no amount of orthodox posturing could counter his experience of undeserved suffering. The modern communications explosion has made instant connections between us in ways that were unimaginable just a few years ago. Why, then, should today's Christians treat our neighbors on the basis of lies, imagining that they will not find out since they live on a different wavelength. The urge to demonize our non-Christian neighbors and ask them to consider us saints, as if they were not intelligent enough to see hypocrisy, is not new, but seems uncomfortably prevalent today. In difficult times prejudices enable many people to orient themselves in the universe. Prejudices, however, foster injustice rather than peace. These are the failures that the gospel ethic of dialogue and of openness toward the strangers among us can begin to correct.

If Christians agree that the Sermon on the Mount is the encapsulation of Jesus' teachings, then we should pay attention to what it says. Of course, through the centuries, Christians have declared the Sermon unrealistic, dated, non-applicable. Usually this is done by differentiating the life of the soul from the life of the body, or the life of personal piety from life in the public square. These distinctions, however, were unknown to the first Christians who transmitted these teachings. The introduction to the Matthean antitheses and the conclusion of the instructions for the life of those who belong to the Kingdom, are at the heart of the Sermon on the Mount. Is there any noticeable difference from what is generally expected if you get along with your neighbor and pray for those who treat you well? Christians are expected to go beyond what is normally expected. They must embrace the other, the enemy. They are expected to do what God does, dealing with others with goodness and generosity. Sending sunshine and rain, God does not compartmentalize humanity. As Paul says, when it comes to Jews and gentiles, "God shows no partiality" (Rom. 2:11).

To live with others the way the Christian God commands is to respect non-Christian history and cultural traditions. As Amos says, God has also been active among them even when in the blindness of our false sense of election Christians failed to perceive God's actions. It is to admit, like the Preacher, that God's ways are not for us to discover, "God is in heaven, and you upon earth; therefore let your words be few. . . . I said, 'I will be wise'; but it was far from me. That which is, is far off, and deep, very deep, who can find it out? . . . As you do not know how the spirit comes to the bones in the womb of a woman with child, so you do not know the work of God who makes everything" (Eccl. 5:2b; 7: 23-24; 11:5).

Coming to terms with our limitations in knowing, a recognition that must be born of humility, is essential to any valid theologizing. It is not difficult to find theological discourse that is pompous and authoritarian. Sometimes it is found where it should most definitely be absent, in classrooms. I must confess a great debt to my Saint Mary's colleague Terence Martin, as the one who helped me to

197

eliminate from my teaching any trace of such discourse. Our friendship began when Terry bought a house and began doing repairs and some remodeling. He knew that a few years earlier I had built the house in which I lived with my family, so he began to ask me for advice concerning materials and tools. After that, he included me in a reading group, and we began to read some ancient Latin authors, some of whom I had used in writing my dissertation. Then, as Terry and I found ourselves writing our own books, we began to give each other drafts of chapters and have lunch together to give each other comments on what the other had written. I was writing a book about theological understandings of the Sabbath among Jews and Christians in antiquity. Terry was writing a book about the use of language by the main figures of the Enlightenment in the eighteenth century. He highlighted the dialogical, tolerant, logical and at the same time serious tone of the philosophers then. Like him, I came to see the need to capture and retain the tone of their discourse. We lamented the myopic ways in which some of our contemporaries were bashing the Enlightenment, ungrateful of the legacy they had inherited. The fact that our areas of expertise were quite different made for lunches that were a bit unstructured yet animated. We always scheduled our lunches at a time when neither of us would have to rush back to teach a class. The intellectual stimulation of our conversations was something that we both, after having spent most of the time trying to interest undergraduates in the details of philosophical or exegetical arguments, enjoyed immensely.

We shared a deep distrust of the way in which theology was becoming spirituality. The arrival of post-modernism did not pose, for us, a particularly serious threat. In fact, many of its features, such as the recognition that absolute objectivity is a chimera, the acceptance of insights and traditions from other cultures, the questioning of European-American hegemony in cultural matters, etc., were quite welcome. Terry and I lamented the post-modern reaction against the Enlightenment and the gains it had brought through its insistence on a rigorous use of the critical faculties.

Now emotional free association was given value as a basis for discourse. Eagerness to give all opinions equal value resulted in a valueless relativism adopted uncritically by most of our students. My lunches and bull sessions with Terry kept me engaged in an ongoing dialogue that was only the expression of our understanding of what characterizes intelligent life. They kept me alive to the need to be thoroughly committed to the life of reason if my theologizing and my spiritual life were to be at all fruitful. Here again I found a mentor in Paul, who admonished his readers repeatedly to look at things, even what Paul was writing to them, with a critical mind. Yes, indeed, the author of Ecclesiastes had it right; while theologizing, our words must be few. But also, again like the author of Ecclesiastes, since our words will be judged by reason and experience we must be fully aware of our limitations.

11

JUSTICE, FAITH, HOPE AND LOVE

My lunches with Terry were social occasions full of intellectual fireworks. We covered a chapter one of us had written, but digressions would take us anywhere. More than once our conversations drifted to the question of whether Christianity was meant to be a religion for the elect few or for the masses. Those dialogues made me reflect on my own sectarian roots. My upbringing was firmly conditioned by a stringent sectarianism. At the time, Adventists were quite certain that only Adventists who believed their pure version of the gospel would enter the Kingdom of Heaven. In this, lamentably and ironically, there was nothing peculiar to Adventism. Salvation was, to a major extent, dependent on holding the right doctrines. Of course, there were also behavioral prescriptions regarding tobacco, the drinking of alcoholic beverages, tea, coffee and Coca-Cola, eating foods classified as unclean in Leviticus 11, and attending dance halls, theatres and cinemas. These restrictions, of course, limited socializing with neighbors and classmates at the public schools.

At the center of the doctrinal edifice and the lifestyle was the Sabbath commandment. It distinguished the church's theological construct and built the most formidable sociological barriers. As Christians who uphold the Sabbath "truth", Adventists have developed a very strong sense of their own distinctiveness and even superiority among Christians. They see themselves as the ones who restored the commandment to its rightful place. In other words, their identity is firmly based on the Protestant tradition. According to them, the reformation of Christianity began with the highlighting of faith by Martin Luther and John Calvin in the sixteenth century, reconfigured and amplified with the emphasis on a life of holiness in the world by John Wesley in the eighteenth, was completed when a non-biblical doctrine was rejected and one crucial element of the Ten Commandments was re-instituted by Adventists in the nineteenth. Adventists are well known for insisting that the biblical Sabbath is not Sunday but Saturday. They are, maybe, less known for insisting on a holistic understanding of the human person, denying that it is made up of a mortal body and an immortal soul. This means that at death the person awaits in sleep until the resurrection. It does not break apart, with one part becoming nothing and another going into hell or purgatory. There is no contemporary human heaven, purgatory or eternal hell in Adventist theology. Knowing that death is just a sleep until the resurrection and the seventh-day is the Sabbath, by the grace of God, gave to those of us who accepted these doctrines a great sense of security.

Sectarian Adventism, self-assured of being the only Christianity in possession of "the Truth," was, as a consequence, marginalized by the other Christians. To them, Adventist efforts to convert Christians of other denominations to the Sabbath truth constituted "sheep-stealing". From the Adventist perspective, of course, missionary efforts among other Christians were demanded by their desire to take others to live in the New Jerusalem. This sectarian missionary outlook was inextricably linked to an implicit fundamentalism. The Ecumenical Movement, which gained momentum after World War II, was seen by Adventists as another sign that the End was near. To this day the denomination is not a member of the Council of Churches.

As someone who was born an Adventist, I too felt secure in the knowledge that I belonged. I must confess, however, that by the time I was in my teens I didn't find the interpretations of the visions of Daniel and Revelation fully convincing. I was amazed

202

when as a result of Adventist evangelistic efforts people joined the church and adopted the lifestyle required of those who were preparing themselves to walk in the streets of gold in the New Jerusalem. Many converts were expelled from the circle of their families and lost their jobs due to their new Sabbath observance. Remember, in Latin America the work week consists of six days. Business and schools function normally, at least half day, on Saturdays. Joining the Adventist church had immediate social and even economic consequences.

Having stood up and suffered on account of one's commitment to keeping the Sabbath holy was considered a mark of special distinction. Since my father worked for the denomination and all my close relatives were either denominational workers or farmers, no one in the extended family had experienced severe hardship on account of the Sabbath. Both of my brothers, Ewaldo and Klinton, took longer completing medical school because they had to wait for months for the final exams in some subject to be offered on a day other than Sabbath. A few times they found a professor who would take into account their religious views, but those were the exceptions. There was always anxiety in our home when the schedules for final exams were about to be posted at the university.

In my imagination, then, I worked hard from an early age to conceive how the time allotted to Sabbaths was ontologically different from the other six days of the week. The distinction between secular and holy time was a matter of life and death, and to fail to recognize the sacredness of the hours of the Sabbath was the most grievous sin. This meant, of course, that all other Christians were living in mortal sin, and the Jews who kept the Sabbath but did not accept the death of Christ as the atonement for the sins of humankind were no better off. Only faithful Christians who keep the Sabbath holy have the ticket to the Kingdom of Heaven. Life within this symbolic universe was comforting for me for a time, but as I matured theologically and spiritually I realized my security was false. Coming to this realization required the adoption of a different symbolic universe.

Getting out of one symbolic universe and constructing another, however, is painful and confusing, but in the end most liberating. What kept pushing me forward was the realization that the false security I had enjoyed was based on un-Christian notions.

Major shifts in the way humans conceive themselves in the universe do not happen overnight, and are never complete. The antecedents to new ways of thinking can be traced to an indefinite past, and in some societies the ancient ways may prove resilient to change. Still, the fifth century BCE is generally recognized as a time when humanity went through major transitions. In terms of the Mediterranean world, two major shifts of perspective have been identified. Prior to this time humans understood themselves as creatures of the earth who belonged to an extended family. The earth was home and their survival depended on future generations. On the other hand, dead ancestors never quite seemed to be absent. Individual identity was located in the tribe. Thus, in the early Biblical texts it is perfectly acceptable for the sins of the fathers to be visited upon their children to the third and the fourth generation. One of the stories from the conquering of Canaan by the Israelites tells that when Jericho fell, the rules of holy war were transgressed by Achan. In holy war, the soldiers could not claim booty for themselves, since the battle had been fought by God. Achan took as booty a Babylonian carpet, two hundred shekels of silver and a bar of gold. Once the crime had been investigated and his culpability established, he and all the members of his extended family were executed as their due punishment. The same principle is at work in the case of David's census. The taking of the census, for the purposes of taxation and military conscription, was condemned by those who wished for the Israelites to be ruled by God through judges, rather than a king, as a grievous sin. The punishment for David's sin is actually inflicted on the people, and seventy thousand died. Apparently everyone agreed this was just.

By the time of the exile, however, when Israelites are told that the fall of Jerusalem is the punishment of God for the sins of previous generations, things had changed. Both Jeremiah and

Ezekiel proclaimed that what used to be could be no longer. The concept of tribal identity as primary was couched in a proverb: "The fathers ate sour grapes and the children's teeth are set on edge." The prophets declare this proverb obsolete. From now on, "the soul that sins, it shall die." This means that Achan's extended family would not be punished together with him. The value of the single individual had come to the fore, challenging the notions of corporate personality characterized by obligations to avenge insults to the honor of the tribe even after many generations. Under the previous conditions the circle of violence could never be broken. Together with the limitation of guilt to the single individual, Jeremiah and Ezekiel also released the people from the obligations of blood vengeance. "Vengeance is mine, says the Lord." It is no longer in human hands.

Probably more important than the shift from a tribal to an individual identity was the shift from understanding the earth as home to thinking that heaven is the human home. Starting with the fifth century BCE, as an individual, each person was the physical manifestation of an immortal soul whose origin and destiny was in heaven; the time passed on earth is just a sojourn. This notion became popular among the Jews who lived in the Hellenized mediterranean world and found its way into the Biblical tradition. Rather than to see ourselves as essentially located in our earthly carnality we came to think of ourselves as essentially an ethereal, immortal soul somewhat in tension with our bodies. While on earth the soul longs to return to its heavenly home. Death is a liberating event that releases the soul for its journey back home, where it belongs. Death is not an enemy that terminates our earthly existence but a welcomed friend. The transferal of our cosmic home from earth to heaven was one of the most significant shifts between the symbolic universe of the Hebrew Bible and that of the New Testament. The Hebrew prophets differentiated between "this age" and "the age to come," but envisioned both on this earth. The apocalyptic book of Daniel also understands that the life of the nation in the kingdom established by divine intervention takes place on earth. In the New Testament, however, the Kingdom of God became the Kingdom of Heaven.

It seems to me that in western culture, where individualism and preoccupations with the place where our soul will live eternally have been predominant, we are today experiencing a swing back to the affirmation of blood ties and family trees, and the recognition of the earth as our cosmic home. In the process we are also coming to see that understanding ourselves dualistically, as a soul in tension with a body, is dehumanizing. The extreme individualism of western culture led eventually to a crisis of identity. Escapism to a home in heaven contributed to the abuse of earth's bounties. The individual soul is showing the effects of the stress put on it by the need to forge a lonesome destiny. A heavenly home has become somewhat hard to imagine as our universe is no longer made up of "the heavens above" and "the waters below".

That such a shift from the heavens to the earth is taking place before our eyes is also noticeable in the efforts of a number of biblical scholars to reconstruct Jesus as a historical figure who did not belong to an apocalyptic movement within Judaism. According to these scholars, the kingdom Jesus preached is one God can only establish on this earth with the help of the disciples. His was not the retributive justice of apocalypticism but the distributive justice of economic equalizing. The special pleading evident in their handling of the evidence is obvious. They want to show Jesus pointing the way to the earth as our home. This places him either in our own times or at a time before the fifth century BCE. That Jesus referred to the Danielic Son of Man is hard to disprove. If Jesus expected the appearance of the Son of Man during his own lifetime, history proved him, at the very least, confused.

In a time when several developments are bringing about a shift in our symbolic universe, on the other hand, evangelical reactionaries find false security in a verbally inspired, inerrant Bible. This longing for a past no longer available contradicts experience. Confabulated conspiracy theories see the present as a crisis in which survival is at stake. But for these "defenders" of the Bible, survival does not mean the survival of humanity. It is the survival of the "elect" in heaven. Such a point of view is based on a selective, capricious reading of portions of the Bible. Read this way, the Bible supports genocide, wars of conquest and the repudiation of millions of human beings.

Doctrines of inspiration based on two or three texts of scripture, while ignoring large portions of the text, lack credibility. A truly Biblical point of view pays attention to every page of the Bible with equal respect and, on that basis, recognizes that the Bible supports diversity of opinions. Monotheism, polytheism, monogamy, polygamy, divorce, slavery, child sacrifices, ethnic cleansing and holy war are referred to with overt or tacit approval in the Bible's pages. Is everything in the Bible morally uplifting? Most people today would draw a line against a god whose worshippers ask of him to "take and smash the little ones [of the inhabitants of Babylon] against the stones" (Psalms 137:9), or who is ready to punish his worshippers for failing to carry out wars of extermination to the last drop of blood (Numbers 33 and 1 Samuel 15).

Being a Christian does not provide one with a supernatural source of information, as many Christians pompously claim. To the one who has faith in God it provides a promise that life is stronger than death. No more . . . no less. God has not forwarded details about eternal life. Humans, of course, have not been reluctant to offer their own visions of eternal life. Isaiah's and Micah's visions of Mount Zion becoming the capital of the planet where lions and lambs nap together; Paul's vision of the Lord Himself coming down from heaven, hovering above the earth and gathering the righteous living and dead in order to take them up to heaven; John the Theologian's vision of two separate resurrections, and of the New Jerusalem and the tree of life (apparently preserved in heaven after its planting in the Garden of Eden) coming down from heaven and settling again on Mount Zion, all these should be taken for what they are: visions

207

constructed by faithful believers according to the frameworks provided by their cultural matrices.

Kierkegaard's "leap of faith" has become a cliché. It has come to mean that one must jump from a cliff into a dark abyss hoping there is a safety net below. Most forget that Kierkegaard lived in flat Denmark and was an aficionado of the royal ballet. When you read about his leap of faith, envision not a cliff, but dancers on a stage. Their leaps are memorable because of the landing, especially if the dancer freezes in a beautiful position as soon as she or he touches the floor. The leap that ends in that beautiful posture is most likely what Kierkegaard had in mind. It allows dancers to integrate themselves as new beings on the stage. Faith makes it possible to transcend to a new posture on life; it brings about its culmination in a new reality.

That is the challenge before the people of faith in the twenty-first century. It has been the challenge of people of faith since the fifth century BCE, when individuals took responsibility for their behavior, rather than taking refuge in the tribe. Basically, it is the problem that the author of the book of Job tackled head on, making the anonymous writer arguably the greatest theologian of the Hebrew Bible. He used the ancient legend of Job as a tool with which to expose the fallacy in the prevalent doctrine of God's retributive justice, which was at the core of the apocalyptic agenda. Even though the long, complicated poem at the center of the book was tampered with over the years by successive generations of readers, even before it was included in the Hebrew canon, the plot in the poem is more or less on the surface. The three visitors who came to comfort Job make, by different means, a single point: Job, your case is dire yet simple. You have sinned, and God is punishing you accordingly. The solution to your problem is obvious and also simple. Repent of your sin. Expiate your sin. God will forgive you and restore you to your health and well being.

The advice does not make sense to Job because he has not sinned! He has no sin to repent from and make expiation for. If the claim were coming from Job's lips alone, readers would be justifiably tempted to think that Job was being dishonest with his visitors and himself. But the narrator affirms in the prologue that, as a matter of fact, Job was an upright person who lived in perfect harmony with God's desires. Job, therefore, was basing his argument squarely on his experience: He was innocent and being made to suffer by the hand of Almighty God.

Given this premise, let's review the options. One way to account for unmerited suffering is by saying there is no god. Things happen by chance. Whether you enjoy the good life or experience suffering instead is a matter of luck. Alternatively, maybe there are gods, and different gods have control over different areas. For things to go well, expiate the appropriate god, probably starting with the goddess of fortune. Or, yet another option, accept that the goddess of fate has cast your lot in life. The stars have it. It is beyond your control, so accept what the gods decided in accordance with their own internal political dealings in the pantheon. You are their pawn.

By the time Job was written, apocalypticism had gained ground within the Israelite community. Its rise was directly related to the new individualism that made it impossible to explain the suffering of the present generation as the punishment for sins committed by a previous one. Apocalypticism put forth two central concepts. First, the sin of Adam and Eve that resulted in their expulsion from Eden coincides with the cosmic falling of heavenly beings that now populate the spheres between heaven and earth. These fallen beings, whose chieftain is Satan, now have power over the lives of sinful human beings. In order to rescue humankind from the grip of Satan, God needs to fight the ultimate battle between good and evil. In summary, apocalypticism introduces the doctrine of the Fall, which allows for the explanation of unmerited suffering as related to Satan's, not God's, activity. Second, apocalypticism introduces the doctrine of the resurrection, of a re-embodied life after death. This makes it possible to affirm that God's rule is just and will be ultimately vindicated in a life after death. In other words, by introducing the present interference of Satan's rule over humanity, apocalypticism dilutes the universality of God's power that had been affirmed by Isaiah. It defends the doctrine of God's retributive justice by transferring its full effect from This Age to The Age to Come. Apocalypticism introduced the doctrine of the two ages as contrasting realities. From the Fall to the resurrection and the final judgment, we are living in "this present evil age", when God's power is somehow not in full control. The Age to Come after the resurrection is the reinstatement of the Garden of Eden before the Fall. In this way, while conceiving it in terms of one cosmic, rather than a yearly, cycle apocalypticism re-appropriates the myth of eternal return.

The author of Job is aware of the apocalyptic use of Satan as an agent of current evil. Very skillfully, however, he keeps Satan under God's control, thus making God responsible for evil. He totally rejects the apocalyptic solution to the problem of the presence of evil in God's world. According to the author of Job, God is nothing if not all powerful. He also rejects the apocalyptic notions of the resurrection and the Age to Come. Job insists that God's justice must be on display now. If God is Almighty, and his experience tells him that his sufferings are unmerited, he draws the only logical conclusion possible: God is unjust. The three visitors surrounding him take turns to argue that God's retributive justice is at work. Obviously, his suffering is due to his sin. The notion that an Almighty God is unjust is, according to them, ridiculous.

The author of Job concludes his exploration of the problem of theodicy with the admission of human limitations in the evaluation of experience. Thus, he agrees with the author of Ecclesiastes, but emerges with a greater insight. Qoheleth reminded everyone that God is in heaven and human beings on earth, therefore their words should be few. Job's author points out that human beings must admit that the god who is available to solve the problem of theodicy is a human creation, not the transcendent God who created the universe. In this way the author of Job, a critic of orthodoxy, is a forerunner of Paul, who was indebted to the Greeks and their critical reasoning. He understood that God's freedom to act is not to be delimited by human notions of what is just.

210

Paul, like the author of Job, would reject the notion that God's ways are discernible in history. The apocalypticists, following up on the argument of Isaiah, argued that the true God is the one who controls the setting up and putting down of kings and nations. Against both the apocalypticists and the author of Job, Paul affirmed that the power of God is manifest in weakness (2 Corinthians 13:7-10). This oxymoron gives him the key with which to open the treasure house of God's love, the love that justifies sinners. The power of God is not revealed by history or nature, but by the love that joins humanity to God in a cross (Rom 5:8).

What could be more contrary to common sense? To begin with, God cannot die, and to see his power in death is beyond absurd. To claim that God's justice is revealed in a historical injustice is to base the Gospel in a logical non-sequitur and a historical irrelevancy. The crucifixion of Jesus did not make history. Christians came to assign significance to it only after the resurrection. There were Christians, however, who rejected this way of understanding Jesus' death. They were not apocalyptically oriented. They understood that Jesus had come to reveal knowledge of the divine realm during his lifetime. As an incarnate divine being by the time his body was being nailed to the cross he had already accomplished his mission and left for the heavenly realms. The soldiers who crucified him were dealing with the "clothing" he had used while on earth.

Like Paul, I believe Christian faith is based on God's action at the resurrection. Faith affirms that as the triumph of life, the resurrection accomplished God's ultimate purpose. The resurrection is not like the historical crucifixion which, in itself, did not "make history". A historian can investigate the evidence for the crucifixion and come to a reasoned conclusion as to whether it occurred. The resurrection, on the contrary, cannot be subjected to an investigation. Still, it "made history". But, it can only be affirmed by faith. Paul compared it, quite properly, to the creation "in the beginning".

One of the bigger steps in my spiritual journey was to realize that Paul moved away from the fetters of a theology centered on a covenant and commandments. Paul understood that God and humanity were connected to each other by a promise. A covenant is a contract that can be accepted by agreeing to its terms. A promise can only be accepted by believing the one making the promise.

The religion of Jesus and Paul was based on faith in The God Who Promised, not on information. The God of Abraham, Isaac and Jacob promised abundant life in the land of promise, a life that is stronger than death. God, however, did not offer details about 'eternal life'. This hasn't deterred humans from envisioning it. Human visions of this life do not add knowledge to faith. They are in themselves expressions of faith.

By transmitting different ways of understanding faith in God's promise, the New Testament points out that we must also find ways of understanding our faith in that promise. Our universe has been in formation for millions of years and the process is in progress still. Creation is still in progress. The earth, or our solar system, is not at its center. Talk about heaven above and water below in this universe lacks reference. The challenge is, therefore, to find ways in which faith in The God Who Promised echoes in our minds, all the time cognizant of the fact that we are not in control of the evidence.

Once I understood that what I needed was not valid information about the management of the plan of salvation in heaven, but rather the best metaphor for how humans relate to God, I finally understood the stakes in the choice of metaphors. For example, scholars of the Hebrew Bible point out that the two main sources of the Pentateuch conceived the relationship differently. The Yahwists make the patriarchal story move forward by means of God's promise to Abraham and to David. The Priestly Authors say Abraham entered into a covenant with God. Then, at Sinai, the people of Israel again entered into a covenant in which the law given at the top of the mountain played a central role. To

212

harmonize the biblical materials into one seamless piece of cloth, conservative Christian theology has cavalierly ignored marked differences, and fundamentalists have denied the existence of sources. Then they pretend to be dealing with information rather than metaphors.

The authors of the gospels and the letters of the New Testament did not engage in a harmonizing effort. This is certainly true in the writings of Paul. Most theologians make Paul a contributor to covenant theology, but to the extent they do distort his message.

Covenants, and covenant theologies, are a matter of actions and reactions: "If you do this, I'll do that." Covenants do not require faith. They require perseverance. Paul understood the radical difference between commitment to the terms of a covenant, and faith in a promise. A covenant obligates two parties to what they agree to. Its success depends on the two parties keeping their side of the bargain. In contrast, God's promise to Abraham depended only on God's faithfulness. It became effective only if Abraham accepted it by faith. The Yahwist reports that "Abraham believed God, and it was counted to him as righteousness." For Paul this phrase was the key to living in the world. With it, he opened the door to an understanding of God's justice as the fulfillment of the promise of life to those who live by faith. His ultimate model was the faith of Jesus, the one who lived by faith even unto death. God then revealed his faithfulness by raising him from death.

Faith enlightens life in a different way from the way a covenant does. Faith brings with it hope and love to form a trinity for life. As a Christian of faith, I live in a universe different from that of a system of doctrines. My symbolic universe does not divide time between the sacred and the profane. Rather, it reorders the past, the present and the future in terms of the trinity for life proposed by Paul. Faith believes God is the creator of life Who promised abundant life, not in giving mental assent to "orthodox" doctrines of creation. The Christian affirms "in the beginning God created." The Risen Christ is the down payment for a new creation, the

213

creation of life in the spirit. Life is a gift from God. Biology can describe it, but cannot explain it, and the resurrection of Christ cannot be confirmed by historical investigations. It is not a matter of knowledge, but of faith. To be a Christian is to anchor one's life on a promise from God and make it the basis for security and identity. True Christian security can only be based on faith. At the core of Christianity stands an oxymoron.

On the basis of my life in the spirit, I can now hope for a future with God. Just as faith is not knowledge, neither is hope. I cannot say how or when God created the earth and all that is in it. I cannot say how or when God will establish justice and peace. By faith and hope, however, I experience His kingdom. My hope is to be eternally bound to God and fully experience the freedom of the spirit. I can imagine such future, and I try to describe it within the bounds of my imagination. My description, however, does not pretend to pass out informative details because it is not based on knowledge. It is my faith finding an outlet. I hope, and my hope gives me reasons for living that transcend selfish inclinations. It is not based on my longings, but on my trust in the God who promised life. The details are totally up to The One Who Promised. My faith and my hope have a common center.

I confess that, even though I have abandoned the symbolic universe that divides time between the sacred and the profane and have adopted a Pauline understanding of time as living in the present with the past, and the future as the sources and the guides for informed decisions, I still retain a particular appreciation for the Sabbath as a tangible metaphor of the connection that humans must have with the source of life. As a time set aside for reflection on, and analysis of the blessings of life, the Sabbath is an incomparable gift. To preserve the Sabbath's significance does not require that I give historical veracity to the story of its origin as the culmination of creation week, and all the baggage that goes along with that story, or to the story of the exodus from Egypt and the parting of the Red Sea. As a time to cease earning a living and to enjoy the blessing of life, the Sabbath is a boon to humanity. As a time to re-orient your muddled thinking, the Sabbath is a compass that points both to the past and the future as a remembrance and an anticipation of God's purposes. As the umbilical cord of the universe that sustains the life of the fetus that is dependent on the body of the giver and sustainer of life, the Sabbath with its glaring mythological garb allows you to express your faith with vividness and effectiveness.

My special attention to Sabbath has, no doubt, several reasons. My reverence for the Sabbath as the day God rests from labor does not at all make me unsympathetic to my fellow Christians who celebrate their Christianity on Sunday. As I see it, my neighbor's observance of Sunday and my observance of Saturday are based on the same traditional notion that human beings give significance to their lives when they mimetically repeat divine archetypal acts. My neighbor and I just happen to pay attention to two different and very specific acts of God. In creation week, God rested on the seventh day; therefore, we rest on the seventh day. On Easter Sunday, God raised Christ from the dead; therefore we are raised to life and worship on Sunday. Both resting on Sabbath and celebrating new life on Sunday are based on the traditional myth of eternal return. They give the weekly temporal cycle a point of reference in the divine eternal world.

Faith in the promise God made and hope in a livable future can become neurotic delusions. The fundamental Christian trinity is the Pauline trinity of faith, hope and love. As the apostle pointed out, the greatest of these is love. When he said this he was not referring to God's love for sinners. He was referring to the love that motivates a Christian to live here and now in a particular way. Christians should live fully and squarely in the present. They don't live by faith and in hope by escaping into the past or the future. Christian life is an enactment of what faith believes about the past and hope anticipates from the future. The best way to live meaningfully and fully is not by following the ancient dictum carpe diem, seize the day. By itself the present is almost non-existent. Its passage is so swift as to make it a will-of-the-wisp. In today's culture

215

of entertainment, where the power of money to create fun seems to be the reigning idol, love is usually conceived in terms of enjoyment, from chocolate to marital bliss and everything in between. Living in the present by love, in this context, can mean almost anything. Seize the day in this context can be very capricious.

What is Christian love? I can only think of it in terms of the Pauline trinity. Christian love is a way of life that is energized, directed and satisfied by faith and hope, by what God did and promised to do. Christians live from the past and the future into the present, performing in love what they believe God did in Christ and hope God will do through him, enacting God's justice and peace.

Christianity is not primarily a matter of doctrines, just as Judaism has never been. Certainly Jesus did not systematize any doctrines. Christianity is a way of life that cannot be reduced to doctrinal statements that are, by the very nature of the human condition, even in the best of circumstances only effective metaphors. Still, a life that enacts faith and hope in love is, of necessity, informed by concepts of the truth. The tension between truth and love, as Paul insisted, must be resolved also by love, a love that reaches all humanity. Confronted by this dilemma, you cannot arrive at a solution by an either/or. You must absorb it as a both/and. Faith in the cross and resurrection and hope for a future of justice must find expression in a love that includes all humanity now. What is the truth of the incarnation if not the truth that in love God is bound to humanity? Is it not true, then, that we must love humanity in order to be bound to God?

Those who worry that love lacks the institutional foundations and structural supports essential to giving Christianity needed sustaining power, fail to appreciate that the demands of love are stronger and more constraining than the commands of any law. Jesus did not issue any laws, but taught using metaphors about forgiveness, repentance, care for the other and compassion. These are nothing if not the expressions of love. Recurrent attempts to give to the Gospel doctrinal and/or ethical shape have proven to be guided by extraneous agendas. The truth of the Gospel which Paul defended with much vigor, if not gallantry, in his Letter to the Galatians was not knowledge of celestial or earthly activities. It has to do with the efficacy of the death of Christ as the revelation of God's justice and love and as the basis of faith. An ancient Chinese proverb encapsulates a significant insight. "Truth is a torch that gleams through the fog without dispelling it." It is high wisdom to recognize that my discovery of the truth does not lift the fog in which I remain entrapped with my contemporaries. To accept the limits of our knowledge is not to endorse relativism. The demands of faith, hope and love are strong and confining, and they insist on humility. To recognize that faith in God must be transposed to life by different people in different cultures and different historical traditions should make one aware that claims to exclusive access to salvation or imperialistic inclusion of others according to our own standards are at best pompous and at worst hypocritical. In our universe these may be the worst sins.

My movement away from doctrines was not a rejection of doctrines. It was toward a better understanding of their function. To recognize that Christianity has primarily to do with a way of life, with the actual business of quotidian living, is also to recognize that right living is determined by the doctrines that inform my decisions. As I see it, my problem had been to prioritize doctrines for their saving power. It was to think that by holding right doctrines I had knowledge of God's mind. In other words, my problem had been to see doctrines as revelatory. Their truth was transcendental, once it was agreed that they were "biblical". Truth, of course, was what one's life was to be about. With this vision, it was quite possible to forget love, a point forcibly brought to my attention by one of my students at Saint Mary's when I had been presenting Paul only in terms of the doctrine of righteousness by faith. Love must ultimately triumph over truth because I can undoubtedly be more certain about the demands of love than about the truth of any doctrine I may have concocted from the metaphors of the Bible.

Once it became clear that the truth of doctrines is to be determined by the conduct they promote, a whole new vision of things opened up before me. I no longer needed to search for the one true interpretation of the biblical text. The voice of each author of Scripture could be listened to for what it had to say. It was no longer problematic to come to terms with the fact that within the Bible there are contradictory statements. Of course, the point of view of each author was subject to different interpretations, several of them with good claims to validity. Their evaluation demanded the setting up of criteria. That was the only way in which the way I interpreted a text could stand. The interpretations of others, with various claims to validity, merited my respect and evaluation.

Ultimately, the process of coming to terms with these insights can only lead to the view that the truth of an interpretation of a biblical author is to be established ethically. One may argue, as some do, that Jesus is the final arbiter of all biblical truth. In other words, he functions as the canon within the canon. He is the standard by which biblical teachings are to be measured. To me this is a copout, a camouflage to hide what is really going on.

When our granddaughter Jacqui was about four we did not see her often. One day when she had been left with us, we decided to go to a popular buffet for supper. Aida's brother and mother also came with us. Once there, Aida's brother offered to serve Jacqui and brought to our table a plate with samples of several entrees that looked most inviting. Jacqui, however found the food unappetizing and refused to eat. Guessing that the reason for her negative reaction was her knowledge of the existence of an ample assortment of desserts at the buffet, I announced that anyone who did not eat nourishing food could not have dessert. As everyone was busy enjoying the meal, Jacqui kept looking out the window at the passing traffic, paying no attention to repeated entreaties to eat her food. Suddenly she turned to us and said: "One day Jesus came by this road and entered here to eat. He was served a plate just like this, and he did not eat it." I could not believe my ears. Jacqui had already figured out that Jesus could be manipulated to serve your need of the moment. More than once I have been under the impression that more sophisticated appeals to the "historical" Jesus are not very different from my granddaughter's childish one. After examining the biographies of Jesus that had been written during the nineteenth century, Albert Schweitzer came to the correct conclusion. The resulting portraits of Jesus say more about the author of the biography and his agenda than about Jesus. This observation is still valid of the more recent attempts to present an authentic Jesus.

The Bible gives us four portraits of Jesus and they are, in fundamental ways, very different and, in important aspects, openly contradictory. At the textual level, which final confession am I to make my own? Mark reports that the centurion at the foot of the cross proclaimed: "Truly this man was a son of God." In this way Mark's gospel puts its seal on the portrait of a human being. John, on the other hand, has Thomas worship at the upper room declaring: "My Lord and my God." This seals his narrative as that of a divine being. For twenty centuries Christians have been trying to hold these two opposing views together without enduring success. I can easily show similar problems in reference to Jesus' teaching. Did he teach that the kingdom of God would be established when the Son of Man came with power and glory with thousands of angels riding on a cloud, as Mark reports? Or, did he teach that, as Luke reports, the kingdom of God was already present among the disciples? Was Jesus essentially an agent of peace who, as he enters Jerusalem, laments: "Would that even today you knew the things that make for peace"? Or, was he an apocalyptic prophet who proclaimed, "I did not come to bring peace, but the sword"?

These conundrums only mean that whatever I say about Jesus and his teaching is established by me. Making him the canon within the canon only serves to obfuscate the fact that I am the canon within the canon. I would rather not assume this role. I also prefer to play with all the cards on top of the table. This is the reason why I acknowledge that judgments have to be made using the criteria of good reasoning. In this way I renounce the temptation of becoming a manipulator of the Scriptures. It is when judgments make sense to a significant number of critical minds that the historical basis for a determination of Jesus or his teachings may be taken more seriously. Charismatic preachers may like to tell others what the Bible teaches, without considering which author is being quoted and who is the interpreter of that author. Their pretensions only persuade the uninformed.

Sermons, like the Bible, do not aim to pass along information. They aim at conversion. That was the cry of the classical prophets of Israel: "Shuv," "Turn," "Convert." The basic meaning of the word is to make a 180 degree turn from the way one was heading. This observation makes my point. Sermons and the Bible are about the direction of one's life. The prophets, moreover, were concerned with the behaviors being displayed. The way in which one travels is just as important as the arrival. In fact, it is determinative of the arrival. The doctrines I hold about all aspects of the journey, the point of departure and of the arrival, are important only in reference to the way in which they shape the journey.

The doctrines I hold are important only in as much as they inform my behavior. The recurrent problem of giving priority to holding the right doctrines, to orthodoxy per se, is that those who hold them often think that they are Christians on account of it. Satisfied with that, they feel free to behave according to cultural mores, personal whims, or the pressure of circumstances. This form of self deception reflects a form of mental laziness and sometimes is sustained by tirades against the fallacies of human reason. It forgets that God placed us on this earth and gave us reason in order to live intelligently.

It has been claimed by many that faith requires the sacrifice of reason (sacrificium intellectus), as if reason were against faith and humans are to make a choice between the two. Nothing could be more deleterious to a healthy life. Unfortunately, however, it is not uncommon to see such religious misconceptions destroying the

220

mental health of individuals. Their schizophrenia is caused by doctrines that destroy the integrity of their minds. Faith certainly transcends reason, but doctrines must never be against reason, just as faith never is. The truth of doctrines is tested by their consequences in human life. What faith demands is not the sacrifice of reason but the employment of reason in order to determine how God's action in Christ is to become my action in the world.

God's justice, the core of the problem of theodicy in the Christian tradition, is not a matter of knowledge, but of faith. Only by faith can I appropriate the meaning of Christ's death and resurrection and make them my own. Faith believes in the death and resurrection of Christ in order to die with him, thus making his death in the flesh my own as a basis for hoping to also experience his resurrection to life in the spirit. In this way, faith makes the past event the foundation for new life. The truth of the Gospel is the necessity of dying with Christ in order to live on the basis of his death and resurrection, making sure that the two are perfectly balanced in my imagination as they inform my behavior. To give to the Christian truth significance in terms of biological, geologic or historical information is "another gospel," which Paul declared to be "anathema." To give to the Christian truth exclusive dominion over God's ways and means is the height of self-righteous false security.

Only when faith and hope are transposed from the realm of language to the realm of being and become effective as love, can the significance of Christianity be understood. To live trying to enact this transposition is the permanent challenge. A great deal of careful thinking and critical judgments is required. The Holy Spirit is needed to enlighten the mind with wisdom that transcends selfish motives and devious rationalizations. The life of love as the enactment of faith and hope can only be carried out under the guidance of God's love. Love is the power that carries one along on the journey to our ultimate home. Living in the past is a waste; living in the future an escape. Living in a present that enacts love

221

informed by the past and the future of Christ is the fulfillment of faith and hope. The community formed by those who have determined to transpose their faith and hope into acts of love is the one that constitutes itself as the body that makes possible the presence of the Risen Christ in the world today. The community amalgamated by the Pauline trinity actualizes justice and peace.

EPILOGUE

Retirement opened a new stage in my life. Some colleagues who retired a few years before me, would come by to visit at the humanities building at Saint Mary's and strongly advise me not to opt for retirement at sixty five. Their repeated advice was to keep working until at least seventy. According to them, retirement was terrible. I never gave their advice a second thought. In fact, retirement has been just wonderful. Besides providing the freedom to write and travel, it has also made it possible to share my life with our grandchildren. While the two youngest live with their parents in Baltimore and we get to be with him only occasionally, the other three live close by and we enjoy their company and support them in their activities much to our delight. I am confident that our doing things together is mutually beneficial.

Being close to my grandchildren has made me aware of how deluded I was when I thought I was close to my sons when they were growing up. Now I see that I actually missed many opportunities, even when I also took advantage of many. I can humbly say that my relationship with my two sons has always been very good, and I have every reason to be proud of them. By the grace of God they survived the struggles of youth and the tensions of young adulthood, and are now healthy and wise members of the human family. I am now confirming, however, what has been often said. Grandparents and grandchildren need each other in ways that are quite different from the way in which parents and children do, and these mutual needs are a blessing.

Looking back at one's life is a profitable endeavor if one can muster the honesty it demands. Memory, as is well known, is quite selective, and can be the servant of delusions. I think it is clear that this is not an autobiography. My recollections here are concerned with only one aspect of my life, my religious experiences and my growth in faith. The narrative I have constructed, moreover, has an agenda. It aims to make an argument that needs to be made at this time.

In America, the insecurity created by the Cold War, and now by the relatively few and primarily Islamic terrorists, is being counterbalanced by a fundamentalism that is distorting our vision of the world. National and international politics are many times based on ideological readings of the Bible, with disastrous consequences. Apocalypticism in all its forms, both religious and secular, is being grasped by many as the key that opens our understanding of the times in which we live. Apocalyptic violence, then, is accepted as normal and even helpful. The use of the Bible as an earlier *Da Vinci Code* that allows us to solve mysteries behind conspiracy theories fosters militant attitudes that only provide false security. In such an atmosphere, legitimate justice and peace are not easily established. Within fundamentalist Christianity, different versions of apocalyptic scenarios of the End Times have gained a strong foothold in the imagination of the Christian masses. The establishment denominations that had gained power in the stolid Victorian era had swept apocalypticism under the rug. Now evangelical fundamentalism finds in political confrontations a means for establishing apocalyptic signposts. Apocalyptic language has become political fodder. Thus, the passage of the Health Care Reform bill was described by a leader in Congress as the coming of Armageddon.

On the other hand, within the academic study of the early followers of Jesus, there has been a strong tendency lately to picture them as untouched by apocalyptic preoccupations. Prominent scholars have been reconstructing the historical Jesus as a Wisdom teacher, or a Cynic peripatetic outsider, who rubbed the Roman authorities the wrong way and had a tragic end. According to these reconstructions, the first followers of Jesus were not Christians in any meaningful way. It was only later that the Cynic wanderer from Galilee of the Gentiles was mythologized into a messianic figure, was framed within an apocalyptic framework and his death was given expiatory significance. It is evident that the gospels report the same incidents or the same words of Jesus with significant differences, and even in contradictory fashion. It is no secret that not every thing written in the gospels happened the way it is reported, if one could decide with certainty which of the alternative reports is to be preferred. Scholars must spend considerable time and effort trying to evaluate all the evidence. In these efforts, however, modern researchers confirm the dictum with which Albert Schweitzer, at the beginning of the twentieth century, concluded his very influential survey of the attempts to write a biography of Jesus between 1780 and 1900. Schweitzer's *The Quest of the Historical Jesus* demonstrated that each biography was more a reflection of the mind of its author than of the historical Jesus. I think this is still true. To counter the prominence of the apocalyptic mentality in our time, Jesus is reconstructed as anything but influenced by the apocalyptic currents of the first century.

Of all the criteria more or less agreed upon by all those attempting to get to the historical Jesus, the one that in my mind is the most important is the criterion "we wish this were not true". In other words, when the Gospels tell things that made the followers of Jesus uncomfortable and caused them to have to give explanations and apologies for it, we can count that it actually happened. For example, no follower of Jesus would have created the story that Jesus died crucified. The cross was undeniable, and the followers of Jesus had to deal with it. They would have given anything for Jesus to have died any other way. The same is true of Jesus' baptism by John the Baptist. John's baptism was for the forgiveness of sins. Those who later came to claim that Jesus was free from sin would never had invented the event of his baptism.

There is no question that Jesus' career was linked to that of John the Baptist. The Gospel of John reports that there was some friction between the disciples of Jesus and the disciples of John. It actually reports that Jesus had begun his mission as a baptizer in competition with John. The historicity of these reports is substantiated by the criterion "we wish this were not true". There is no question that Jesus himself had an apocalyptic mindset, his disciples also had it, and early Christianity grew primarily in contact with Pharisaism, which also had an apocalyptic mindset.

The way to combat the violence of the modern fundamentalist Christian mindset sustained by apocalypticism is not by re-writing history to our liking, but by finding within the tradition alternatives more in keeping with the exigencies of our times. Technology has brought us many blessings, but it has also given us the capacity to be violent to the point of annihilation. The apocalyptic mindset in this brave new world is not one the authors of the biblical books could possibly envision. We must find ways to transform this mindset. In the first century, anyone wishing for an end of the unjust world of violence and death could imagine this as possible only by God's hand. Today, thanks to scientific advancements, this can be carried out by human hands. This historic difference must make us re-think apocalyptic discourse.

We need to do today what Paul did in his day. He was a Pharisee concerned with living according to the Scriptures. For him religion was relevant to daily living. As a Pharisee he conceived history in apocalyptic terms. This means that the world will exist in two distinct time periods: This Age and The Age to Come. The coming of Messiah will accomplish the passage from This Age to The Age to Come. In This Age, now, humans live in weak bodies of flesh. In The Age to Come humans will live in incorruptible spiritual bodies in the very presence of God. All the righteous dead will be raised to participate also of life in The Age to Come. Having this as the framework within which to understand human reality, Paul saw the life, death and resurrection of Jesus as the event that set in motion the turning of The Ages. The cross of Christ put an end

226

to the weak world of flesh under the power of sin and death. The resurrection of Christ inaugurated The Age to Come, the Age of the Spirit and Divine Power. The risen Christ is the second Adam. Believers in Christ are given life by the Spirit who raised Christ. Believers have been raised to life in, and according to, the Spirit.

Paul understood the significance of the cross and the resurrection of Christ in apocalyptic terms, but in the process transformed apocalypticism from a blow by blow account of the future violent destruction of the forces of evil in the world to a means for understanding what had already taken place in an uneventful, weak, past event. His faith was fixed on the God who had acted in the death and the resurrection of Christ. Jesus had died on a cross, but the resurrection was not the resuscitation of Jesus and his death was not just one more criminal execution in an empire where crucifixions and violence were common place. The death and the resurrection of Christ was an apocalyptic cosmic event. On account of it, it is now possible for humans not to live under the power and the condemnation of sin. The resurrection has brought about life in the Spirit for the benefit of all humanity. The creation of a Second Adam marked the beginning of the New Creation. Paul's life as a Jew now became open to be shared with all human beings on account of the cosmic significance of the cross and the resurrection of Christ. This made his fellow Jews, many of whom were, like him, Christian Jews, consider him an apostate.

After the dawn of the nuclear age, when the termination of history, or of all life in the planet earth, is no longer God's exclusive prerogative, we are again in need of transforming our apocalyptic visions and no longer use them as forecasts of violent things to come which, if possible, we must help to bring about. Like Paul we need to place ourselves within a cosmic framework and reinterpret its significance in the light of what is taking place in the shrinking global village. Messianic delusions of grandeur too often serve to give justifications for irrational acts of violence. These are in evidence these days among believers in the three religious streams that flow from Torah: Judaism, Christianity and Islam. Too many of my fellow humans see themselves as messianic agents, warriors for God, or "The Truth." Those who see themselves as God's Warriors are not the agents of peace, bridges that allow for the free transit of peoples and ideas in God's world for the benefit of all of God's creatures.

More than ever, this world needs agents of justice and peace. We can learn from apocalypticism that symbolism and allegory can be useful to our feeble attempts to say something meaningful about our living in God's world. We can learn that God is concerned with the whole of the universe, not just our parochial concerns. This must induce us to also become concerned with the welfare of the universe. We can learn that yes, there is evil in the world. We must, therefore, not be naïve. Yet, this is God's world. We must, therefore, not despair. Apocalypticism is primarily concerned with the affirmation that God's justice will triumph. It did it by a retrieval of the cosmogonic myths of creation. We must also be concerned to establish the justice of God. Rather than reading apocalyptic language as if it were prophecy, in our scientific atomic age we must renounce cosmogonic violence and speak the message of justice. My purpose in writing a memoir of my faith journey, and in my other various activities, has been, precisely, to be an agent of peace, more specifically, peace within Christianity. I can't think of a better way to spend my retirement.

Index

A

B

229

232

233

S

T

U

More from Energion Publications

Personal Study

The Jesus Paradigm	$17.99
When People Speak for God	$17.99
Holy Smoke, Unholy Fire	$14.99
Not Ashamed of the Gospel	$12.99
Evidence for the Bible	$16.99
Christianity and Secularism	$16.99
What's In A Version?	$12.99
Christian Archy	$9.99
The Messiah and His Kingdom to Come	$19.99 (B&W)
(an EnerPower Press title)	$49.99 (Color)

Christian Living

52 Weeks of Ordinary People – Extraordinary God	$7.99
Daily Devotions of Ordinary People – Extraordinary God	$19.99
Directed Paths	$7.99
Grief: Finding the Candle of Light	$8.99
I Want to Pray	$7.99
Soup Kitchen for the Soul	$12.99

Bible Study for Groups

Learning and Living Scripture	$12.99
To the Hebrews: A Participatory Study Guide	$9.99
Revelation: A Participatory Study Guide	$9.99
The Gospel According to St. Luke: A Participatory Study Guide	$8.99
Identifying Your Gifts and Service: Small Group Edition	$12.99
Consider Christianity, Volume I & II Study Guides	$7.99 each

Politics

Preserving Democracy	
	$14.99

Fiction

Tales from Jevlir: Oddballs	$7.99
(an Enzar Empire Press title)	
Megabelt	$12.99

Generous Quantity Discounts Available
Dealer Inquiries Welcome
Energion Publications
P.O. Box 841
Gonzalez, FL 32560
Website: http://energionpubs.com
Phone: (850) 525-3916

CPSIA information can be obtained at www.ICGtesting.com
Printed in the USA
LVOW132052151212

311806LV00002B/120/P